Vegetarian America

Vegetarian America

A History

KAREN IACOBBO and
MICHAEL IACOBBO

Foreword by Andrew Linzey

Westport, Connecticut
London

Library of Congress Cataloging-in-Publication Data

Iacobbo, Karen.
  Vegetarian America : a history / Karen Iacobbo and Michael Iacobbo ;
  foreword by Andrew Linzey.
      p.   cm.
  Includes bibliographical references and index.
  ISBN 0–275–97519–3 (alk. paper)
  1. Vegetarian history. I. Iacobbo, Michael. II. Title.
TX837.I22   2004
613.2′62—dc22   2003027344

British Library Cataloguing in Publication Data is available.

Library of Congress Catalog Card Number: 2003027344
ISBN: 0–275–97519–3

First published in 2004

Praeger Publishers, 88 Post Road West, Westport, CT 06881
An imprint of Greenwood Publishing Group, Inc.
www.praeger.com

Printed in the United States of America

The paper used in this book complies with the
Permanent Paper Standard issued by the National
Information Standards Organization (Z39.48–1984).

10 9 8 7 6 5 4 3 2 1

To the pioneers, especially Sylvester Graham,
Rev. William Metcalfe, A. Bronson Alcott, and
William Andrus Alcott, M.D.

Contents

Foreword:
Veggie Pilgrim Fathers

Andrew Linzey

In 1817 a small band of pilgrims sailed from Britain to the New World. Like the original Pilgrim Fathers, they sought escape from persecution and hoped to propagate their faith. They were a godly lot. They took their Bible seriously—and one bit especially: Genesis chapter one, verses 29–30, which commands that humans eat only herbs and vegetables—a wholly vegetarian diet. This, they maintained, was God's original will. Unsurprisingly, they called themselves the Bible Christian Church (BCC) and vegetarianism was a practical condition of membership. Armed with this vision, they were determined to escape the persecution of the barbarian British and help establish a new, vegetarian world.

To say their mission was ambitious would be an understatement. During the eleven-week voyage, conditions were so desperate that more than half of the original group abandoned their vegetarian principles. Only eleven adults and seven children remained true. It was hardly an auspicious beginning. And yet mindful of John Wesley's comment that "with six true Christians I could convert the whole of England," this handful began their task of converting America.

Of course they failed. Even the open intellectual climate (which they so valued) of the New World could not easily embrace the vegetarian gospel. But, astonishingly, they lasted and prospered, and did not fade away without celebrating their centenary, and then some decades more.

And yet—in another sense—success did not elude them. Their toils fertilized a new Anglo-American movement. Within a few decades the first

British vegetarian society was established in Manchester—their city of origin—and was quickly followed by its American counterpart. The BCC was eventually disbanded and consigned to history, but its vision of a non-violent diet has, despite many setbacks, prospered in remarkable ways both in Britain and the United States. There are now more practicing vegetarians, demi-vegetarians and vegans in Britain than there are practicing Roman Catholics.

Although the BCC can be confidently judged to be the forerunner of the modern vegetarian movement, it did not of course "invent" vegetarianism. That accolade—if it is appropriate—probably belongs to the Greek philosopher, Pythagoras, whose own religious community made vegetarianism compulsory—like the BCC centuries later. Vegetarianism was first known—in the Western world at least—as "the Pythagorean diet." Neither did the BCC bring vegetarianism to America. Previously there were small communities and notable individuals who espoused the "higher" way. But what the BCC did was to help transform the vision into an organization; with considerable BCC support, the American Vegetarian Society was founded in 1850.

If the reader is wondering why they have never heard of the BCC, its leading lights like the Reverend William Cowherd and the Reverend William Metcalfe, or the biblical command to be vegetarian, the answer should be obvious. The omnivores who have written history have largely written vegetarians out of it. Indeed, the vegetarian voice is almost absent from all human studies whether of history, science, ethics, or theology. That is why this book is so important. It is one of the few—perhaps even the first—history of vegetarianism written from the perspective of vegetarians. It provides what other accounts have not—a sensitive understanding of vegetarian ideals and an empathetic insight into the people who have adopted them.

History, it has been said, is the province of the winners. Overwhelmingly the omnivores have won, and have, perhaps unconsciously, written history from their point of view. But another reading of history is possible—one that gives voice to those who have fought for a more humane world and have sacrificed much in the endeavour. Now is the time for vegetarians to fight back, to reclaim their history, their leading lights, and their powerful philosophy of non-violence. Our veggie pilgrim fathers who suffered obloquy in one age deserve recognition in another. In your hands is a fascinating, insightful, even humorous work, which begins to do just that. It may be a first; we must ensure it is not the last.

When I became a vegetarian in the 1960s, I was told that it would not be long before I met my Maker. Medical professionals told me that vegetarian diets did not provide, *inter alia*, "first class" protein. Clerics told me that the Bible said that animals were put here for human use. Philosophers told me that we owe animals nothing morally. Economists told me that widespread vegetarianism would mean that all modern agriculture would come to a halt. It is difficult now to recount these warnings without smiling, but they were all intended to be serious. I hope the reader will understand if I say that I have subsequently become inured to "expert advice." In my case, the rejection of "expert" guidance has been the beginning of wisdom.

The climate of opinion has now thankfully changed, but as this book shows it has been—and still is—an uphill struggle. The old enemies—indifference, prejudice, and ignorance—largely remain, and to them we now have to add the immense influence of multi-nationals, the vested interests that sustain factory farming, and what I have called the all-prevalent "power of misperception" displayed in the media. In the light of this, understandably, the title of this book may appear an oxymoron—a conjunction of seeming contradictoriness, like "God-less Christianity." America, after all, has become synonymous with hamburgers and the sale of cheap animal flesh. But it has also an intellectual climate that is uniquely capable of responding to moral change, to public opinion, and to the demands of the market. Thus the factors, which continue to keep animals enslaved in factory farms, may be the very factors that will eventually liberate them. Consumers have the power in their hands to make moral choices every day for the sake of the animals.

It is not impossible that one day most people will connect the food that they eat with the violence done to other sentient beings. And that the same culture which has countenanced violence will one day come to a different view of it—and also the implications for the human beings who perpetrate it. The vegetarian ethic is as simple as it is profound: when we can live without killing we have a moral obligation to do so.

The point was made by one of the pioneers of the American Vegetarian Society, Ernest H. Crosby, in 1900, and remains true over a century later: "Death is natural, I own, and without it this world would be cursed with life, but...when death is made the chief end of life, and life becomes the handmaid of death, and nature is prostituted to the express manufacture of fattened corpses, then death is hideous indeed."

The Reverend Professor Andrew Linzey is a member of the Faculty of Theology at the University of Oxford, England, and holds the world's first post in the ethics and theology of animal protection at Blackfriars Hall, Oxford. *He is also Honorary Professor of Theology at the University of Birmingham, England, and Special Professor at Saint Xavier University, Chicago. His first book* Animal Rights: A Christian Assessment *(1976) heralded the modern animals rights movement, and his later works, notably* Animal Theology *(1994),* Animals on the Agenda *(1998) and* Animal Gospel: Christian Faith as if Animals Mattered *(1999) make the case for an enlightened Christian view of animals and for adopting a vegetarian diet.*

Acknowledgments

A special thanks to Rev. Professor Andrew Linzey, Ph.D., D.D., for helping to keep alive the two-centuries-old tradition of American and English vegetarians working together for one great cause.

Thanks to our editor Heather Ruland Staines, Emma Bailey, Cynthia Harris, the team at Impressions Book and Journal Services, and Kathy Saideman. Our appreciation to Erica P. Jurgensen for organizing us and making us laugh. A special thank you to family and friends for their support, encouragement, and patience, especially our parents, Ludovico and Gloria Tomasso and Guido and Carol Iacobbo. Thanks to Doris A. Bridgehouse and Jeffrey R. Callahan for their contributions. Thank you to the following generous individuals and organizations for sharing their archives, stories, or suggestions: Connie Salamone, Marcia Pearson, Freya Dinshah, and the late Jay Dinshah, of the American Vegan Society, Jeanne Toomey and the Millennium Guild (Last Post in Great Falls in Connecticut), Dorothy Bronson Wicker and the A. Bronson Alcott Society of Monroe, New York, James Gould, Nellie Shriver, Muriel Golde, Joann Scanlon, Colman McCarthy, Dr. V. Vetrano, Alex Hershaft and F.A.R.M., Vegetarian Resource Group, People for the Ethical Treatment of Animals, Physicians Committee for Responsible Medicine, Mary Shearer of the Victoria Woodhull & Company, Gene and Lorrie Bauston of Farm Sanctuary, Seventh-Day Adventist Church, William Dailey, Wilfred Rauper, Victoria Bidwell at GetWellStayWellAmerica.com, the late Mervin G. Hardinge, M.D., Unity School of Christianity, Salvation Army, Jeff and Sabrina Nelson at VegSource.com, and Pam Rice at VivaVegie for publishing our articles on history.

To conduct research for this book required not only our resourcefulness but the expertise or permission of the following people or libraries: The staff at the Providence Public Library, particularly Margaret A. Chevian, Kathryn M. Blessing, Lynn Harris, William Schneller; Dean Helena F. Rodrigues, D.A., and Elizabeth Anne Nelson at the Johnson & Wales University Library, the reference staff at the American Antiquarian Society, Joan Hackett of the Harmony Library, Rhode Island, Pennsylvania Historical and Museum Commission (Ephrata Cloister), The Free Library of Philadelphia, John Hay Library at Brown University, University of New Hampshire Library (Milne Special Collections), Indiana Historical Society, State Historical Society of Wisconsin, University of Rhode Island Library, Forbes Library, North Hampton Historical Society, Dansville Area Historical Society, Vermont Historical Society Library, Rhode Island Historical Research Library, Swarthmore Peace Collection, Dartmouth College Library, Francis A. Countway Library of Medicine, Schlesinger Library, Widener Library and Countway, and the University of Michigan's Bentley Historical Library.

In remembrance of Robert Newton Cool—historian, friend, mentor, vegetarian.

Introduction

Vegetarian America presents a fair and accurate account of the vegetarian movement in the United States, and the obstacles it faced, over the past three centuries. The book offers the first history of vegetarianism in the United States, and a record of a neglected part of America's history.

The path that vegetarianism traveled from the eighteenth century to the present was not a straight road, but a twisted and rocky one. Like the ebb and flow of tides, vegetarianism has experienced three major waves, each beginning roughly 70 years apart. The first washed across America in the 1830s and 1840s, the second from approximately 1900 to 1930, and the current wave began about 1970.

The advocates who rode the tumultuous movement created the waves that became modern vegetarianism. The pioneering figures such as Sylvester Graham and William Alcott were strongly rooted in their Christian beliefs, unlike most of the advocates today, who do not bring religion to the movement. But they and their counterparts of all eras had other motivations for rejecting meat eating. Some of these motivations include animal rights, aesthetics, health, environmental or economic concerns, and physiological reasons. The arguments for not eating meat have varied little over the centuries.

Vegetarian America makes clear that vegetarians have played a major role in changing America's eating habits. After all, vegetarians seeking to improve America's eating habits developed the first flaked and ready-to-eat cereal, and the first shredded wheat cereal; hence they were largely responsible for starting the breakfast revolution. They were also integral to the movements for abolition, temperance, peace, women's rights, environmentalism, feeding the world, simple living, alternative and preventative medicine, organic foods, nonviolence, and animal liberation.

Some past crusaders of vegetarianism might have had characteristics deemed odd by today's standards. John Harvey Kellogg, M.D., for example, could be seen as being concerned with the colon and its role in health. He also was considered one of the world's top surgeons in his day, and he was one of the top advocates of vegetarianism of all time.

The great advocates of vegetarianism must be viewed in the context of their times. Sylvester Graham, for example, has been denounced for his views on sexuality. However, Graham's views were not unheard of in the society he lived in.

The book chronicles vegetarianism through the centuries, but does not offer amateur psychoanalysis of its advocates. It does offer, however, a look at the contributions made by men and women advocates of vegetarianism. Most vegetarians and nonvegetarians have no knowledge of these people and their contributions.

- A vegetarian is a person who dines upon the foods of the plant kingdom; that is, a person who eats no flesh of any animal. (A vegetarian might also eat eggs, cheese, and cow's milk.)

- A vegan exclusively eats foods of the plant kingdom. A vegan is also a vegetarian since the term originally meant vegan.

- Some vegans—those who abstain out of ethical concern for animals—choose to use no products or services derived from animals or that exploit animals.

To contact the authors, go to www.vegetarianamerica.com, www. vegetarianmuseum.com, or write to Vegetarian America, 409 Pine Street, first floor, Providence, RI, 02903.

Chapter 1

Seeds Are Sown

Vegetarian America has existed since at least the 1700s. Practiced by small pools of people during the eighteenth century, the meandering stream of vegetarianism would burst forth like Niagara Falls by the late twentieth century. Vegetarianism has crossed the chasm of obscurity, of mockery, and of misunderstanding and moved into the mainstream of society. But it took more than one hundred and fifty years, and the tumultuous journey over the rapids of cultural change is not yet complete.

Vegetarianism in the United States did not sprout from a Sixties California commune. The seeds of the modern vegetarian movement were firmly planted in the nineteenth century by Christians. Vegetarianism in the United States dates to even before it was a nation.

Speculators suggest, and even some evidence holds, that at least two Native American tribes practiced vegetarianism.[1] One explorer, Captain Fremont, in the narrative of his travels through the Rocky Mountains, noted a robust Indian tribe that lived on the nuts and seeds of a species of pine tree and traded exclusively in pine nuts.[2]

What is not speculation regarding vegetarianism is that among the population of non-Native people, that is, the Europeans who inhabited the thirteen colonies during the eighteenth century, were a few groups and an unknown number of individuals who abstained from animal flesh.

The most famous of these individuals was Benjamin Franklin, who became a vegetarian at the age of 16 after reading the writings of Thomas Tryon, a seventeenth-century English author whose books include *The Way To Health, Long Life and Happiness; or, a discourse of temperance and the things requisite for the life of man* and *Wisdom's Dictates; or, aphorisms and rules, physical, moral, and divine; for preserving the health of the body, and the peace of the mind.*

A vegetarian dinner served by Franklin to famous guests was described in *The Stirling Observer*. His dinner guests included George Washington, Benjamin Rush, M.D., and John Hancock. Franklin served cucumber, a pot of butter, a jug of spring water, a loaf of bread, lettuces, leeks, a cheese, and foaming beer "more brisk than strong."[3]

One of the founding fathers of the nation, Franklin had decided to not eat meat when he was 16 years old. He "refused to eat the flesh of any animal that had been slaughtered," historian Charles C. B. Seymour reported in 1858.[4]

Franklin was a vegetarian for a time, but he decided not to remain a vegetarian while on a sea voyage. At the start of the trip, Franklin considered the lives of the fish: "Hitherto I had stuck to my resolution of not eating animal food, and on this occasion consider'd, with my master Tryon, the taking of every fish as a kind of unprovoked murder." But Franklin was tempted by the aroma of the cod fish as it was cooked, and decided to eat it after seeing smaller fish taken out of the stomachs of larger fish.[5]

He noted in his autobiography: "thought I, If you eat one another, I don't see why we mayn't eat you." From then on, the statesman ate meat, returning "now and then to a vegetable diet." Franklin explained his rationale: "So convenient a thing it is to be a reasonable creature, since it enables one to find or make a reason for everything one has a mind to do." Evidently, although he ate meat, his reservations about doing so remained.[6]

Franklin was not the first to choose the vegetable diet, as vegetarianism was known, over one containing animal flesh. The practice and philosophy of vegetarianism is at least as old as antiquity, and possibly practiced by some Antediluvians. History records that in the East, vegetarianism was practiced and promulgated by Hindus, Buddhists, and Jains. Pythagoras was called the father of vegetarianism in the West. Scholars like Franklin were familiar with the classics, including wisdom attributed to Pythagoras, and writings by others who advocated vegetarianism such as Seneca, Plato, Porphyry, and Plutarch. The idea of vegetarianism was ancient, and although it seems to have never been widespread for as long as history as been recorded, the practice of it in the West seems to have waxed and waned for centuries. It is difficult to determine what percent of the European population declined to eat meat, for whatever reasons, during the centuries that preceded the eighteenth century.

Part of the problem in determining demographics of the past is that just as the history of war has been written by the victors, the recorded history of vegetarianism in the United States, scant as it has been, has usually been written about as not only an anomaly, but as a quirk of individual people's personalities, rather than as a significant aspect of the past to be studied.

Poor Richard (a.k.a. Franklin) knew of at least one other vegetarian, and he likely knew at least a few more. Johann Conrad Beissel, a German immigrant who in 1732 founded the Seventh-Day Baptists and their community of Ephrata Cloister in Lancaster County, Pennsylvania, and his followers settled in Pennsylvania in 1721.

Followers joined him and together they built Ephrata as a sanctuary against the corruption of the world and as a spiritual retreat for preparing for a better life in the next. Beissel called for a vegan diet for the community, a diet featuring wheat, buckwheat, potatoes, cabbage, greens, fruits, and no meat, milk, cheese, eggs, or honey. Beissel believed that meat eating harmed the soul. "For it is certain that all meat dishes, by whatever name known, quite discommode us, and bring no small injury to the pilgrim on his way to the silent beyond." He believed in a vegan diet with water to drink and that eating became necessary by human beings only after Adam and Eve were banned from Eden for sinning. Whether the community was consistently vegan is unclear. But evidence suggests that they were meat free.[7]

"Beissel and his friends may have also avoided meat because they regarded it a sin to kill another living creature," wrote one historian. It seems that meat eating was considered sinful by Beissel, and kindness to animals good. The community used oxen and horses, but treated them kindly. Beissel's community was also renowned for helping people, sheltering them and healing them with herbs.[8]

Beissel, his community, and others who were baptized in the water were known as the Dunkers. They were described in a 1940 history of the area: "Some were odd-appearing, it is true, like the vegetarian Dunkers whose black beards hung ruggedly over their long white gowns, who abhorred worldliness—some of them thought buttons sinful—and communed with spirits." Very likely this was a description of Beissel's followers since the other Dunkers were not known to have been meat abstainers.[9]

The Ephrata Cloister residents believed human beings could better serve God if unmarried, and they are said to have practiced celibacy, asceticism, pacifism, and vegetarianism. They lived simply and grew lush orchards and gardens. They were renowned as talented artists and skilled craftsmen. Beissel was a gifted musician who composed religious hymns, likely the first published in the colonies. He set to music portions of the Bible and the sect's religious texts. Beissel created his own system of composing that included syllables he deemed masters and servants, which was described in Thomas Mann's 1947 novel *Doktor Faustus*.[10]

Born in Eberbach, Germany, in 1691, Beissel emigrated to Pennsylvania in 1720, as did thousands of Europeans escaping religious persecution. A leader of a Brethren church (Christian) for several years, Beissel in 1732 went into the wilderness, for solitude, and others followed. After his death in 1768, his community changed and ceased to exist when the last member died in 1813.

It is known that at one point Franklin had in his possession Beissel's 1746 Ephrata Community hymnal *(Die bittre Gute, oder Das Gesäng der ein-samen Turtel-Taube)*. The book is today considered one of the American Treasures of the Library of Congress, in Washington, D.C.

Although it is not clear how many other religious communities, or individuals, living in the colonies practiced vegetarianism, there is a record of at least one other community, one founded by William Dorrell.

VEGETARIANS IN VERMONT

Born to a farm family of Yorkshire, England, on March 15, 1752, Dorrell became a soldier and went abroad to the colonies to fight in the Revolutionary War. After the British had been defeated, Dorrell resided in Petersham, Vermont, where he married Polly Chase. In 1794 the couple moved to the town of Leyden.

Dorrell has been described as more than six feet tall, robust, personable, well-spoken, and, although illiterate, keenly intelligent, with a memory powerful enough to recall vast portions of the Bible that had been read to him. He began preaching in 1794 and was soon known throughout Vermont as Reverend Dorrell the earnest "apostle, prophet, seer, revelator, and translator" of the religious sect and community he had established at Leyden, which became known as The Dorrellites.[11]

The British-born preacher's Christ-based message was similar to the message espoused by modern day vegans in regard to animals: "The doctrine at first declared was founded upon the principle that man should not eat flesh, and should not cause the death of a living creature. The doctrine was carried to the extent that no member might wear shoes, or use harnesses (for horses) made of leather or use the skins of animals for any domestic purposes."[12] Some prominent people of Vermont were among those who initially embraced Dorrell's radical message, including the belief that Jesus Christ taught followers to raise themselves above sin to a spiritual life, and that he was not raised from the dead. What was more, Dorrell taught that human beings had no need to pray; they must abide only by God's law and not by man-made laws of church or state. Although these ideas likely raised eyebrows in eighteenth-century Vermont, they seem to have been tolerated by a good number of non-Dorrellites.

What was not tolerated was Dorrell's belief that a man and woman need not marry before making love. Perhaps solely due to this doctrine, rumors circulated outside of the small community that Dorrell and followers engaged in wild sexual activity. By 1798, under pressure from outsiders, some members left his community. Perhaps also due to the alleged drinking bouts of Dorrell, the community disbanded. Whether or not rumors about Dorrell and his community were true is not as important as the pioneering efforts they made as vegans in a culture at large that was, one can assume, decidedly nonvegetarian.

Dorrell was not the only religious man of eighteenth-century America concerned about the ethical treatment of animals. Consideration for God's creation—which included the animals people ate—was also on John Woolman's mind. His thoughts about animals and humanity's obligation to them are well known. They appear in the humble Quaker's most famous work: *The Journal of John Woolman,* which is a record of his spiritual life from 1720 until the 1770s. "I believe," wrote Woolman, "where the love of God is verily perfected, and the true spirit of government watchfully attended to, a tenderness towards all creatures made subject to us will be experienced, and a care felt in us that we do not lessen that sweetness of life in the animal creation which the great Creator intends for them under our government."[13]

In his Journal Woolman also stated: " I was early convinced in my mind that true religion consisted in an inward life, wherein the heart does love and reverence God the Creator, and learns to exercise true justice and goodness, not only toward all men, but also toward the brute creatures; that, as the mind was moved by an inward principle to love God as an invisible, incomprehensible Being, so, by the same principle, it was moved to love him in all his manifestations in the visible world; that, as by his breath the flame of life was kindled in all animal sensible creatures..."

Perhaps Woolman's belief about how God-loving people should treat animals can best be summed up in one sentence from his Journals: "To say we love God as unseen, and at the same time exercise cruelty toward the least creature moving by his life, or by life derived from him, was a contradiction in itself."

The son of a Quaker who had settled in New Jersey, Woolman was a crusader against slavery. He might not have been a vegetarian, but the ideas he forwarded about animals, that they deserve kindness and respect, are today part of ethical vegetarians' values.

Advocates of vegetarianism of Woolman's era believed that food from the plant kingdom was the proper food for men and women, as stated by God and recorded in the Book of Genesis in the Bible. The new idea of ethical treatment of animals, professed by the Dorellites and Woolman, was found in the Bible.

Another proponent in America of this idea was Herman Daggett. In his Providence College (now Brown University) commencement speech of September 1791, Daggett, who earned a master's degree, stopped short of calling for vegetarianism, but condemned cruelty to animals and hoped for a new golden age (an era of vegetarianism and peace among people and animals, wrote Hesiod):

I cannot close these observations, without indulging myself, for a moment, in the pleasing anticipation of that time, which is fast approaching, when there shall, no longer by any disposition, in mankind, to hurt the peace of one another, or to wage war with innocent nature: "For the earnest expectation of the CREATURE, waiteth for the manifestation of the Sons of God"—the joyful period, when the groans of this lower creation shall have an end:

When lambs, with wolves, shall grace the verdant mead,
And boys, in flowery bands, the tyger lead;
The deer and lion at one crib shall meet,
The smiling infant, in his hand, shall take
The crested basilisk, and the speckled snake,
Pleas'd, the green lustre of the scales survey,
And with their forked tongue, and pointless ring shall play.[14]

A few years later, in 1809, another American, L. Du Pre, called directly for vegetarianism as an obligation that fulfilled God's covenant with humanity, as described in the Bible. In the Old Testament are several of God's covenants with humanity. It seems likely that Du Pre was referring to Genesis or Isaiah. In the first is the mandate for vegetarianism (veganism) and for people to have dominion over animals, meaning to care for them. Isaiah contains the promise of a future for humanity and animals of peace when the lion shall dwell with the calf "and a little child shall lead them." In his book titled *The Principles of a New Covenant, or Social Compact; for the Animal Creation,* Du Pre argued that as part of the covenant, human beings could take the milk of the cow, but only if the cow was given a better life in return; for example, if people created rich pasture for her to enjoy where once there had been forest. If instead, human beings devoured her calf, and then, when she no longer produced milk, slaughtered her and ate her carcass, God's covenant with humanity would be violated.[15]

Another advocate of vegetarianism of the era became an American folk hero by traveling far and wide planting apple trees. But Johnny Appleseed was much more than a sower of seeds—he was on a spiritual mission. He was born John Chapman in Leominster, Massachusetts, in September 26, 1774. Little is known about Chapman's early years, but scholars trace the start of his saga to the late 1790s. Chapman gathered seeds from cider presses in western Pennsylvania, put them in bags, and carried them into the wilderness of Ohio and neighboring territories and states. He bought and sold land for use as orchards and seedling farms. Chapman ventured as far west as Indiana, and as far north as the northern lakes, but spent many years in Ohio. He was respected by settlers, and even by Indians hostile to other white people.

Most of the time Chapman, who was a small and wiry man with long, dark hair and a beard, walked barefoot, but occasionally he wore hand-me-down moccasins or shoes that he received for payment for his seeds. Chapman ate fruit, nuts, berries, and other delicacies of the woods, and sometimes he accepted food from settlers.

The bearded traveler was a follower of the teachings of eighteenth-century Christian mystic and vegetarian Emmanuel Swedenborg. Chapman carried copies of *Heaven and Hell* and other Swedenborg writings on his journeys, and shared the writings with all he met. Chapman refused to harm any animal, and it has been said that he would prematurely extinguish fires that he started to keep warm because the light attracted bugs that might burn if they got too close to the flames.

An account of Chapman's life published in an 1871 *Harper's New Magazine* stated: "His diet was as meager as his clothing. He believed it to be a sin to kill any creature for food, and thought that all that was necessary for human sustenance was produced by the soil."[16]

American vegetarianism was not yet an organized movement during the colonial era or in the early years of the new nation. Yet the idea of abstinence from animal flesh would continue to blossom in the nineteenth century. Like their predecessors, most advocates of vegetarianism of that century would have a connection to Christianity. They, like Woolman's contemporary, Joshua Evans of Jersey, abolitionist and vegetarian, would tend to believe, "I considered that life was sweet in all living creatures, and taking it away became a very tender point with me. . . . I believe my dear Master has been pleased to try my faith and obedience by teaching me that I ought no longer to partake of anything that had life."[17]

Chapter 2

Abstinence from Fleshfoods: Christian Vegetarians, and the English Connection

At least a small number of individuals and groups practiced vegetarianism during colonial days. When the new century emerged like sunlight out of the shadows, the numbers who did not eat meat started to increase. By the teens, this slight wind of change was beginning to blow stronger in America and would bring new ideas about food, about animals, and about Christianity.

The winds of change brought in the American Vegetarian Movement, which originated in England early in the nineteenth century. The rise of romanticism created fertile ground for vegetarian values by ushering in a world view of imagination, intuition, and egalitarianism. Romantics glorified the simple, rural life, communed with nature, and believed in kindness toward fellow humans and animals. They challenged revered ideals and institutions. Eschewing meat appealed to the romantics, politically, aesthetically, and morally.

One romantic, perhaps the most romantic of them all, poet Percy Bysshe Shelley, in his poem *Queen Mab*, told of the horrors human beings had inflicted upon each other and the world—and of a coming age of nonviolence when people and animals would live in peace. That age would include vegetarianism. Wrote Shelley:

…no longer now
He slays the lamb that looks him in the face,
And horribly devours his mangled flesh, Which, still avenging nature's broken
    law,
Kindled all putrid humours in his frame,
All evil passions, and all vain belief,

Hatred, despair, and loathing in his mind,
The germs of misery, death, disease, and crime.
Flee from the form of man; but gather round,
And prune their sunny feathers on the hands
Which little children stretch in friendly sport
Towards these dreadless partners of their play.
All things are void of terror; man has lost
His terrible prerogative, and stands
An equal amidst equals…

In Shelley's *Notes to Queen Mab,* the poet explained ethical, economic, and health arguments for excluding meat from the diet. Shelley, who had witnessed cruelty toward animals, was influenced by the writings of ancient philosophers, like Plutarch, and by a friend, Dr. William Lambe, author of *The Doctor's Moral Inquiries on the Situation of Man and Brutes. On the Crime of Committing Cruelty on Brutes, and of Sacrificing Them to the Purposes of Man, etc.*

Other works published during the Romantic era that contained arguments for vegetarianism included: George Nicholson's *The Primeval Diet of Man: Arguments in Favor of Food; with Remarks on Man's Conduct to [Other] Animals* (1801), Joseph Ritson's *Essay Upon Abstinence from Animal Food as a Moral Duty* (1802), and *John Oswald's Cry of Nature: an Appeal to Mercy and to Justice on Behalf of the Persecuted Animals.* (1793).

Another more direct contribution to the growth of the vegetarian movement in England was the work of the newly established Bible-Christian Church. Bible-Christians abstained from animal food (meaning flesh) and alcoholic drink. Reverend William Cowherd, a former Swedenborgian minister, founded the church in Salford in 1807, and was likely among the first to publicly lecture on the health and spiritual aspects of the vegetarian diet. The size of the church's membership fluctuated, and at times numbered as many as 400 people.

Whether in the UK or the United States, vegetarianism in the early 1800s was an oddity. The majority of people were ignorant of its benefits, and it was considered unnatural as well as heretical by some. However, even negative attention given to vegetarianism was attention to the fact that at least some individuals eschewed meat in lands where menus featured lamb, beef, or pork. It can be speculated that this attention led more people to vegetarianism.

Cowherd, born in Ambleside, England, believed that optimal health could be obtained by respecting the body as the temple of the Holy Spirit. He believed it was the "duty of mankind, to abstain from the use of animal food, and intoxicating liquors as a religious requirement; or, in the language of the Apostle Paul, 'It is good not to eat flesh, and not to drink wine.' "

In 1809, the decision of one young Englishman in his early 20s to join Cowherd's unusual church, and then as a Bible-Christian no longer dine

William Metcalfe: Bible-Christian and early promoter of vegetarianism.

on meat, eventually led that young man to the United States of America, where he would become one of the greatest advocates of vegetarianism the nation has ever known.

Born in Ortin in 1788, William Metcalfe decided to reject meat eating after reading correspondence on the subject given to him by his neighbor Joseph Wright—a member of the church. The letters, evidently from Cowherd to Wright, were the catalyst that led Metcalfe to vegetarianism and to the Bible-Christian Church and school, where he was educated. In 1810 Metcalfe married Wright's daughter Susanna, who was also a vegetarian. A year later, the bridegroom was ordained as a minister in the church.

In June of 1817, Metcalfe and Susanna, along with 40 other members of the church, journeyed across the Atlantic to the United States. Eighteen remained vegetarian. They settled in Philadelphia, Pennsylvania, to establish the Bible-Christian Church. The year Metcalfe arrived, America was at war with Seminole Indians and regular steamship upon the Mississippi River began, as did the building of the Erie Canal.

From his pulpit Metcalfe preached the Bible-Christian practice of abstinence from animal flesh and intoxicating drink. Down from the pulpit, he
faced a challenge. Jobs were scarce, so most of the church members who
had come to the new country were forced to move away to find work.
Worse, they deserted the church and its creed of abstinence, reverting to
meat eating and wine drinking. Metcalfe might have been disappointed,
but he was also determined.

The minister revealed how he felt upon this desertion, and why he
maintained his vegetarian crusade: "As a minister in this little community,
you will readily conceive, I felt much discouraged; but believing in the
truth of my views, and considering it a duty to endeavor to diffuse the
doctrines I had espoused, and to promote a cause which I believed then
and still believe to be calculated to add to the physical, mental and spiritual well-being of mankind, I determined, with the blessing of God, not to
give up in despair."[1]

Metcalfe, according to his son and biographer Rev. Joseph Metcalfe,
believed "there is a desolation wrought in the soul by the sin of flesh-
eating *more fearful* than any outward ghastliness, but which cannot be
understood, because of the long and unlimited prevalence of the custom.
Hence a constant and self-sacrificing devotion was needful on the part of
those who were enlightened in the principles of Vegetarianism, to awaken
the public to its enormity."[2]

The new church also faced financial difficulties, but Metcalfe told the
remaining members that the Lord would provide. The church continued
to exist, and although never a large congregation, it thrived for a time. It
became widely known in Philadelphia that the Bible-Christians didn't eat
animal flesh, whether from a cow, chicken, pig, fish, lobster, or any other
being. Metcalfe reached out to the public, writing articles on vegetarianism for the *Philadelphia Gazette*, the *Saturday Evening Post*, and other publications. He corresponded with all who showed even slight interest in the
subject.

The Bible-Christians believed that vegetarianism was God's law, and
that Jesus had been a vegetarian. This was contrary to the prevailing belief
of Christians of that time, which held that, according to the Bible, God
permitted people to eat meat, Jesus had fed a group of 5,000 people fish,
and that Jesus ate meat.

Metcalfe preached that this conventional belief that Jesus fed fish to the
people and ate it himself was based on a misunderstanding of the Bible.
The term *fisherman*, during the era when the Gospels were written, Metcalfe explained, was applied to many occupations, ranging from fishers of
pearls, coral, and marine plants to those who hunted fish. Metcalfe
explained that the word for fish used in the Gospels did not translate as an
aquatic animal, but meant some other, nonanimal food that was served
with bread.[3]

The commandment "Thou Shalt not Kill" had also been misunderstood. "Who has authority or presumption to limit this precept to killing men?...May we not reasonably believe that its application was benevolently intended to reach the animal creation?" the minister preached in *Abstinence from the Flesh of Animals,* his 1821 tract.[4]

These unorthodox beliefs of the Bible-Christians, together with their other equally unpopular beliefs, including abolition and pacifism, evoked criticism. A newspaper labeled Metcalfe a pretend reformer, and on the street, some people called him "Infidel!" Despite the animosity, Metcalfe was not without friends. His young church was impoverished, but his new, well-to-do, Philadelphian friends urged him to discontinue teaching vegetarianism and temperance. They even offered him a ministry of a nearby affluent church, if only he would mend his ways. He refused.[5]

Due to social pressure, practicing vegetarianism, and preaching it from the pulpit, was not easy in the early nineteenth century—in Philadelphia or in England. Before coming to the United States, Metcalfe had been ridiculed by friends. It was common for the meat-eating majority in England and the United States to believe that vegetarianism led to emaciation, emasculation, feebleness, insanity, and death.

My friends laughed at me, and entreated me to lay aside my foolish notions of a vegetable diet. They assured me I was rapidly sinking into a consumption, and tried various other methods to induce me to return to the customary dietetic habits of society;...Some predicted my death in three or four months...and others...hesitated not to tell me I was certainly suffering from mental derangements, and, if I continued to live without flesh-food much longer, would unquestionably have to be shut up in some insane asylum...." Metcalfe was not swayed by his friends' predictions. "Instead of sinking into consumption, I gained several pounds in weight during the first few weeks of my experiment...my mental operations have, up to this day, been such that I have never even seen the interior of any insane-institution.[6]

Instead of succumbing, Metcalfe survived. His small American parish faced obstacles, and several times almost perished. However, Metcalfe and his parishioners became the organizers of a vegetarian society open to the public, likely the first such organization in the nation. Susanna collected recipes from church members, and published them as the Bible-Christian cookbook.

To sustain himself, his family, and the church, Metcalfe founded a school and published newspapers, and he also became a homeopathic physician. Metcalfe stayed in touch with his peers in England and inaugurated the alliance between the American and UK vegetarian movements, which has endured for nearly two centuries. His vegetarian advocacy in Philadelphia continued for many years, and he went on to establish, in 1850, a national vegetarian organization.

But two decades before that would happen, vegetarianism in America would take a giant leap forward through the efforts of another charismatic man. Metcalfe was preaching in Philadelphia when a traveling temperance reformer, who, like the Bible-Christians, called for abstinence rather than mere moderation in use of alcohol. He had already made a name for himself as a reformer and came to the city to lecture and meet members of the church.

It was 1830 and the Presbyterian temperance reformer—Sylvester Graham—learned that church members—all vegetable eaters (a term for vegetarians)—had escaped a cholera epidemic that had recently ravaged the city and the nation. This gave Graham, who had been reading books on health to add to his moral- and religious-based argument against use of alcoholic drink, another reason to continue his studies of physiology and anatomy. He had read works of history and anthropology, as well as the Bible, literature, and books on vegetarian philosophy. Apparently, Graham became a vegetarian during this time, perhaps only after becoming acquainted with the Bible-Christians.

Reverend William Metcalfe had prepared the ground and planted some seeds of vegetarianism in the Philadelphia region, but it was Graham who would spread the seeds that would take root far and wide in America. For the father of American vegetarianism was not William Metcalfe, but this other Christian, a Presbyterian minister without a permanent parish. More than a decade had passed since the Bible-Christians had settled in America when Graham began his great crusade for the vegetable diet.

Chapter 3

Sylvester Graham, Grahamism, and Grahamites

The Father of Vegetarianism, Sylvester Graham, planted seeds of change. The abundant harvest, of more widely accepted and practiced vegetarianism, would not be reaped until well into the next century. Meanwhile, during his own time, vegetarianism in the United States would slowly grow under Graham's cultivation. Today, neither America nor the vegetarian movement has recognized Graham's contribution.

Sylvester Graham's life was from the start one of hardship. He was born in West Suffield, Connecticut, in 1794 to a family of 17 children. His parents were John Graham, age 70, and his second wife, Ruth.

John Graham died when Sylvester was two years old, and Ruth apparently suffered from mental illness and was unable to effectively care for her son. So Sylvester was shuffled from home to home and raised by relatives and friends of his family. As a young child he lived for a time with a tavern owner who had the boy help out with chores in the bar. Early exposure to drunkenness made an impression on the boy that lasted a lifetime. An unstable home life was not young Graham's only trouble. He was a sickly child who suffered from bouts of illness. His early struggles for health would also play a role in his future.

Graham's erratic home life and battles with sickness deprived him of a complete formal education, but people observed that he was a talented writer of poetry and painter of pictures. He was also, by his own description and that of others, a highly sensitive and passionate person. These characteristics, combined with his unusual upbringing and his at times feeble health, made him stand out as different from his peers. When he was in his 20s, he stood apart from them because he did not drink liquor

Sylvester Graham: Father of Vegetarianism in
the United States.

in an era when it was expected, even demanded, that a young man
drink.

As much as his constantly deteriorating health permitted, Graham
worked as a teacher, farmer, and a variety of other jobs. As an adult in his
late 20s he briefly attended Amherst Academy in Massachusetts, where he
studied to become a minister like his father and his grandfather before
him. During his short stay at the preparatory school, it became evident
that Graham was an outstanding, if unusual, orator. He was labeled a
stage actor—which was an insult during those days.

This odd but evidently appealing young man was popular with the
young ladies of the town but not appreciated by his male peers at the
school, who, it has been said, were envious. A conspiracy was devised
among them to get rid of Graham. One or more lied that Graham had
acted improperly towards a young lady.

He was forced to leave school. He was devastated; his health failed,
and he apparently suffered a nervous breakdown. Stricken with physical
and mental exhaustion, Graham moved to Rhode Island to recover. He

recovered in 1826; that same year, on September 19, he married one of his caretakers, Sarah Earle of Compton, Rhode Island, the daughter of a sea captain.

Despite the trials he had faced before his marriage, Graham continued his studies and was soon ordained as a Presbyterian minister. It was still 1826 when he and his bride moved to Bershire Valley, New Jersey, where he was appointed minister of a congregation.

The Reverend Graham was well liked by his congregation. That was until he began vigorously advocating abstinence from alcohol. At the time, alcohol consumption was likely more prevalent than today. It was acceptable to most for people young and old to imbibe at daily dinner as well as at baptisms, weddings, and funerals—at every social occasion. It was considered antisocial to not offer liquor to one's guests. A social lubricant, liquor was also hailed as good medicine for many maladies—including what is now called stress. It was not unknown, and not unacceptable, for a physician to have a drink before surgery to calm his nerves, and for college students to indulge before exams for the same purpose. Young men, even teens, were encouraged by their peers, and by adults, to drink. Alcoholic beverages were accepted virtually everywhere, and partly in reaction to this rampant use of beer, wine, and whiskey, the temperance movement began to thrive during Graham's day.

In 1830 he left the church, but not the ministry, and was hired by the *Pennsylvania Society for the Suppression of Ardent Spirits* to lecture to the public on the health risks and moral evils of drinking alcohol. Graham was convinced that alcohol was harmful to the body as well as the soul, an unusual idea at a time when most medicine contained a large percentage of alcohol. Immediately Graham made a reputation for himself as an outstanding orator, and as a self-educated man knowledgeable about health. So self-educated was Graham on the subjects of health and diet, and anatomy and physiology, that people began to refer to him as Dr. Graham. His attributes as a speaker and a thinker and his way with words, the very qualities he had been criticized for as a youth and that had alienated him from peers at school, would propel him to national prominence.

CHOLERA EPIDEMIC

In 1832 a cholera epidemic swept across the nation like a tidal wave. Panic gripped the nation. The epidemic was front-page news; newspapers were daily reporting the death toll, and doctors were advising the public on how to stay out of the path of the deadly disease. The consulting physician of Boston, at the request of the Mayor and Aldermen, offered instructions on treatment and on how to avoid the Asiatic Cholera. He advised that those afflicted should be given 50 drops of laudanum in a wine glass of hot brandy, an injection of gill of starch, arrowroot, and one teaspoon of laudanum, and that bags of hot sand and poultices of mustard must be applied to their bodies.[1]

The consulting physician of Boston prescribed a dietary regimen to prevent the disease. It was heavy on meat, contained some vegetables and scant fruit, and was flavored with religious instruction—typical recommendations of the day. "The best articles of food are bread, eggs, fresh meat, fresh fish, and rice. Perfectly good and thoroughly boiled vegetables stand next, as potatoes, asparagus, etc. All uncooked vegetables, as salads, are dangerous. Fruits, unless very fine, had better be avoided. Strawberries, taken by themselves, or with the addition of a little wine, are the least likely to do mischief.... We recommend a good conscience, and a fearless performance of duty, as the best of all preservatives against the disorder.... We (therefore) strongly urge on our fellow citizens, a perfect confidence in the wisdom and goodness of God, and a full assurance that those who perform His will, by the devotion of their labors to the sick and suffering, are taking the surest means to escape the attack of this disease."[2]

Other physicians made recommendations regarding diet to prevent cholera. One, Dr. Rhinelander, had been sent by officials of the city of New York to Canada to determine how doctors there dealt with the disease. The result was that Rhinelander prescribed to the people of the United States port wine as a preventive medicine against the disease. Dr. Felix Pascalis added dietary advice to the prescription. He stated cholera outbreaks were the most severe in regions of the globe where people ate little or no animal food; Pascalis told the press the disease had decimated large populations of people in those regions.[3]

Thus, it became widely known in America that one should eat large portions of meat and drink plenty of port to cheat the cholera. It was well known, too, that vegetables and fruit should be largely avoided, since it was believed that eating them caused cholera. The sale of fruit, salad, and any uncooked vegetable was banned by several cities and, in August of 1832, the federal government backed the ban.

The U.S. Board of Health prohibited the sale of many foods for 90 days. On the list: apples, apricots, beans, carrots, cherries, coconuts, corn, cucumbers, eggplant, lemons, melons, peas, peaches, plums, pumpkins, squashes, turnips, and watermelons, as well as ice cream, fish, and shellfish. The Board of Health warned that onions, potatoes, beets, and tomatoes should only be eaten in moderation.[4]

The ban on sales of produce through the important harvest months must have been a hardship for farmers. That fruits, vegetables, even peas and beans, were prohibited from the diet was likely detrimental to the health of at least some people, since science now knows these foods provide important vitamins to boost the human immune system, and at the least, the foods provide essential fiber in the diet.

Another health belief in the age of the cholera epidemic was that sickness was a mystery, and that it was sent by God. Numerous Christians, who comprised the vast majority of the nation's population, held this opinion. U.S. Senator Clay and Congress called for a day of humiliation and prayer—a National Fast—to beg for divine intervention to end the cholera epidemic.[5]

GRAHAM'S PREVENTIVE MEDICINE

Sylvester Graham had other ideas about how to safeguard the population against cholera, ideas quite opposite of what people believed in those days. His father and grandfather had been ministers, and they were also physicians. Although not formally trained as a doctor, Graham followed their example by becoming a minister who crusaded for health. His mission was to teach Americans to think twice before plunging a fork into a slab of meat, eating a slice of denatured bread, and drinking alcohol. He succeeded in his mission—to a degree.

In his lectures against the use of alcohol, delivered in Philadelphia, Graham talked about the health effects of drinking, and he said the eating of meat led to the craving for liquor. With the rise of the cholera epidemic, Graham was suddenly in great demand as a lecturer. He heeded the call and, as he and not a few of his fellow citizens perceived the situation, came to America's rescue. Graham lectured up and down the northeastern United States and attracted crowds. As many as 2,000 people attended his lecture in New York City. Overnight, millions became familiar with the name Sylvester Graham.

In his lectures, he called for newspapers to cease sensationalizing the epidemic and frightening the country. He believed a potentially significant numbers of cases of the cholera had been caused by fear mongering. "By often hearing the acounts of the Cholera, ... filled with fearful anxiety, disease could result," Graham said in his oft-repeated series of talks titled and published as "A Lecture on Epidemic Diseases Generally and Particularly the Spasmodic Cholera." This lecture was likely the first in U.S. history that identified anxiety (stress) as harmful to health.[6]

In his lectures, Graham identified more than anxiety as the problem; he explained that the "primary and paramount" reason disease afflicted a person was due to the condition of the human system, resulting from the violation of the laws of organic life. The germ theory, that was proposed much later in the century, and which is the basis of modern (allopathic) medicine, would not have impressed Graham. Although he might have agreed that germs spread disease, he would have likely argued that the germs could have no effect if the body was in a state of health, rather than broken down by constant bad health habits.

He instructed his audiences the way to good health was adhering to the laws of life. Graham also told his audiences to beware of the treatments administered by the allopaths, that is, the regular doctors who administered medicine, which he considered ineffective at best and lethal at worst. "Drug and grog shops are yawning at every corner...like so many craters of hell, to vomit out the lava of death."[7]

To prevent cholera, people must avoid worry over contracting it and avoid the doctors who claimed to cure it, said Graham. More importantly, people must follow the laws of life: they must bathe frequently, exercise, take plenty of fresh air, and drink plenty of pure water. Even more essential, they must exclusively eat foods of the plant kingdom, including whole grain and not white bread, and avoid all forms of meat, alcoholic drink, and tobacco.

This radical advice—lifestyle as preventive medicine—was the crux of what Graham considered the laws of life that were given by God to keep human beings strong and healthy. Graham's recommendations were anathema to the advice of the allopathic doctors of the day.

He was controversial almost from the start, for his style as well as his ideas. Graham's rhetoric was colorful and filled with allusion to his background as a minister. His talent as an orator was also apparent in his lectures and subsequent books.

One sample of his use of language comes from the series of lectures he presented in New York, Philadelphia, and several northern cities during 1832. Graham said: "In the whole career of the Epidemic Cholera, dietetic intemperance and lewdness have been the grand purveyors of its devastating rage.... debility, by whatever cause, or in whatever manner induced, always predisposes to the cholera; and hence, again, "a generous system of diet" (including a free use of animal food, and of wine, and even brandy)..."[8]

Although others had proposed it earlier, the vegetarian crusader in his popularity introduced America to the idea that sickness was the body's way of attempting to correct conditions arising from violation of the laws of life. Thus, symptoms were not caused by God and did not arise mysteriously, but were reactions to repeated irritation—debility—of the tissues or organs, such as from meat eating and drinking liquor, which resulted in disease, and if not corrected or if the violation occurred often enough, led eventually to death.

Graham's approach to teaching these ideas made him an original in the history of health. Rather than get sick and die, he stated, people could do much to save their health by taking control over their bodies through their habits, particularly what they ate and drank. A few others preached similar ideas, but it was Graham who popularized them.

That one could take control of one's health was good news to an apparently significant number of Americans, but some others met it with skep-

ticism and even hostility. Graham attracted a sizable following as his reputation as health savior spread. Neighbor told neighbor that his system
worked, and little by little it became known that he was teaching people
not only how to prevent cholera, but how to regain health. Through Graham's efforts, word of vegetarianism—that it existed, that it was beneficial—grew in America.

Graham's talent as an orator certainly helped him attract the public's
attention. One person who attended a lecture noted this ability in a letter
to the slavery abolitionist newspaper *Genius of Temperance, Philanthropist
and People's Advocate,* "On his first rising he observed that he had not prepared a set address for the occasion, but wished only to speak to them in a
colloquial manner. I was sorry to hear this,.... (then I was) almost aston-
ished. Such an extemporaneous address I had never heard. In physiology
he is perfectly at home..."[9]

Another person who attended Graham's lectures, William Goodall, editor of *Genius of Temperance,* an abolitionist newspaper, likely spoke for a
good number of Americans when he stated of the vegetarian crusader:
"And the Kind Providence that has thus far shaped the course of this won-
derful Reformation, seems to have provided Mr. Graham, just such a
leader as was needed, and at the very moment when his labors were most
wanted."[10]

Letters of gratitude poured into Graham's mailbox. The letters came
from grateful people who had been invalids for years but after heeding
the crusader's advice were in a short time back on their feet in full health.
His followers became known as Grahamites, and Grahamite soon became
synonymous with one who partook of the vegetable diet. Vegetarian, a
word known at that time, was rarely used.[11]

WHY VEGETARIAN?

Graham's main source for his teachings on health came from his observation of people and their habits. Like the French scientist Bichat, whose
theory on health he had read, Graham believed disease resulted from
debility of the body. Meat was a stimulant to the body, and repeated stimulation, that is, irritation, caused debility; therefore, meat was injurious,
reasoned Graham. He also thought that the way farmed animals were
raised—confined and fattened—further caused their flesh to be harmful
food for humans.

Like Reverend William Metcalfe and his Philadelphia church, Graham
also looked to the Bible for instruction on humanity's diet. "For according
to Moses the Lord God planted a garden, and caused every tree that is
pleasant to the sight and good for food, to grow out of the ground; and he
took the man whom he had formed, and put him into the Garden of Eden
to dress it and to keep it and to subsist on its fruits. Such then, is the food

which adapted to the highest and best condition of human nature," Graham told his audiences.[12]

He had also looked to literature and folklore which, like the Bible's book of Genesis, told of the Golden Age when all men and women were vegetarians and lived in peace with each other and with animals. "Peutrescent carcasses of dead animals" were not on early human's menu, Graham said.[13] He also said human beings of Antediluvian times lived extremely long lives, hundreds of years, and were robust in health.

Graham took into consideration the history of eating habits around the world, from the wise intellects of the Ancient Greek philosophers to the powerful physiques of the Roman soldiers, and noted meat was not in their diets.

Other sources of Graham's teachings included works on natural history, anatomy, and physiology. In these books he found facts coinciding with the Bible on diet. Graham consulted the works of Cuvier and other naturalists, who had believed that human beings were not designed to eat flesh. These books taught that the human animal was not a carnivore, as was the fanged, clawed lion of lightning speed and an appetite for raw, fresh flesh, and was more like the ape.

After analyzing evidence from comparative anatomy, such as the shape of the human jaw and teeth, in contrast to that of the lion, Graham concluded human beings were neither carnivore, omnivore, nor herbivore. "The whole evidence of comparative anatomy goes to prove that man is naturally a frugivorous animal."[14] *Frugivorous* literally meant "fruit eating" and connoted also the eating of vegetables, nuts, and grains.

He conceded people could obtain nourishment from meat; he said God was merciful and would not want people to starve when other foods were unavailable. However, Graham explained, meat was not the food for which man was designed, and therefore, eating it, over time, would result in negative consequences.

Since meat was a stimulant, and eating it made one thirsty, it created the physical craving for alcoholic drink. Remove the meat from the menu, and the need for strong drink would dissipate, Graham stated, offering hope to those addicted, and a way for them to break the habit.

He also offered advice on the subject of bread. Although he thought his campaign for better bread (including improved farming methods to grow it) that would make healthier Americans was nearly futile, Graham felt it was his responsibility to speak out just the same.

(Yet) If some one does not raise a voice upon this subject which shall be heard and heeded, there will soon reach us, as a nation, a voice of calamity which we shall not be able to shut our ears against, albeit we may in the perverseness of out sensualism, incorrigibly persist in disregarding its admonitions, till the deep chastisements of outraged nature shall reach the very "bone and marrow" of the human constitution, and fill our land with such a living rottenness, as now in some other portions of the earth, renders human society odious and abominable.

Whether, therefore, my voice shall be heard and needed or not, I will obey the dictates of my sense of duty, and solemnly declare that this subject demands the prompt and earnest attention of every agriculturist and of every friend to the common cause of humanity; for it is most certain, that until the agriculture of our country is conducted in strict accordance with physiological truth, it is not possible for us to realize those physical, and intellectual, and moral, and social, and civil blessings for which the human constitution and our soil and climate are naturally capacitated.[15]

Meat and bad bread were the most obvious errors in the diet, but not the only errors, Graham believed. Among his specific advice: raw foods from the plant kingdom were provided by God, and when it wasn't possible to eat raw foods, the next best choice was unadulterated foods—including whole grain wheat bread and plain meals made without the use of condiments. Pepper, vinegar, mustard, and other condiments, like coffee and tea, were stimulating (irritating) to the body, as was meat, and therefore injurious when used over time, taught Graham.

Andrew Combe, M.D., physician to the king and queen of the Belgians and a Fellow of the Royal College of Physicians of Edinburgh, who was highly regarded and much read by leaders of the vegetarian movement for his position on diet in those days, had, like Graham, stated that "stimulating condiments are injurious to the healthy stomach."[16]

Vegetarianism and use of whole grain bread were two essential parts of Graham's system of health, and they were the parts for which he was becoming famous—and infamous. Many people learned of Graham's teachings secondhand, either from newspaper accounts of his lectures, or from friends or relatives who had attended his talks, and did not hear the actual words of the crusader. Confusion about his system resulted, prompting Graham to publish his lectures and his closest followers to eventually create a newspaper entirely devoted to Grahamism.

So incorrect had been some depictions of Graham's system, by those who did not actually know it, that the crusader had to explain that his system was more than abstaining from flesh foods.

I wish to be clearly understood on this point however;—I do not affirm that the mere abstinence from animal food and living on vegetable food exclusively, without any regard to a proper regimen, will better enable our bodies to withstand the action of foreign morbific causes, than a mixed diet, under good regulations. I continually insist upon it, and wish it to be distinctly remembered, that vegetable food can be made incomparably more pernicious than plain, simple animal food in temperate quantities. It is infinitely better to subsist on a mixed diet of vegetable and animal food under a good general regimen, than to live wholly on vegetable food, badly selected, viciously prepared, and eaten in ordinate quantities, while at the same time, we live in the violation of almost every other correct rule of health.... To this question I reply, unhesitatingly, that both physiological science, and facts prove that the pure vegetable diet is the safest and the best; because it is best adapted to the organization and the physiological properties and powers of the human body.[17]

However, Graham emphasized that vegetarianism was integral to good health. "I am convinced that as a general and permanent rule, the whole human family would do best—after a certain period in very early life, to subsist entirely on the products of the vegetable kingdom and pure water."[18] Food had to be in a natural state, and if it was not, eating it brought ill effects: For example, Graham explained, obstructions and disturbances in the stomach, bowels, and other organs of the abdomen resulted from "the use of superfine flour is among the important causes of these and numerous other difficulties."[19]

Graham had a steep mountain of adversity to overcome in changing America's eating habits. He moved slowly upward, and constantly encountered obstacles. Nevertheless, he encouraged like-minded individuals to lead their unphysiologic, meat-eating neighbors up the mountain, and he believed that, eventually, all would reach the peak.

JACKSONIAN ERA: DINING HABITS

The time was right for Sylvester Graham. It was the Jacksonian era, a time when Americans examined the promises of Democracy, and found them lacking fulfillment. Reformers (activists) were everywhere. They were critical of much, including slavery, women's inequality, oppressive working conditions, prisons, education, taxation, and the medical profession.

Industrialization brought rapid and dramatic change to America. Forests were felled, buildings were constructed, trains puffed along tracks, and a system of dirt roads connected state to state. A long exodus began of farm families from bucolic towns to noisy, frenetic cities where smokestacks pumped pollutants into the air. Men were leaving the farm for the factory, and women were purchasing white bread at the bakery, instead of baking their own whole grain loaves. Dyspepsia, a group of symptoms affecting the gastrointestinal area, was a common complaint among Americans.

Dining at restaurants of the day was an adventure in grease and booze. Buffets containing as many as two dozen types of flesh foods (heavily spiced with pepper or mustard) and mounds of pastry were washed down with gallons of liquor. Portliness and gout were common among men, as was fainting among women, who were restricted in bone-deforming corsets and heavy skirts. To overeat was common, to be overweight was considered healthful, and dyspepsia was not connected to diet in most people's reasoning.

Several writers of the era described American eating habits, which were far removed from Graham's ideal of light meals of foods from the plant kingdom, raw or lightly cooked. In the widely read book *Domestic Manners of the Americans*, author Mrs. Frances Trollope, who visited the United States in 1828, observed that: "the 'tea' is announced, when they all console themselves for whatever they may have suffered in keeping awake, by taking more tea, coffee, ("white" flour) hot cake and custard, hoe cake, Johnny cake, waffle cake, and dodger cake, pickled peaches and preserved cucumbers, ham, turkey, hung beef, applesauce, and pickled oysters, than ever were prepared in any other country of the known world."[20] Trollope also noted the American love affair with meat:

They consume an extraordinary quantity of bacon. Ham and beef-steaks appear morning, noon, and night. In eating, they mix things together with the strangest incongruity imaginable. I have seen eggs and oysters together; the sempiternal ham with apple-sauce; beef-steak with stewed peaches; and salt fish with onions. The ("white") bread is everywhere excellent, but they rarely enjoy it themselves, as they insist upon eating horrible half-baked hot rolls both morning and evening. The butter is tolerable, but they seldom have cream as every little dairy produces in England; in fact, the cows are roughly kept, compared with ours.[21]

Other foods Trollope noted as prevalent on American tables: Indian corn as hominy, served green, or as flour made into cakes; rock and shad fish; canvas back ducks; and desserts. "They are 'extravagantly fond' to use their own phrase, of puddings, pies, and all kinds of 'sweets,' particularly the ladies.... " explained Trollope. Water was drunk with meals, and coffee or tea was served at teatime, she wrote.

Another well-known author, Harriet Martineau, who visited America in 1834, wrote that in South Carolina she had dined on "broiled venison, the ham collops and eggs, and apple-sauce; the infusion which is called tea or coffee; and the reeking corn-bread." At another home: "the dinner is plentiful, including of course, turkey, ham, and sweet potatoes; excellent claret, and large blocks of ice cream."[22]

In New Orleans, Martineau saw more of the same: "Excellent coffee, French bread, radishes, and strawberries at breakfast; and at dinner, broth, fowls, beefsteak, with peas, young asparagus, salad, new potatoes, and spinach, all well cooked; claret at dinner, and coffee worthy of Paris after it..."[23]

GRAHAM BREAD

More than 150 years before modern medicine would prove fiber necessary in the diet, Graham published his *Treatise on Bread, and Bread Making*. In it he explained that Americans made two major errors in diet: they ate meat and they ate white flour. He stated that the body required fiber (although he did not use that term), and removing the bran from the wheat, and adulterating it in other ways, made it injurious to health. Today it is widely known that fiber in the diet is beneficial; for example, nutrition authorities recommend dietary fiber to help prevent some diseases.

Graham taught that bread from the bakery should be avoided, and instead bread should be home baked from coarsely ground whole wheat flour. This type of flour was deemed Graham flour after the crusader who advocated it. Thus, crackers made with the flour became known as Graham crackers. Although Graham could have become financially prosperous if he attached his name to any product, he believed he was on a mission from God to help humanity, and even though he was frequently in dire financial straights, did not promote any product.

Social upheaval caused by industrialization brought the increasing adulteration of food—including additives in bread such as lime and sawdust. Graham advised that bread be baked at home by the mother for assurance that the bread was not tainted.

Rather than wanting to retreat from society, Graham's "hearty and fervent desire" was to benefit his fellow human beings by teaching them to improve their diet and their health, and therefore gain happiness. Graham attempted to reform society by offering Americans self-empowerment at a time when they were ignorant of how their daily habits affected their health.

He thought the bread of America had become a symbol of sickness, not of life; the germ was removed from the bread, it was whitened, and other additives were mixed in. Graham believed wheat should be grown in virgin soil that had not been debauched by use of manure.[24] Graham thought the quality of wheat and other crops could be improved if his physiological principles were applied to farming, such as the use of green manure, meaning nitrogen-rich cover crops, as fertilizer.

Graham knew his health crusade went against the grain of society. The greater public lived to eat, and gave little or no regard to the consequences of a bad diet. Moreover, meat eating and the eating of bad bread were inextricably melded, Graham believed. He also believed bakers cared more about cash than the quality of bread or the health of Americans.

Regarding commercial bakers' use of additives and removal of the bran, Graham was not optimistic that the practices would soon cease. He wrote: "I have very little expectation that proper attention will be paid to this subject, so long as the dietetic habits of society continue to be what they are. While the various preparations of animal food constitute so important a portion of human aliment, the quality of bread will be greatly disregarded and neglected, and people will continue almost universally to be cursed with poor bread."[25]

Graham was convinced poor eating habits were so entrenched in the culture as to be practically impenetrable. He explained this in *Treatise on Bread, and Bread Making:* "(But) while the people of our country are so entirely given up as they are at present, to gross and promiscuous feeding on the dead carcasses of animals, and to the untiring pursuits of wealth, it is perhaps wholly in vain for a single individual to raise his voice on the subject of this kind. The farmer will continue to be most eager to increase the number of acres, and to extort from those acres the greatest amount of produce, with the least expense of tillage, and with little or no regard to the quality of that produce in relation to the physiological interests of man; while the people generally, are contented to gratify their depraved appetites on whatever comes before them, without pausing to inquire whether their indulgences are adapted to preserve or to destroy their health and life."[26]

JACKSONIAN ERA: MEDICINE

Not only had humankind gone down the wrong path of eating, they were all mixed up about health in general, thought Sylvester Graham. People believed sickness came about mysteriously, striking at the whim of God.

"At a time when Christians in general viewed disease as a divine punishment for sin, health reformers indicated that disease was generally caused by man himself. They had adopted the rationalistic principle of cause and effect. Whatever one sows he shall reap, both morally and physically. Health reformers attributed the major cause of man's suffering to transgression of God's laws—the moral laws in the Decalogue and the physical laws of nature," wrote historian Gerard P. Damsteegt.[27]

Graham taught that sickness did not strike at random, or out of God's malice; rather, Graham warned that people brought sickness upon themselves by unwittingly violating God's laws of life. The solution to sickness, and the way to living a long, happy life, then, was to change one's habits and prevent poor health. This was a radical view, but it attracted Americans.

That era was marked by a general dislike and distrust of doctors. The doctor was regarded "as more than half a sorcerer," wrote William Alcott, M.D., in 1859.[28] When a man could not succeed at practical skills needed for other trades, people laughingly pointed out that he should become a physician. Although they tended to avoid, and fear, doctors, when they were sick enough or suffering in pain, some forsook home remedies and sought to be cured by a physician and his loathsome potions and other treatments.

It is debatable what Americans feared more: diseases like cholera or doctors. The drugs and treatments administered by the doctors were frequently worse than the symptoms they purported to alleviate. Graham and other reformers of the day contended the doctors were deadlier than any disease.

Jacksonian Americans, educated by reformers, were critical of their country's social inequities, including its established medicine, and they wanted a remedy. Graham and his generation deeply believed in democracy and demanded it be applied to all professions. "Jacksonian Democracy made them suspicious of pretenders to exclusive learning or supporters of monopolistic professions," wrote John B. Blake, Chief of History of Medicine, National Library of Medicine.[29] The allopathic medical profession required elitist credentials, and it even employed legislation to protect against competing forms of medicine—factors that more reform-minded Jacksonians deemed antidemocractic.

Reformers questioned the medical profession, as had some allopaths themselves, including Benjamin Rush, M.D., likely the most influential doctor of the day, friend of Thomas Paine, and a signer of the U.S. Constitution. Rush had stated "unless we put medical freedom into the Constitution, the time will come when medicine will organize into an undercover dictatorship.... To restrict the art of healing to one class of men and deny equal privileges to others will constitute the Bastille of medical science. All such laws are un-American and despotic...and have no place in a Republic.... The Constitution of this republic should make special privilege for medical freedom as well as religious freedom."[30]

Benjamin Rush was a champion of bleeding to treat ailments—a common practice criticized even within the allopathic circles—but he was skeptical of the medical profession's drugging and dosing, as it was termed. Later in the nineteenth century, one of the most illustrious of critics against drugging and dosing was Oliver Wendell Holmes. He stated, "If the whole materia medica, as now used, could be sunk to the bottom of the sea, it would be better for all mankind,—and all the worse for the fishes."[31]

The *materia medica* was the list of substances used by doctors on their patients. Health crusaders were opposed to these typical medical remedies and other treatments of the era, which included such practices as administering powerful purgative agents, bleeding people (sometimes using leeches), cauterizing (burning) them, and even withholding water when the patient had a fever.

At least one American, Yale-educated Isaac Jennings, M.D., of Connecticut, conducted his own experiment regarding the effectiveness of medicines. Concerned that the medicines did not help his patients, and that they instead caused harm, without the patients' knowledge he gave them placebos—bread shaped like pills.

To Jennings's surprise, the placebos worked; his patients, some who had been sickly for years, recovered. The doctor figured out a number of laws that he believed governed the human body, laws that kept it healthy and caused it to heal itself when needed, and he believed that when the laws were broken the result was sickness and eventual death.[32]

Jennings kept his let-alone system of healing a secret. He prescribed vegetarian diet as part of his system, and became a vegetarian, having been convinced by evidence provided by his colleague, health reformer William Alcott, M.D., on the benefits of a flesh-free diet.

When Jennings's bread pill secret was revealed, his patients and some colleagues were extremely displeased. The patients insisted that the doctor then provide medicine. He would not, and his career was damaged. Jennings kept to his system (he named it Orthopathy) and published books on the subject such as *The Tree of Life; Or Human Degeneracy: Its Nature And Remedy, As Based On The Elevating Principle of Orthopathy.*

Americans might not have been aware of, or approving of, Jennings's study, but, stated historian Blake, people were "deathly sick of calomel, they turned in droves to the minute doses of homeopathy, the 'vegetable' drugs of the Thomsonians and eclectics, or the pure cold water of the hydropaths. Others turned to prevention…to state action…to individualistic, moral reform."[33]

Alternative forms of medicine—including that which relied on the body to heal itself without drugs, which was a rejection of medicine, not an actual alternative—were apparently rising in use during the days when Graham's fame was growing. Proponents of alternatives, or no medicine at all, tended to be more open, even favorable, to Graham's ideas, including the avoidance of flesh food.

In short, conditions in the nation were ripe for a crusader like Sylvester Graham. Into the chaos over the cholera epidemic came Graham, bursting onto the national scene like a tornado, upturning common notions about health and sickness. Yet what Graham offered the panic-stricken, petrified nation was a life preserver. His basic message was one of empowerment. Rather than waiting fearfully for God to strike with the cholera, people could take measures, especially in diet, to prevent sickness, Graham said. That human beings caused their own sickness was a strange new notion to most in Jacksonian America, but one that apparently made sense to a significant number of people. Graham reassured the public that they need not fear drugging and dosing doctors, because they would not need them, if they took preventive measures.

Graham became famous. His lectures attracted thousands. It was not uncommon for a Graham lecture to be attended by more than 2,000 people, which occurred in Rochester, New York, and New York City. He evoked strong reactions: some saw him as a savior of America's health, and others, as a threat to health or business, an ultra to be ridiculed, challenged, and stopped.

That Graham generally commanded attention and respect from some is evident from press accounts of his lectures, as well as from letters about him published in newspapers and journals. One editor, in announcing the crusader's forthcoming lecture series, wrote: "Mr. Graham's lecture, tomorrow evening, will be on the subject of the sensorial power of the nervous system and peculiar organization of the brain, as connected with the intellectual and moral faculties and manifestations of man. The first series of these Lectures has been attended by a large and respectable class, who, so far as we have learned, have listened to them with undiminished interest and satisfaction. We are desired to say that the Lecture to-morrow evening will be at Masonic Hall."[34]

Initially discovered by the upper classes of society, the masses of Americans eventually learned of Graham. In his lectures, and later in his writings, Graham advised those seeking health to abandon all medicine, liquor, coffee, tea, meat, butter, and milk (the latter not preferred and allowed only in small quantities and diluted). They were to drink water, toast water, or water gruel; eat food in its natural state, unspiced; and especially eat bolted wheat bread and fruit for regularity. Cleaning and exercising the skin with a brush was also advised.

Graham thought it necessary to compile testimonials from people who benefited from his system, especially because of accusations against it and him. Graham compiled comments from admirers who had been helped by his system into a book, called *Aesculapian Tablets of the Nineteenth Century*.

No one knows exactly how many Americans considered him a hero. But one of the people grateful to Graham was Temple Fay of New York, who had written to the crusader in February of 1833. Fay had for more than two decades suffered from recurring, severe headaches. Then, a few years prior to 1833, he had also developed chronic dyspepsia.

He explained in his letter to Graham: "I ate flesh quite freely.... I was extremely fond of gravy, which I used plentifully. I assure you. I also ate pudding, pies, etc., drank tea and coffee, and smoked plenty of cigars..." Several doctors had advised Fay, and each offered different advice including to eat cassia, use dyspeptic bitters, take epsom salts, use plenty of mustard on meat, and drink brandy and water with dinner. Yet another doctor had advised Fay to abstain from animal flesh, while still others told him to eat less food, or to eat more food.[35]

Then in August of 1831, Fay, who had debated with friends against Graham's system, especially the diet, attended the crusader's lecture series. To Fay's astonishment, despite his admitted prejudice against Grahamism, "I found my opposition so shaken, that I was unable to bring into existence one argument..."[36]

By May of 1832, Fay "left off using coffee, tea, flesh, all kinds of spices, peppers, mustard, preserves and the like; and in great measure dispensed with all kinds of pastry, and discarded entirely, alcoholic beverages of every kind, and even went beyond your instructions and quit the use of salt." Fay's diet then consisted of "rice and milk, hominy, and wamp and milk, etc...Graham bread, potatoes, turnips, squashes, beans, cabbages, etc..."[37]

He stated all of this in his letter to Graham, and explained the result of his dietary change: "Almost as soon as I commenced living on your system, my health began to improve, and I continued to grow better very fast, until all my symptoms and ailments left me, and I was restored to good health; and since then I have enjoyed the most perfect, uninterrupted health, to the present moment; and in no one instance have I felt the slightest indisposition, that I could not trace immediately to the violation of your rules."[38]

In a statement similar to those made by others who proclaimed their health had been saved by Graham, Fay told the crusader: "Please accept, sir, this statement, imperfect as it is, as a cordial tribute of respect and gratitude, from him who is, and I trust ever will be, your humble, sincere, and devoted servant."[39] Evidently, with such devotion offered, and so many in desperate need, Graham could have exploited the sick for financial gain.

In his book, Graham explained that countless people approached him seeking an instant cure for their health woes. He told them that he had none to offer. Rather than attempt to make money off of the sick by offering some cure-all, Graham chose to teach them what he believed would enable them to help themselves. Graham was on a spiritual mission of saving souls and bodies and not working a get-rich-quick scheme.

He wrote: "I have no specific to sell; and therefore no money to make or lose, whether these statements are believed or not. But the cause of humanity has an immense interest in the issue of this matter. The vis medicatrix which I contend for, is none other than the renovating and conservative power of nature's own vital economy. The remedy which I propose, is in the reach of every human being, and demands no price. The appropriation of it to ten thousand individuals, would not enrich me a farthing, save in the grateful satisfaction I should experience, from the consciousness of having been the means of alleviating the suffering of my fellow-creatures."[40]

Graham urged people who had benefited from his system to come forward and tell their stories. "The cause of humanity demands this, and they ought not to withhold their testimony."[41] Today testimonials are considered part of quackery, especially since they were used by sellers of patent medicines (snake oil salesmen), and therefore the veracity of the testimonials was questionable. The writers of letters to Graham were likely in earnest. They included some well-known, highly regarded individuals such as Asenath Hatch Nicholson, who established a Graham boarding house about 1832 in the impoverished Five Points neighborhood of New York City—the poorest neighborhood of the metropolis. She was later author of a book on health and vegetarianism titled *Nature's Own Book*. Still later, Nicholson would make a name internationally ministering

to the poor of Ireland, where she preached Christianity and taught vegetarianism. About humankind's meat-eating practice, Nicholson wrote in
Nature's Own Book: "he eats for the low purpose of gratifying a morbid
appetite, regardless of consequences, and then complains of the cruel,
unavoidable curse."[42] Vermont-born Nicholson stated:

Let us go back to first principles, and, while bewailing the curse entailed upon us
by our first parents, see how far this curse would have affected us, had we obeyed
the original laws of nature. When God placed man in the garden, he said: "Behold,
I have given you every herb bearing seed, which is upon the face of the earth, and
every tree, in which is the fruit of a tree, yielding seed; to you it shall be for meat;
mark, he did not say, every animal in earth, sea and air shall be your meat—nor
did he make one distant allusion to the necessity of eating any. But what followed?
Eve committed the first sin, by eating prohibited food, and the curse ensued, the
natural consequences of disobedience; and now let us not mistake the nature of
this curse. God did not pass an irrevocable decree, that man should be miserable if
he followed the original laws of nature...facts in all ages prove, that when man
has obeyed those laws, he has been universally healthy, cheerful, and more happy
than miserable.[43]

Another writer who advocated Grahamism was Dr. John Burdell, a den-
tist. Burdell argued that human teeth had not been designed to chew meat.
He wrote on diet and digestion in *The Health Almanac,* a periodical that
featured articles about vegetarianism. Burdell's views were published in a
book *Observations on the Structure, Physiology, Anatomy and Diseases of the
Teeth; in Two Parts.*[44] Burdell, who illustrated his writings on the teeth and
anatomy, also wrote on this topic and vegetarian diet in the pages of
Youth's Cabinet, a popular children's magazine.

GRAHAM IN THE PRESS

People everywhere were writing about Grahamism. The crusader's
name was now attached to the coarsely ground whole wheat bread he recommended—there was Graham bread, Graham meal, and Graham flour.
Even the eminent and popular Transcendentalist philosopher and lecturer
Ralph Waldo Emerson referred to Graham. He crowned him "prophet of
bran bread and pumpkins," a title not necessarily meant as ridicule.

During January of 1834, when Graham was lecturing in Providence,
Rhode Island, some merchants noted his presence in the city in newspaper
advertisements for their wares. For example, J.F. Crocker announced in an
ad for his food store: "Just received, Graham meal; and Buck Wheat Flour,
free from grit."[45]

Not everyone in Providence was pleased with Graham. Some who were
displeased felt compelled to note this in their advertisements. W. Din-
neford in an ad for his Confectionery and Pastry store offerings was defi-

ant. The ad read in part: "Among the delicacies which he has in store for the epicure (Doctor Graham to the contrary notwithstanding)..."[46]

Another merchant, that is, one who sold meat, announced in an ad: "Hams—Hams—Hams—Samuel Young, has just taken from the smoke house, a prime lot of yellow hams, not Grayhams, as he does not deal in that article—also on hand, smoked Beef, just cured, pickled salmon; No. 1 Mackerel; sounds and tongue; salt Pork; butter, cheese and lard. He invites all his friends—but those especially not fond of Grayhams, to call and exchange their cash for any of the above artifacts..."[47]

Graham's regimen had become known to Americans through his extensive lecturing across the Northeast, through word of mouth, and through reports published in newspapers and magazines. Graham, and a few others who espoused eschewing flesh and other health reforms and who taught how the human body functioned, became known as physiologists. The word was also at that time used as a synonym for a teacher of Grahamism; that is, an advocate of vegetarianism who taught that the human body was best suited to digest food from plants, and that meat and other stimulating substances had an adverse effect on the body.

"By 1835–36, the newspapers were full of Graham's preachments, often poking fun at the master's oracular dogmatism, yet spreading the knowledge of his regimen, too," wrote historian Gerald Carson in *The American Heritage Cookbook and Illustrated History of American Eating and Drinking.*[48]

Newspaper articles about Graham's system forwarded the fledgling vegetarian movement. People in areas far from cities where Graham lectured learned from the press that he was preaching a way to prevent disease that required rejection of meat eating. For most of these individuals, this was likely the first they had heard that human beings could, and should, live without meat in their diets.

A typical article on Grahamism was published in *The Boston Palladium* newspaper, and later published in *The Hampshire Gazette.*

As there are a variety of opinions on the Lectures of Dr. Graham, which were delivered in this city, during the last winter; and as many of your readers have received much knowledge from them, it is desirable that the substance of them should appear in your journal.... Although man can adapt himself to almost any and every kind of aliment, there are certain kinds which are better suited to his real physical wants, to health and long life. So far as man deviates from Nature, he becomes more liable to disease, short life, etc. The best manner of living in civil life is as follows:—The chief food should be vegetables and fruit, to be eaten in as near their natural state as possible. Bread should be made of unbolted wheat (that being in natural state) is the best, although if made of rye or Indian, it would answer, if unbolted. Rice, sago, Etc, are very wholesome, if plainly cooked. Butter should be used sparingly and cold, and none but fresh and sweet—cream is a good substitute. Milk, eggs and honey are substances somewhat of the nature between animal and vegetable, and are allowed if desired ....[49]

Graham explained in his lectures that if one were to eat meat, and he did not recommend it, then it should only be the flesh of animals who lived naturally. The flesh should be eaten plainly cooked, without spices, frying, or gravy, and not served in soup. He said that invalids and others who were sedentary must never eat meat, and that everyone should avoid pastry (pastry in those days was usually made with lard and adulterated flour). Graham also advised people to masticate food thoroughly, drink only water, eat regular meals (no more than three a day), not eat large quantities of food, bathe regularly in warm or cold water, avoid overly soft beds, dress in loose clothing that is not too warm, and ventilate their homes.

Before the decade would end, people could read Graham's teachings. His *Lectures on the Science of Human Life,* in two volumes, was published in 1839. He planned a separate volume on vegetarianism in the Bible but did not complete it.

WILLIAM ALCOTT

Sylvester Graham was not alone in his attempt to awaken America to the vegetarian message. Others appeared on the regional and national platform, and although they had an effect, they evidently never evoked as strong a reaction as did Graham. Yet they made their own contributions to the movement.

Of these advocates, William Andrus Alcott, M.D., appeared on the vegetarian scene almost simultaneously with Graham. After Graham, Alcott was apparently the nation's second most influential health reformer. If not for the fact that Graham's fame—and notoriety—overshadowed Alcott, Alcott might today be the father of American vegetarianism.

Before advocating abstinence from animal foods, Alcott was a prominent progressive educationalist, and a leading health reformer. The doctor reached people with his message of health through the magazines he published. One was titled *The Moral Reformer and Teacher on the Human Constitution,* which he established in 1835 in Boston, where he practiced medicine. In the first year of publication the magazine addressed "the causes of vice and disease in the errors of the family, the school, the factory, the counting room,—indeed in all the varied employments and modes of life." The publication also covered "the multiplied evils connected with eating and drinking improper substances and improper quantities of wholesome substances, but also those connected with quackery, dosing, exercise, dress, and improper mental and moral habits."[50]

Alcott wrote on these health reform topics and more for his magazine, and in most of his 113 published books and booklets. "Dr. Alcott's works have been very popular," reported writer Samuel Austin Alliborne in 1859 in his *A Critical Dictionary of English Literature and British American Authors.*[51]

William Alcott: *Vegetable Diet* author. Courtesy of
William Dailey.

In an article for *The Moral Reformer* titled "Fifty Years Ago" Alcott
explained why the subjects he addressed urgently needed America's
attention: the health of the people was deteriorating. He stated that a half
century earlier "few of the hardy sons and daughters of New England:
wore flannel and leather under-garments; used umbrellas to shelter the
head from the sun and rain almost unknown...; (they were) travelers—(in
the) habit of either walking or riding on horseback; (there was) little muf-
fling up in close carriages, either public or private; houses, too, were very
far from being so tight and hot as to (not) admit a breath of cold air, even
in midwinter."[52]

Alcott asked his readers, "Were our ancestors of fifty years ago less
healthy and happy than we of the present generation? Have bodily and
mental vigor and moral progress, kept pace with the introduction of
stoves, and carpets, and flannel, and India rubbers, and umbrellas, and
covered carriages? Do men live longer, as well as happier, than before?

Have we less consumption, and rheumatism, and liver complaint, and fever?"[53]

Life had changed and was continuing to change at an even quicker pace then when Alcott was a boy, and it alarmed him to observe what he thought was decline in the physical and moral strength of New England and the nation. Like Graham, Alcott was not seeking a return to primitiveness, but to help Americans be healthier and stronger, and therefore, the reformers reasoned, happier.

A transcript of a conversation on vegetarianism published in his magazine, *The Moral Reformer,* between Alcott and a stranger, which occurred in 1836 near Boston, provides an account of the typical questions asked of vegetarians of the day.

The meat eater, after ascertaining that Alcott ate no meat, fish, butter, or cheese, asked him "But do not the teeth and intestines indicate that we are formed to use a mixture of animal and vegetable food?" Alcott replied "They do not," and said that man was naturally frugivorous, meant to eat fruit and nuts. The stranger then brought up a common perception of the era that vegetarian populations are feeble.[54]

AMERICAN PHYSIOLOGICAL SOCIETY

Alcott and Sylvester Graham pooled their talents as leaders of the American Physiological Society, an organization founded in 1837 by Colonel John Benson, a Grahamite. The colonel was typical of the APS's members. According to Alcott, most, if not all of the members suffered from chronic disease and no longer ate meat. Benson, who was a prominent, prosperous Boston merchant in his 50s, became a Graham devotee after attending the crusader's lectures.

The APS was established for the teaching of physiology, anatomy, and especially diet. Due to the focus on diet, it soon became known as a Grahamite, that is, vegetarian, society. Many members of the APS suffered from physical ailments—near invalids long in search of health. That APS members were sickly, and that a few of the members died while involved in the organization, did not improve the image of Grahamism. It only reinforced the cultural belief that refusal to eat meat led to emaciation, feebleness, and death.

The formation of the APS was a milestone for the vegetarian movement. Not attached to a religion, as was the Bible-Christian's vegetarian events, the APS was likely the first exclusively vegetarian organization in the United States. It was also likely the first natural hygiene organization in the nation.

The APS was a platform for the promulgation of the ideas of Graham, and those of Alcott. The Society taught people about the human anatomy and physiology—and the principles of Grahamism and Dr. Alcott's work.

"Graham's work...was really scientific in the sense that it included the current physiology as well as hygiene; it having always been his contention that the latter must rest on a rational basis of 'physiological principles.' For this reason he became an ardent advocate of the popular teaching of physiology, and his followers were perhaps the first group to urge its introduction in the public schools," stated historian Richard Harrison Shyrock.[55]

The society held its first meeting on March 7 in Boston and named Alcott as the first president, David Cambell as the secretary, and Nathaniel Perry as treasurer. Benson served as a vice president.

The APS hired Mary Gove (later Nichols) to present lectures to women. As a youth, Mary Sargeant Neal, born 1810 in New Hampshire, had been plagued with poor health, and experienced the ineffectiveness and unpleasant side effects of the typical medical treatments of the time. Sickly but uncommonly smart, young Nichols had an appetite for books, including those on health, and became a health practitioner. After studying with allopaths and finding their methods unsatisfactory, she studied water cure techniques, and, after experimenting with the techniques on herself, began treating others.

About 1837, Mary Gove became a vegetarian after reading Graham's works. She attributed her good health—that is, her recovery from lingering consumption—to her simple vegetarian diet. "I have no doubt that, other things being equal, human life is lengthened by a vegetarian diet."[56]

Soon after becoming a vegetarian—a Grahamite—she began lecturing for the Ladies Physiological Society, an offshoot of the American Physiological Society. Gove was the first woman in America to lecture on topics of anatomy and physiology and she included lessons on vegetarianism, and prevention and cure of sickness. On vegetarianism Gove stated: "I have seen cancer checked in its progress and cured, or at least rendered inactive through a life of many years, by the use of a simple sparing diet without flesh, grease of any kind, salt, or irritating condiments. I have seen many severe cases of indigestion cured in the same manner."[57]

She lectured to audiences of approximately 200–700 women in cities such as Boston, New York, and Providence. Gove illustrated her lectures with charts provided by medical doctors, and later with models of internal organs she had created for her talks. Accounts of Gove's lectures were published in the *Graham Journal of Health and Longevity*.

Gove had some allies in the medical profession who applauded her educational efforts, but was criticized by other medical professionals and by newspaper editors. Despite criticism, Gove was influential. Later, in the next decade, other women would lecture on anatomy, physiology, and plant-based diets.

Gove empowered women to take control of their health. She taught women that physical strength was integral if they were to become inde-

THE

GRAHAM JOURNAL

OF HEALTH AND LONGEVITY.

HE THAT STRIVETH FOR THE MASTERY, IS TEMPERATE IN ALL THINGS.—Paul.

VOL. III.]   BOSTON AND NEW YORK, SATURDAY, FEB. 16, 1839.   [No. 4.

MORAL AND PHYSICAL REFORM IDENTICAL.

[The following interesting letter is from the pen and heart of a clergyman, formerly a physician, who is an indefatigable laborer in every good "word and work." After the usual address, and acknowledging himself "under much obligation" to us for favors to which he is thrice welcome, the writer proceeds.—]

Most heartily, dear sir, do I wish you success in the great work to which your Journal is devoted. What the Gospel is to the Moral, such is the cause you espouse, to the Physical world of Mankind. And as the Gospel of our Saviour, acting directly upon the soul, and through that medium, indirectly upon the physical constitution, forbids and prevents practices destructive of health and life—so the principles of Physiological Reform, acting directly upon the physical constitution, in preventing or reforming such bodily habits as weaken the virtuous faculties and strengthen the corrupt propensities, indirectly bless the soul. The connections between physical and moral evil are numerous, close, and mighty. It is plain that the redemption of the moral world, and the redemption of the physical constitution of mankind, must proceed together. The promotion of one, is, in general, the promotion of the other of these great interests—if, indeed, they may be regarded as being, to some extent, distinct interests. Extinguish the Gospel, that Sun of the Intellectual world; and what would become of physical temperance! Let temperance cease—let the laws of our physical nature all be disregarded and violated; and what becomes of the influence of the Gospel! Ah, there is an inseparability here, an identity, so close and so important, that description seems all powerless for the delineation, and the mind is overwhelmed beneath the considerations so vast and numerous, flowing from a contemplation of these subjects and their connections.

Although educated to the Medical profession, I had paid very little attention to the laws of health, until having been several years in practice. This may seem to some a paradox. Well, then it is a paradox which attaches to that noble profession generally. Here is the solution: the profession study the laws of disease, rather than the laws of health. I have termed it a noble profession: so I regard it, although no longer of it, practically. And I am expecting it to become far more excellent. If, while the profession regards little else

The Graham Journal of Health and Longevity.

pendent and attain equality to men. Gove was a leading advocate of women's rights, having had a difficult marriage to Hiram Gove that ended in divorce, and for a time lost of custody of their child. Only after tremendous effort and many years did Gove regain custody of her child.

Paulina Wright Davis, a leading feminist and editor of *Una*, a women's rights magazine, founded the Physiological Society in Providence, not long after Gove lectured in that city. On March 28, 1838, Gove founded the Graham boarding school for young ladies on Broad Street in Lynn, Massachusetts (board $2.00 per week, tuition $2.00 per quarter), where she lectured and also taught needlework (a talent which had financially supported her and her spouse).[58] In 1840 she studied with Joel Shew, the acclaimed hydropathist. When not studying, teaching, or lecturing, Gove was editing vegetarian health magazines and writing fiction. No less a literary figure than Edgar Allan Poe praised Gove's fiction, which she wrote under the name Mary Orme. One of her works of fiction was a novel based upon her life.

THE VEGETABLE DIET

Like Gove, Alcott was a prolific writer. Several of his books promoted vegetarianism; one, *Vegetable Diet: As Sanctioned by Medical Men, and by Experience in all Ages* was a compilation of the doctor's and the vegetarian movement's reasons for choosing grains, vegetables, fruits, and nuts instead of meat.

Alcott's book also provided information on ancient cultures such as the Pythagoreans and Essenes that ate no meat, as well as information on the Bible-Christians and the American Physiological Society. *Vegetable Diet*, apparently a popular and influential book, presented seven arguments used by Alcott and other members of the vegetarian movement:[59]

- Anatomical: The teeth, based on evidence from Cuvier, and the length of the intestine, favor foods from the plant kingdom.

- Physiological: Vegetable eaters need less food, and less often, claimed Alcott, and have "a more quiet, happy and perfect digestion than the flesh-eater." Vegetarians perspire less, tend not to have dry skin, smell better, suffer less thirst, will not crave alcohol, and have better temperament.

- Medical: Vegetable diet best promotes and preserves perfect health. Grahamites are less likely to get cholera: "There is abundant testimony to be had, going to show that a vegetable diet is a security against disease, especially against epidemics, whether in the form of a mere influenza or malignant fever," he wrote.

- Political: "Political economists tell us that the produce of an acre of land in wheat, corn, potatoes, other vegetables, and fruits will sustain animal life 16 times as long as when the produce of the same acre is converted into flesh by feeding and fattening animals upon it."

- Economical: It costs much less to feed a family on the vegetable diet than it does to raise animals for them to eat.

- Experience: Most people in the world are vegetable eaters out of necessity rather than choice. "Over half of the 800 million of human beings which inhabit our globe (are vegetarian); or, if they get meat at all, it is so rarely that it can hardly have any effect on their structure or character."

- Moral: "How can it be right to be instrumental in so much unnecessary slaughter. How can it be right, especially for a country of vegetable abundance like ours to give daily employment to 20 thousand or 30 thousand butchers? How can it be right to train our children to behold such slaughter? How can it be right to blunt the edge of their moral sensibilities, by placing before them, at almost every meal, the mangled corpses of the slain; and not only placing them there, but rejoicing while we feast upon them?"

Alcott gave much credit to Graham for educating the public. Alcott stated in *Vegetable Diet* that Graham "has probably done more to reduce the subject of vegetable dietetics to a system (ital) than any other individual,—though he makes much use of all (ital) the rest, especially the moral and medical,—appears to dwell with most interest on the physiological argument. This seems to be, with him, the stronghold—the grand citadel. And it must be confessed that the point of defence is very strong indeed..."[60]

Like Graham, the doctor had studied the diet of human beings and the other laws of human health. For example, he wrote books on the health and moral evils of use of tobacco, coffee, and tea. In 1832, he anonymously published a pamphlet on his observations and ideas on diet titled "Rational View of the Spasmodic Cholera."[61]

A year later, the Boylston Medical Committee of Harvard University offered a prize for the essay which best addressed the problem of "What diet can be selected which will ensure the greatest health and strength to the laborer in the climate of New England—quality and quantity, and the time and manner of taking it, to be considered."[62] The prize was awarded to Derry, New Hampshire physician Luther V. Bell, M.D. Alcott had planned to offer a dissertation, but instead, months later, he learned that Dr. Milo L. North, "a distinguished professor of medicine in Hartford, Connecticut," was attempting to survey vegetarians.

Diet was very much on the minds of those in the medical community, and evidently enough people were rejecting meat for North to want to study the results. Also, stories were circulating in the medical community and in society that Grahamism was causing people to become weak, sick, insane, and it was even killing some of them. North wanted to either verify or dispel these rumors.

His survey questions were published in the *Boston Medical and Surgical Journal (BMSJ)* in February of 1835, and in the *American Journal of Medical of Medical Science,* as well as in a plethora of newspapers. North stated his reason for conducting the survey: "Reports not unfrequently reach us of certain individuals who have falled victim to a prescribed course of regimen. Those persons are said, by gentlemen who are entitled to the fullest confidence, to have pertinaciously followed the course, till they reached a point of reduction from which there was no recovery. If these are facts, they ought to be collected and published....There are, in our community, considerable numbers who have entirely excluded animal food from their diet. It is exceedingly desirable that the results of such experiments, so difficult to be found in this land of plenty, should be ascertained and thrown before the profession and the community..."[63]

During that same time period, Dr. Bell's prize-winning essay was published in *BMSJ* and garnered much attention. The doctor had stated that human beings did best on a mixed diet, meaning one that included meat. Graham, who had also entered an essay into the contest, was evidently not happy that he lost. He believed that the vegetable diet was the key to health, and he explained this in a letter to *BMSJ*. The letter drew criticism from medical men.

Meanwhile, replies to North's vegetarian survey were received from around the country, mostly from doctors. North had asked 11 questions, such as how excluding animal food had affected strength, thinking ability, digestion, existing infirmities, or incidence of colds, and if the health of laborers or students would be improved if they quit eating animal flesh.

North took sick before his work was finished, so Alcott continued it and added to it. The result was his book *The Vegetable Diet*. Alcott presented replies from North's survey and evidence of the benefits of the diet from renowned physicians and scientists of his time and of the past, such as George Cheyne, William Lambe, Professor Lawrence, and Baron Cuvier.

The Vegetable Diet apparently found an appreciative audience, but the book also caused Alcott, a highly esteemed physician, to become, like Graham, an object of suspicion and scorn by some within the medical community. The two crusaders' work was a catalyst for people to think about vegetarianism, even if most then dismissed it.

One writer in a *BMSJ* article, after mentioning that meat-eating New Englanders were perfectly hearty people, and would have long ago ceased to exist had the vegetarians' claims of the injuriousness of an animal flesh-based diet been true, stated that he wanted to know how Alcott would reconcile such a fact "with the dogma he preaches. Will he attempt to reconcile them—or will he not rather lead us aside to hear Mr. Graham's opinions, and then endeavor to amuse us with some practical illustrations of the effects of the bran-bread and dried apples, spreading out before us his own case, and then, in long array, the cases of half a dozen gaunt, wry-faced, lantern-jawed, ghostly-looking invalids, who, he declares, are so many walking proofs (those that are able to walk) of the beautiful results of his system?"[64]

The writer claimed that not only the invalids, who had eschewed meat eating to better their health, were weaklings, but nearly all vegetarians were weak, as well as neurotic: "...it is almost universally the fact that the vegetable-eaters among us (I do not forget what Dr. Alcott says of himself) are a very complaining sort of people. They are delicate, nervous, dyspeptic, and universally susceptible to all sorts of influences. They have sallow or pale countenances, a lax fibre, little muscular strength, and are incapable of any fatiguing or laborious employment. These characteristics of the vegetable-livers are, doubtless, very often the result of inadequate nourishment, depending on feeble digestive powers and in nutritious diet."[65]

The criticism of Alcott's book and character continued in long articles published in several more issues of the journal. Alcott responded to the articles by stating that he ordinarily ignored personal attacks, but since the attacker was a medical man he respected, he felt obliged to reply. He criticized his critic for failing to understand the subject of vegetable diet.

William Andrus Alcott was born on August 6, 1798, in Wolcott, Connecticut, to a farm family. As a young man, he had suffered from a number of ills, including consumption, but managed to earn the medical degree from Yale University in 1826.

Alcott's road to vegetarian advocacy began in the late 1820s, when he decided to place his health into his own hands. Allopathic physicians of the era were expected to use bloodletting, purging, and medicines such as calomel, but Alcott took a different path that included diet. The Connecticut doctor, according to William Penn Alcott, had suffered from the ill effects of medicine he had been prescribed. At first, he took control of his health by giving up liquor, cutting down on his meat intake, and exercising daily.

Determined to regain his health, he was well on his way to vegetarianism before he had even heard of Sylvester Graham. By 1830, Alcott was eating meat only two or three times a year, and a few years later, he was a vegetarian. Dr. Benjamin Rush's advocacy of a simple diet, free from stimulating food and drink, and the foremost American physician's noting of cases of vegetarianism likely influenced Alcott to a degree. But Alcott was likely more influenced by reading about Benjamin Franklin's experiment with vegetarianism. Among Alcott's reasons for advocating vegetarianism was his belief that in the Bible, in the book of Genesis, God provided foods of the plant kingdom for food.

It was likely that Alcott was a vegan, eschewing all foods derived from animals. He was noted for his seemingly endless energy and his strong physical condition. It was typical for Alcott to rise at four A.M., bathe in cold water, work in his garden, and work late into the evening, but only after praying with his family, writing his books, and treating his patients.

Alcott, trained as a regular (allopathic) doctor, was expected to use the poisons, burning, purging, and other methods of physicians of his time period; after gaining experience as a doctor, he decided those methods were injurious to his patients, so he began emphasizing the body's own healing ability, brought on by proper health habits, including omitting meat from the diet.

Vegetarianism became his number one cause. Initially renowned for advocating educational reform and as a teacher of progressive ideals, Alcott had also worked to improve the unhealthy conditions of school-houses by pioneering improvements in ventilation.

Alcott's *Vegetable Diet,* and other books of his like *The Young Housekeeper* (Boston: George W. Light, 1 Cornhill, 1838), contained arguments for not eating meat. The former book on vegetarianism caused controversy; the *Boston Medical and Surgical Journal,* a publication by colleagues who had respected Alcott, assailed his every argument.

Criticism did not deter Alcott or Graham. At an 1839 meeting of the American Physiological Society, Graham explained that if members could not persuade their neighbors to change their habits to preserve their health, then the members must use moral power to compel people to change, just as abolitionists were using such power to try to change the public's attitude on slavery.

Members of the APS became a community within Boston. They purchased food at the organization's Provision Store, likely the nation's first natural foods store and first vegetarian store. The store, which was located close to the Boston Common, sold a variety of grains such as rye, rice, oats, and corn. Graham flour was always on hand. Beans, tapioca, milk, dyspesia bread, and produce grown on virgin soil not contaminated by manure fertilizer were also sold. Boston became a center of the vegetarian movement.

Within the area between Boston Common and Washington Street were a number of other places that were part of the vegetarian community: the Marsh, Capon and Lyon book publisher and seller, the office of the Graham Journal of Health and Longevity, the site of a lecture hall where Graham spoke, Bronson Alcott's Temple school where he also lectured, and William Alcott's office.

The APS branched out and applauded the coed Physiological Boarding School of Derby, Connecticut, which offered classes in chemistry, astronomy, rhetoric, and English, and served simple vegetarian meals. APS local groups were formed in several cities. In Providence, the society led by Paulina Wright Davis drew hundreds to lectures.

In 1839, Boston APS members listened to a lecture by Asa Mahan, who cofounded Oberlin in northern Ohio with Charles Finney. The founders of the progressive school, Oberlin Collegiate Institute, as it was then known, were Christians intent on creating a training ground for the next generation of reformers. Oberlin was the site of a vegetarian dining hall experiment—one that did not go over well with parents who had heard rumors that students were starving because they were not fed meat or pastry. Behind this experience in meat-free dining was David Cambell, member of the APS, and Alcott, who had spent a few days on the Oberlin campus discussing diet.

Students formed a Graham club. One student contended that his mind burst forth from "debasement and reassumed its pristine vigor" after eliminating meat from his daily diet. Another called vegetarianism, "a cause which lays just claim to the aid of every Christian and philanthropist, and one which must prevail." Some Oberlin students lauded their increased vigor under the vegetable diet. Others ridiculed their schoolmates' self-imposed dietary restrictions:

Venison is vile, a cup of coffee curst,
        And food that's fried, or fricaseed, forgot;
Duck is destruction; wine of woes is worst,
        Clams are condemned, and poultry's gone to pot;
Pudding and Pork are under prohibition,
        Mustard is murder; pepper is perdition.[66]

Nevertheless, Grahamism—that is vegetarianism—spread to other college campuses, including Weselyan in Connecticut.

DR. MUSSEY

Alcott was not the only prominent physician aligned with the APS. Reuben Dimond Mussey, M.D., L.L.D., crusaded against the use of alcohol and for vegetarianism, and became known as an ardent Grahamite. Early in his career, he became renowned in the medical world for his experiments on himself. In one of them, Mussey immersed himself into a bath of madder and other chemicals to prove, among other theories, that the skin absorbs. His conclusion contradicted the teaching of the eminent Dr. Rush.

Mussey, born in 1780, held an array of titles and distinctions, including chair of Theory and Practice at Dartmouth Medical College, and the fourth President of the American Medical Association. He became a vegetarian in 1832 after learning that both Cuvier and Lawrence had pronounced the vegetable diet natural for human beings.

After suffering from dyspepsia, which caused chronic headaches, the doctor abstained from use of liquor, coffee, and tea. He also abstained because it eased his nervous condition that otherwise caused his hands to shake during surgery. Then, in 1848, Mussey developed a severe illness, and at the behest of friends concerned for his health, ate fish and drank a few drops of brandy.

He would later permanently eliminate meat from his diet after developing a cancer on his face. Mussey's father had died of such a cancer. The

Reuben Mussey: Vegetarian who served as president of the AMA. Courtesy of Dartmouth College Library.

son eschewed fish eating, and his cancer disappeared. Although Mussey
had no scientific proof that vegetarianism had led to the healing of his
body, he no longer ate the flesh of fish or any animal. He believed avoiding meat was overall beneficial to his health, and he began an investiga-
tion into why that was so. Other leaders of the vegetarian movement used
the evidence he gathered favoring vegetarianism in an attempt to assure
the public that a diet free of meat was nutritious and natural.

Mussey's studies had led him to conclude that humans were anatomi-
cally and physiologically much more similar to the vegetarian Great Apes
than to carnivorous animals. Naturalists had earlier observed that apes
who ate flesh became sick and some died. Mussey wrote: "The whole ali-
mentary apparatus in man and the orangs is strikingly alike...If in one
this organization is indicative of particular food as best suited to health, is
it not a reasonable inference that the same intention is denoted in the
other?"[67]

The influential physician also looked to the Bible for evidence that man
and woman were meant to partake of foods from the vegetable kingdom
and not the slaughterhouse. Adam and Eve, Mussey realized, were veg-

ans, and that only after the Fall did humanity devour animals. Moreover, Mussey noted that people of certain ancient cultures had been vegetarian and had lived lives far longer than that of his contemporaries. Longevity, Mussey learned, was common until the ancients began eating meat. Like William Alcott, Mussey also wrote against the use of tobacco and alcohol.

He became a Grahamite and leading advocate of vegetarianism, especially in New England, where it was said numerous people, including his medical school students, followed his example. One of Mussey's methods of convincing people that the foods of the vegetable kingdom provided nutrition enough to build strong human bodies was to showcase his teenage son, who was over six feet in height, and, Mussey proclaimed, had never tasted animal flesh.

The doctor was not known for charisma, but he was held in high esteem for his intelligence, leadership, and especially his Christian character. Mussey was also known for his dedication to scientific truth. He would not recommend to others what he did not first approve for himself.

One obstacle confronting Mussey, his colleagues at the APA, and similar groups in New York and Philadelphia was the growing rumor that they planned legislation to compel people to stop eating meat. Graham told his audiences that there was no such plan. "No man living can show an instance in which we have attempted to force on the people our peculiar views, or compel others by moral despotism or any other means, to conform to our dietetic regulations. Had we the power to effect all our purposes we should have no desire to compel the people of this country to submit to our dictum, or unwillingly to change any of their habits," stated Graham.[68]

He further explained that those who did not conform to dietetic regulations were not rendered "disreputable and odious." Graham said that vegetarian leaders ask people to think for themselves and investigate until they find the truth, then "we wish them to communicate it to us and the world, for the common good of the human species."[69]

Another rumor rampant in America was that Grahamites were all dead: they had succumbed to cholera because they refused to eat animal flesh. Graham's ideas were gaining adherents despite rumors and ridicule. Although the crusader was lauded for his work by many people, he was not receiving funding necessary to sustain him as a full-time lecturer and writer. Graham spent time and money on preparing his lectures. He drew and hand colored high-quality posters, styled after illustrations he had seen in French medical textbooks.

A writer in *The Genius of Temperance* informed readers of this situation. "Mr. Graham has spent much time and money in preparing himself for his particular work, and his whole soul is enlisted in the cause of humanity. Ought he not to be sustained and encouraged, and can there be no plan devised to keep him that field of labor, for the cultivation of which he is so admirably qualified?" At one point Graham appealed to Gerritt Smith, the wealthy abolitionist leader and friend of vegetarianism, for financial assistance. Evidently Smith did not reply in the affirmative.[70]

Initially Graham's lectures had garnered praise from the prestigious *Boston Medical and Surgical Journal*, which would eventually be renamed *New England Journal of Medicine*.

We listened attentively, too, for more than one hour and a half, to a discourse that would have reflected honor upon the first medical man in America.... he simply exhibited himself to be a fearless, independent, benevolent expounder of this difficult science, which he seems to be endeavoring to make plain to the comprehension of all classes of intelligent, reflecting people. We are utterly amazed at the ridicule with which this gentleman has been assailed in other places, if, what we have heard is the type of what is to follow. With such strict regard to the positive indications of nature as he exhibits, based upon known physiological laws, there is no denying his propositions. Both his language and his illustrations were in strict accordance, in our humble apprehension, with the best medical authors.[71]

The praise from the medical publication was not without condition, and the condition was that Graham's credibility would be demolished were he to, in a subsequent lecture, prove himself a quack or a fame seeker, or "attempt to prove that man is not omnivorous, or that raw vegetables are more conducive to health and longevity than roast beef and mutton."

Graham was admonished more than once in the pages of the prestigious publication. He wrote to the journal to clarify his point of view, and to express displeasure. "Personal abuse and obloquy and ridicule can serve no good end; and no one, of correct principles and refinement, can reflect on them, as manifestations of the qualities of the human heart, without painful regret," wrote Graham, who was still a Christian minister.[72]

Nevertheless the attack continued. "The new-born fanatic of the Graham creed leaps for joy under the buoyant influence of his airy diet—glories in the victory achieved by intellect and conscience over sensual appetite—revels in the new fountains of vigor and felicity" stated a writer in the *Boston Medical and Surgical Journal* letter titled "Emasculation the first fruit of Grahamic fanaticism."[73]

Another example of attack was an editorial on the use of fruit and the vegetable diet—and the character of those who advocated it: "In the scheme of creative wisdom, the indications are clearly manifested that man is omnivorous; and it was not until muzzled by the opinions of one, and perplexed by the ridiculous hypotheses of another, touching the subject of his food, of which he is himself better qualified to judge than the most learned physician in Christendom, that he relinquished in his nature, to become the football of those who raise themselves into a short-lived notoriety by giving to unfounded theories the character only belonging to well-established facts."[74]

Dr. Lee, a prominent physician, writing in the pages of *BMSJ* specifically attacked Sylvester Graham and Grahamism. "I can only regard it as atheistical in its tendency, and destructive in its operation." By destructive, Lee had explained that a diet without flesh led to insanity in his patient.[75]

Graham, who suspected a plot existed to destroy his character and distort his message, responded to the claim that his teachings on diet led people to lose their minds. He replied to the accusation in the medical journal, and in his book *The Aescepulian Tablets*.

About Lee's contention regarding his delusional patient, Graham stated: "We are invited to believe that this deluded pedestrian was saved from imminent insanity by giving 'his bread a heavy coating of butter, eating freely of eggs, and occasionally of fresh fish.' " Graham proposed a challenge to Lee: "Let all the cases of insanity that Dr. Lee can bring forward, with the help of all those whom he calls upon, be fully given in every particular, of parentage, life, habits, circumstances, employments, events, etc., and if I cannot show to the satisfaction of every candid and intelligent individual, that the 'Graham System' is wholly free from any blame in each and every case, then let that system and its humble advocate stand convicted before the world, of all their errors, and receive all the censure they deserve. I do not fear for my reputation, for the present and for the future, rest on the issue."[76]

THE GRAHAM JOURNAL OF HEALTH AND LONGEVITY

Information regarding the teachings—and the character—of Sylvester Graham had become convoluted by rumor and inaccurate news accounts, according to David Cambell. To set the matter straight, and give the crusader and his followers a forum to express themselves, Cambell established in April of 1837 *The Graham Journal of Health and Longevity*.

"Those who have never heard Mr. Graham's instructions from his own lips, can form no just idea of their importance; and from this cause, as well as from the unbounded misrepresentation that have been made of his doctrines, an almost total and universal error of opinion and prejudice of feeling have gathered around his course and exceedingly retarded the progress of his great enterprise of philanthropy," wrote Cambell in the premiere issue.[77]

The first issue was eight pages long and included testimonials on the power of Grahamism to transform health. It also featured a survey. The publisher wanted to learn of others who followed the system, and how they had benefited from abandoning meat, alcohol, and other stimulants and adopting habits like regular bathing and exercise. Cambell published the magazine from the office on Washington Street in Boston.

The premiere edition provided accounts of Grahamism in Providence, Rhode Island, a reprint of an anti-Graham article published in the *Boston*

Medical and Surgical Journal, and advertisements for Graham's upcoming lectures, as well as ads for books such as *Nature's Own Book* by Asenath Nicholson, who operated a Graham Boarding House in New York City. The price of *The Graham Journal of Health and Longevity* was three cents per copy and one dollar for a year. Local agents in several states sold the journal.

Health was a motivation for most Grahamites, but they were not unconcerned about the fate of animals deemed dinner by human beings. This latter reason for rejecting meat especially evoked ridicule. The following brief article about this topic was published in the Journal on March 3, 1838.

We "Grahamites" are often charged with ultraism in our notions; and among other things, in regard to abstinence from animal food. We do rather try to awaken and cherish a feeling and horror at the shedding of blood. We do look upon the lives of animals as being their own, as much as ours are, and that we may not, for the mere gratification of what we hold to be a depraved appetite for blood, bite, murder, and devour them. If it is necessary to sustain the life of the individual, or promote the welfare of the human race, that we should not, perhaps, hesitate to do it; but we believe that there is no such necessity. On the contrary, we believe, that welfare of man would be almost infinitely better promoted, if another drop of blood should never be swallowed, and though as a mere dietetic question we regard flesh eating as one of the least modern abominations upon physical, social and moral character, we do strive "To view with tenderness all living forms—Our brother emmets and our sister worms."

But we did not intend to enter into an argument upon this subject. Our only object in alluding to it is to make an extract from the journal of Mr. Newton, missionary of the Presbyterian church, in Northern India, which we find in the Missionary Herald. The faqir leaves us Yankee Pythagoreans in the background. Perhaps, however, we shall come to this extreme bye and bye.

Faqir. "He (a Faqir, or priest) is an old man, goes bare headed, and keeps a square cotton rag tied before his mouth to prevent the inspiration of insects and animalculae. It seems to be the chief part of his religion to destroy no animal life...(he) carries a soft brush to remove all insects from the path...takes a pitcher of boiled water that he may quench his thirst (without risk of swallowing any animal substances)."

There's consistency, equal to some of us, Grahamites; revolting at the idea of swallowing a living animacule, but scalding them to death, and then swallowing their dead carcasses by the quarts.[78]

Graham was not involved in the publication of the *Graham Journal.* However, his speeches were excerpted in it and he contributed articles. He was busy conducting lecture tours—series of lectures lasting several nights—in the many northeast cities and towns he visited. He also gave lectures for various organizations and events. For example, while on tour in Providence he met with the Providence Physiological Society and was awarded a silver bowl in appreciation of his crusade.

On May 30, 1838, when the Grahamites, that is, the American Physio-logical Society, held their American Health Convention at the Marlboro Chapel in Boston, Graham was a featured speaker. Alcott and Mussey were also participants. The convention was a gathering of the friends of physiology—the term commonly used by Grahamites and other vegetari-ans to describe themselves. The president of the Committee of the Con-vention was Amasa Walker.

The convention was likely the first of its kind in the nation where lay-men discussed the laws of health. The people gathered at the convention believed a "great revolution is needed in the dietetic habits of mankind," and they wished to "commence such a revolution."[79]

William Alcott announced the following resolution: "That we view with gratitude to Almighty God, the formation of Physiological and Health Societies in this country; and that their efforts to promote knowledge and health by means of lectures, tracts, periodicals, infirmaries, & etc deserve the serious attention and vigorous support of the entire community."[80]

In addressing the gathering, Alcott spoke on the progress of the Ameri-can Physiological Society: membership grew to 250 members, including 60 females; the group held monthly meetings featuring lectures or discus-sions; the organization had accumulated a library of American and Euro-pean books; and members tended to be patrons of the GJHL and Alcott's own *Library of Health*. The APS, according to Alcott, was working on estab-lishing an infirmary in Boston based upon physiological principles. Gra-ham announced another resolution at the convention: "That a knowledge of the human constitution and of its laws and relations is of vital impor-tance to the cause of sound morality and true religion."[81]

Crusader Graham's orations on the dangers of dining on meat and on bakery-made bread caused heated reactions. The meat makers and com-mercial bread bakers, fed up with the vegetarian and whole wheat bread crusader, plotted to stop their nemesis, according to press accounts. In 1837 at the Marlborough, a new temperance hotel in Boston, a mob awaited Graham's arrival. But unknown to them, Grahamites on the upper floors of the hotel let loose a pile of lime and the would-be assailants scattered.

Graham escaped the mob, but was assaulted on another day with words rather than fists. The *Boston Medical and Surgical Journal* published a lengthy unsigned letter from a medical doctor who stated that it was common sense that human beings were designed to eat meat. But, he stated sarcastically, if instead the famous vegetarian crusader was correct, then "Let every association of men, especially the literary, scientific, moral and religious, pass resolutions and send forth eulogies in his praise. And let America, proud America, boast a Washington, a Franklin and a Gra-ham!" The Graham system "must be abandoned," commanded the physi-cian. After attending a Graham lecture, the doctor declared that Graham had "demonstrated evidence of 'excessive irritability and excitability, emotion and feeling.'" The physician also said if he had met Graham in an insane asylum, he would have "pronounced him insane."[82]

Evidently it wasn't just Graham who was looked upon with suspicion for signs of insanity and sickness; it seems all vegetarians were suspect. According to the doctor's account, a 19-year-old man eliminated meat from his diet and became emaciated, feeble, and deranged. The doctor further explained that the young man's condition worsened until he wet the bed, and "was in fact in a state of extreme mental and bodily imbecility." The doctor stated that he immediately went to feed his ailing patient meat, but it was too late. The vegetarian had died.

Perhaps such doctors who attempted to save a vegetarian patient by administering animal flesh were in earnest, and simply abiding by accepted beliefs about diet. Or perhaps some of the doctors had a more personal motivation for vigorously speaking out against removal of meat from the diet.

For the harsh criticism Graham evoked from the orthodox medical profession (the regulars) was based on more than just his dietary advice to the masses. He provoked the physicians with his passionately and publicly stated conviction that the American people, particularly physicians, were deluded about what caused and wrecked health.

For example, Graham had written in *The Aesculapian Tablets:*

With the universal opinion, that all their diseases and sufferings were the direct and arbitrary and even vindictive inflictions of their God, or gods, mankind have cherished no other fear of disease than that which grows out of their gross superstition—a fear that God would send sickness and death upon them, independently of any laws which he has established in relation to health and disease. Therefore, as a general truth, it has never occurred to them that there is any relation between their own voluntary habits, customs, and indulgences, and the diseases with which they are afflicted. Consequently, they have never sought to find the causes of their diseases within the precincts of voluntary conduct; and have never taken any care to prevent disease by avoiding the causes. The whole drift, therefore, of the human world, in all generations, has been to this one point, on this subject,— the ascertainment of remedies for disease have been in every form.[83]

Graham did not stop there. Instead, he went further and explained that this belief meant symptoms—not causes—were studied in the ceaseless search for remedies. The result, wrote Graham, was that disease was considered distant from its cause to the point that symptoms were treated with little or no reference to cause. Rather than look to the cause, allopathic doctors relied on medicines. Graham must have raised not a few hackles within the medical community with such comments.

His passion combined with his powerful use of language —he was after all, a poet—left no doubt what he thought of doctors who dispensed potions and powders: they were deluded. Wrote Graham, "Such a delusion necessarily has led to the deeper and more fatal error, that there is in medicine an intrinsic health-giving virtue; that it has the power absolutely to take away or kill disease and impart health! And this has led the way to the wide-sweeping evil which has spread, more calamitously than all the plagues of Egypt, over the whole civilized world:—the eternal and suicidal drugging! drugging! drugging! of mankind."[84]

AN EXPERIMENT

The Yankee preacher wasn't at a loss for confidence, and Horace Greeley, the editor of the influential *New York Tribune* newspaper, described him as a "fluent and forcible" man who had "a considerable knowledge of physics, metaphysics, and theology, along with a healthy ego."[85]

As Graham's fame grew, he was reported to have said, "No man can travel by stage or steamboat or go into any part of our country...and begin to advocate a vegetable diet...without being immediately asked...What! Are you a Grahamite?"[86]

He had reasons to be self-confident, at least about his health and diet message—people told him his system restored them to health. That it evidently did many good did not escape public attention.

One of the earliest examples of Graham's regimen apparently restoring health and preventing disease took place in the Orphan Asylum of Albany, New York. The orphanage had opened in 1829 and four years later a number of the children had died during the cholera epidemic. The children's diet had consisted of fine bread, rice, Indian puddings, potatoes, vegetables, fruits, milk, "and to these was added flesh or flesh soup once a day." Many of the children were sickly. Then in 1833, physicians Dr. James and Dr. Green, who had learned of Graham's teachings, tried an experiment and took the meat out of the youngsters' diet. They also adapted other Graham principles for the youngsters, including regular exercise and bathing.[87]

By 1836, a report noted that the 80 or so children who had been following the Graham diet for three years were well. It was also reported that newcomers to the orphanage who were sickly soon grew strong, active, and cheerful under the Grahamite regimen. In 1837, when a smallpox outbreak struck the orphanage, it was reported that it was so mild that it hardly interrupted daily activities. Praise was heaped upon Graham for this success and others.[88]

Upon the publication of Graham's work, *Lectures on the Science of Human Life*, a reviewer in *Bell's Select Library and Eclectic Journal of Medical Science* wrote: "The physiological views they contain are, in general, correct, and expressed with perfect clearness.... the natural food of man appears to consist of fruits, roots and other succulent parts of vegetables."[89]

GRAHAMITES AND ANTI-GRAHAMITES

Opposition to Grahamism grew with his fame. Graham's vegetarianism, with his edicts that people must eat less food, and that plain, uncooked food was best, as it was most natural, provoked comments in publications beyond the BMSJ.

For example, although A. Curtis, M.D., editor and publisher of the Columbus, Ohio-based *Botanico-Medical Reporter,* was open to Graham's ideas because they were truth, he also published letters critical of the system. *Botanico-Medical Reporter* primarily published articles on the use of plants in medicine and opposing the regular method of medicine.

A commentary published in the *Reporter* explained that people followed Graham, adhering to his dietary and health principles, at least to some degree, and those who did tended to be classified in the press as Grahamites. However, not all were Grahamites.

In advocating the peculiar views of Sylvester Graham, we do it not because we call any man master, and least of all that man who has spent his life, as it were, that men might understand and think for themselves. We advocate these views because we believe, with a confidence not to be shaken, that they are immutable, eternal truth. If men choose to call us Grahamites, so be it. We will promise to hold our way unmoved. We are pledged to principles not men. If Graham should prove to those principles for which he has suffered in no common manner, we shall still hold our way. Words can never make a truth an ism.[90] Men may talk of Grahamites and Grahamism, but why should we be disturbed at terms which they choose to designate or reproach truth?[91]

One of the critics of Graham's system was J.J. Flournoy of Atlanta, Georgia. In several lengthy letters to the *Botanico Medical Reporter,* Flournoy addressed areas of contention between vegetarians and meat eaters.

The following excerpted letter contains a partial list of claims against Grahamism/vegetarianism during the Jacksonian era, including: that it was heretical; that the supposed long-lived, plant-eating antediluvians were barbarians; that vegetarians wanted humanity to return to a state of primitiveness; that they were depriving people of food; that they would make Americans physically weak; that meat eating had no connection to one's health, and that meat made men strong.

Wrote Flournoy:

The Graham faction cannot convince me that God forbade flesh-eating, when his word of allowance to Noah is plainly written.... Was it sympathy or pity for the suffering of animals in the agonies of death, that determined Mr. Graham's course? They that be predestined for the table, cannot, under Providence, feel pain so acutely as man...Grahamites dwell frequently on the argument, that the antediluvians lived long and were giants, that ate only vegetables. To this I answer, they were filled with violence.... If Mr. Graham will carry out his system to completeness, he must...forbid fire to warm his zealots, and make their ones wear loose tunics! Why, beasts that eat grass, do not want fire. Cannot we imitate them thus far! Presently will some lean and cadaverous disciple, propose moonshine as our simple aliment, and the fumes of the fog for our only medicine. We cannot tell how far they will go if humored in their folly of restraining the appetite of hungry children, and advising men to measure food by the eye, and not by the stomach! Food, sir, ought to be cooked to tempt appetite; and then a sated stomach will refuse even dainties. Let little children have plenty of good fare, and their health will be insured, if they do not actually surfeit. Starve then to simple bread and mush, and a little of each too, and you make a nation of "pigmies to be warred upon by cranes." Give the strong, large, hale men, and we shall have better sailors, workmen and soldiers, and majestical Christians.[92]

The tide had not entirely turned against Graham, but the going was rough. Graham believed his opposition was attempting to poison the waters by ruining his reputation as a gentleman and scholar, and by misrepresenting his ideas. It probably did not help the cause that the last number of the *GJHL* was issued in 1840. (The magazine was, however, renamed *Health Journal and Advocate of Physiological Reform* by the new editors, Mary Gove—now Nichols—and her husband Thomas Low Nichols, M.D., who later would be named a vice president of the *American Vegetarian Society*.)

Although a tempest of controversy swirled around Sylvester Graham, threatening to destroy his reputation and the fledgling vegetarian movement, supporters of Grahamism were galvanized.

Praise of Graham, which was largely in defense of vegetarianism, also grew with his fame. *Botanico-Medical Recorder* publisher Curtis offered a lengthy reply to Fournoy's letter, stating in part:

We do not recollect that he uses the suffering of animals in the slaughter-house, as an argument against flesh-eating.... The rest of friend F.'s article, being intended as pleasant raillery than positions for refutation, we omit further notice at present, only assuring him that we shall join him in opposition to living without fire, or subsisting on moonshine as aliment, when ever any one seriously proposes it.... (Regarding) his statement respecting "cooking food so as to tempt the appetite" and "sating the stomach" to make "strong, large, hale men" After he has suffered as much from dyspepsia as we once did, he will be better qualified than he is now, to discourse on the propriety of "cooking to please the taste," and eating to satisfy...[93]

Although Metcalfe, Alcott, and Graham had people talking about abstinence from animal flesh, the type of meals served at most hotels and restaurants—and in most private homes—had not changed. There was an increasing number of vegetarian households, but there was no doubt that meat still dominated dinner plates.

Charles Dickens, upon his visit to the United States in 1842, observed American dining habits: "breakfast would have been no breakfast unless the principal dish were a deformed beef-steak with a great flat bone in the centre, swimming in hot butter, and sprinkled with the very blackest of all possible pepper."[94]

Dickens, almost a decade after Harriet Martineau observed American food habits, described breakfast, and then the dinner served aboard a canal boat near Pittsburgh, "At about six o'clock, all the small tables were put together to form one long table, and everybody sat down to tea, coffee, bread, butter, salmon, shad, liver, potatoes, pickles, ham, chops, black-puddings, and sausages."[95]

In Cincinnati, Dickens boarded *The Messenger*, a steamboat, and noted:

There are three meals a day. Breakfast at seven, dinner at half-past twelve, supper at six. At each, there are a great many small dishes and plates upon the table, with very little in them; so that although there is every appearance of a mighty "spread," there is seldom really more than a joint: except for those who fancy slices of beet-root, shreds of dried beef, complicated entanglements of yellow pickle; maize, Indian corn, apple-sauce, and pumpkin.

Some people fancy all these little dainties together (and sweet preserves beside), by way of relish to their roast pig. They are generally those dyspeptic ladies and gentlemen who eat un-heard of quantities of hot corn bread (almost as good for the digestion as a kneaded pin-cushion), for breakfast, and for supper.[96]

ABOLITIONISTS AND TRANSCENDENTALISTS

Americans were still eating plenty of meat, but that didn't deter Mary Gove Nichols and Englishman Henry Wright from publishing in 1842 another vegetarian magazine—the *Health Journal*, which had a short run and was succeeded by *Independent Magazine*, also briefly in existence.

The year 1843 was a notable year in vegetarian history. Wright, who had been an editor of *The Healthian,* an England-based vegetarian and health magazine, had come to the United States to help establish a vegetarian community in Massachusetts with his countryman Charles Lane and their American associate, A. Bronson Alcott. This other Alcott, a first cousin to Dr. William Alcott, was also a leading advocate of vegetarianism, and other far-reaching reforms.

His contemporaries knew philosopher Bronson Alcott as the American Plato. Alcott, an admirer of Sylvester Graham, with whom he was acquainted and whose lectures he attended, became a vegetarian in 1835. Alcott wrote in his journal about Graham: "He is the prophet of physical renewal; and as was John the Baptist to Jesus, so is he to the revealer of the doctrines of Spiritual Restoration."[97] Besides Graham, Alcott was also influenced by the life of Pythagoras, which he had read in the biography by Iamblichus.

A. Bronson Alcott: Transcendentalist and vegetarian advocate. Courtesy of Concord Free
Public Library.

Whenever possible, Alcott avoided leather, wool, and lamp oil made
from the remains of whales. He called leather "an invasion of the rights of
animals." But vegetarianism was more than a personal choice for Bronson
Alcott.

Like Graham and cousin William, he considered it an essential step
towards the perfecting of humanity. Alcott believed if humankind were ever
to regain its position of spiritual and physical perfection it enjoyed before the
Fall, purity in all things, including diet, was needed. He strived to model his
life after Jesus Christ. One historian had named Alcott a New England Saint;
another wrote that Ralph Waldo Emerson played Plato to Alcott's Socrates.

Amos Bronson Alcott was born in 1799 and raised on a farm in Connecticut. As a teenager, he traveled to the South with his cousin William;
they peddled goods to support themselves while looking for jobs as teachers. Bronson taught penmanship to children of plantation owners. He fed
his appetite for knowledge by reading the books in the libraries of the
homes where he taught.

After returning north in 1828, Alcott embarked on a career in education,
and became known as a reformer. Alcott's innovations earned him the title

of the American Pestalozzi, after the famous Swiss progressive educator. The Yankee teacher believed that children were good, not evil, and he did not believe in using the hickory stick or any other method of punishment. Learning by repetition and memorization was in vogue in those days, but Alcott believed that learning should be more. Alcott introduced many changes into a one-room schoolhouse in Chesire, Conneticut, including the Socratic teaching method, student government, art, gymnastics, a library, parent–teacher meetings, and no corporal punishment. These reforms were lauded by progressive educators but rejected by some townsfolk. So Alcott, also rejected, continued his teaching at the Boston Temple School. However, some Bostonians were outraged when he allowed a black girl to join his class, and possibly also because he had invited Sylvester Graham to lecture. They swiftly withdrew their children from his school. *Record of a School,* a book by Alcott assistant teacher Elizabeth Peabody, which was a transcript of and commentary on Alcott's school, caused greater controversy due to Alcott's transcendentalism.

His name is not often recognized today; when it is, it is for several reasons. He was the father of Louisa May Alcott, author of *Little Women.* Alcott was a leader of New England transcendentalism—a form of pure idealism philosophy. He was the only one of the recognized leaders of transcendentalism to consistently abstain from meat. Alcott was also originally considered the leader of the New England transcendentalist movement, according to Octavius Brooks Frothingham, who knew Alcott.

Frothingham wrote: "To Transcendentalism belongs the credit of inaugurating a theory and practice of dietetics which is preached assiduously now by the vegetarian physiologists. The people who regarded man as a soul, first taught the wisdom that is now inculcated by people who regard man as a body.... The materialist prescribes temperance, continence, sobriety, in order that life may be long, and comfortable, and free from disease. The idealist preaches them, in order that life may be intellectual, serene, pacific, beneficent."[98]

Alcott, on having to go to the market to buy meat for his wife Abigail May (who seems to have later become a vegetarian) wrote in his journal: "What have I to do with butchers? Am I to go smelling about markets? Both are an offence to me. Death yawns at me as I walk up and down in this abode of skulls. Murder and blood are written on its stalls. Cruelty stares at me from the butcher's face. I tread amidst carcasses. I am in the presence of the slain. The death-set eyes of beasts peer at me and accuse me of belonging to the race of murderers. Quartered, disembowelled creatures on suspended hooks plead with me. I feel myself dispossessed of the divinity. I am a replenisher of graveyards. I prowl, amidst other unclean spirits and voracious demons, for my prey."[99]

The father of *Little Women* lived for many years in Concord, Massachusetts, with his family at Orchard House. Alcott's neighbors in Concord included his two closest friends, fellow transcendentalists Ralph Waldo Emerson and Henry David Thoreau. Thoreau wrote about vegetarianism in Walden, perhaps reflecting on his friendship with Alcott. In Walden, Thoreau praised Alcott, calling him the sanest man he had ever known, but without identifying him by name.

Biographer Odell Shepard explained that Bronson Alcott was known as the after-dinner member of the Saturday Club, a prestigious literary club that met in the Parker House Hotel in Boston. Members of the club included the poet Henry Wadsworth Longfellow and Nathaniel Hawthorne, who was another of Alcott's Concord neighbors. Alcott arrived "for the best of the feast—the nuts, the apples, the wit and the philosophy abounding—after the abominations were removed."

Once, while Alcott sat at Ralph Waldo Emerson's dinner table, his host discussed the savagery of cannibalism. Emerson was carving a roast as he told his tale. Alcott joked with his nonvegetarian friend: "But Mr. Emerson, if we are to eat meat at all why should we not eat the best?" Legend has it that Emerson experimented with cutting meat from his diet, but it didn't last.[100]

Alcott promoted vegetarianism in his "Conversations," which were informal talks on spirituality and other topics of the day which he gave in Massachusetts and as far west as Missouri. After discussing vegetarianism at the Roxbury, Massachusetts, transcendental community called Brook Farm, more of the members chose to dine at the Grahamite table, according to historian Lindsey Swift. Alcott also talked with children at Emerson's house on the topic of animal liberation. It was said that the children agreed that choosing the vegetable diet was a way to be just and kind to animals.

Alcott's vegetarianism was also based on nonviolence. Massachusetts professor James Warren Gould, expert on peacemakers, credits Alcott as the first person to develop a theory of nonviolence and resist the violence of the state. Gould crowned him the Grandfather of Nonviolence.

In a conversation, Alcott stated,

Human institutions bear no fruit; if you plant them, they will yield nothing. Divine prohibitions and commands now stand for nothing. "Thou shalt not kill," which is a history recording to sense what the divine law of purity suggests in every unperverted heart, is held binding by none. "What shall I not kill?" asks the butcher, the poulterer, the fishmonger; and he answers, "All things in which I do not trade." And what shall the soldier not kill? All men, except his enemies. These exceptions make the law nugatory. The command is universal only for the pure soul, that neither stabs nor strangles. The laws of man inculcate and demand slaughter. Nor will they exculpate rebellion on the ground that holiness has rendered obedience impossible. But we must ignore laws which ignore holiness. Our trust is in purity, not in vengeance.... Together with pure beings will come pure habits. A better body shall be built up from the orchard and the garden.... As he who seizes on civil liberty with the hand of violence would act the tyrant if power were entrusted to him, so he whose food is obtained by force or fraud would accomplish other purposes by similar ignoble means. Tyranny and domination must be overcome when they first take root in the lust of unhallowed things. From the fountain we shall slake our thirst, and our appetite shall find supply in the delicious abundance that Pomona offers. Flesh and blood we will reject as the "accursed thing." A pure mind has no faith in them.[101]

"We must ignore laws which ignore holiness," believed Alcott, who was arrested for refusing to pay a tax that funded war and a country that accepted slavery. Without his permission, one of his fellow townsman paid the fine, and although he was brought to the local jail, Alcott was not imprisoned.

The vegetarian philosopher's efforts inspired Henry David Thoreau, who was 18 years younger than Alcott and did not initially support his Concord neighbor's act of conscience. But three years later Thoreau was arrested and did go to jail for refusal to pay the tax that he then found unconscionable.

Thoreau wrote about his beliefs in the powerful essay *Civil Disobedience*. Years after Thoreau's death, another advocate of vegetarianism, Englishman Henry Salt, author of *Animals' Rights* and founder of The Humanitarian Society, wrote about the arrest in his biography of Thoreau. He also briefly mentioned Bronson Alcott's arrest. Salt's account was read by a young acquaintance, a vegetarian from India then living in England. The young man was deeply impressed by Thoreau's words and actions. That man was Mahatma Gandhi, future leader of India, whose life, it is said, was an influence on Dr. Martin Luther King, who employed nonviolence in the struggle for civil rights in the States.

For many decades Thoreau's works have been among the most widely assigned works of literature in American high schools and colleges, and although his vegetarian mentor is rarely mentioned, the moral influence of Bronson Alcott is apparent.

Transcendentalist leader Alcott also wrote about animal liberation: "The Soul's Banquet is an art divine.... I would abstain from the fruits of oppression and blood, and am seeking means of entire independence...our wine is water,—flesh, bread;—drugs, fruits..."

The philosopher had been invited to help establish Brook Farm but declined, in part because the community raised pigs for slaughter and profit. Orson S. Murray also expressed disapproval. Although, like Alcott, not a member of Brook Farm, Murray was known to the farmers as an ardent abolitionist and as a person who abhorred the killing of animals.

Alcott, who seemed to be more appreciated in England than in America, sailed to England in 1842 at the invitation of James Pierrepont Greaves, founder of a vegetarian and transcendental community in Ham Common,

Surrey, which included a school. Greaves honored Alcott and his principles by naming his community Alcott House.

While at Alcott House, Alcott lectured on the connection between violence against animals and the violence human beings inflict upon one another. With William Lambe, M.D., and surgeon J.N. Sherman, Alcott formed a vegetarian society named the *Physiological and Health Association.* This vegetarian organization, perhaps the earliest established in England, predates the still existing *Vegetarian Society of the United Kingdom,* which was founded in 1847.

Lambe was a renowned physician in the UK and across the Atlantic in America. A letter he wrote in defense of vegetarianism, published in *The Lancet,* was also published in *The Bulletin of Medical Science,* a Philadelphia-based periodical edited by John Bell, M.D.

The doctor wrote: "I apprehend it to be impossible for you not to know that the experience of all ages has proved that the healthy man can be perfectly nourished without using a particle of animal food. I will fearlessly assert, from long experience, that vegetable food is much more salubrious than mixed diet in common use, in which, however, animal matter commonly enters in the smallest proportion. Numerous instances may be cited of persons who have lived for years in very good health without animal food..."[102]

Englishman Lambe explained that since 1804 he had been a vegetarian—"induced to this by severe bodily suffering." Lambe, who was in his late 80s when he wrote to *The Lancet,* stated that he had been healthy the past 38 years due to his vegetable diet.

Lambe's countrymen Charles Lane and Henry Wright of Alcott House accompanied their new American friend philosopher Alcott back to Massachusetts, where the three planned to establish a transcendentalist-vegetarian community of their own.

FRUITLANDS

In 1843, the same year that he was arrested, Alcott founded Fruitlands, a vegan community in Harvard, Massachusetts, with Lane. They were joined by Wright and Lane's son. Alcott's wife and daughters, and several others participated in the Consociate family, as it was called. Outside the tiny community, Charles Lane, for his outspoken opposition to the slaughter and eating of animals, was labeled violent vegetarian by some whom he apparently offended with his direct manner.

However, William Ellery Channing referred to Lane and Alcott as America's Essenes because, like that sect that existed at the time of Jesus Christ, they did good works for humanity; were, as spiritual people, in the world but not of it; lived nonviolently; and were vegetarians who opposed the slaughter of animals.

Alcott firmly believed that he and his fellow Fruitanders were planting a new Eden and that New England was the promised land. The community members, male and female, wore tunics and pants designed by Alcott. The garments were made of linen, not cotton, which was a product of slavery. The Fruitlands farmers' daily fare, which was vegan, consisted of Graham bread baked by Alcott, apples, potatoes, and other foods from the garden and orchard. Alcott knew that simple vegetarian meals required little to no cooking, unlike meat, and he held that this liberated woman from the kitchen. Historian Dorothy Bronson Wicker, a descendant, and founder of the A. Bronson Alcott Society of Monroe, New York, says that Alcott, before any other transcendentalist, signed a petition in support of women's rights. Alcott was a lecturer for at least one women's rights convention.

On the topic of farming, Alcott, like Sylvester Graham, thought the use of manure was filthy. Animal-based agriculture and plowing with oxen depleted the soil, while using green crops for fertilizer enriched the soil, he stated.

Our present modes of agriculture exhaust the soil, and must, while life is made thus sensual and secular; the narrow covetous which prevails in trade, in labor, in exchanges, ends in depraving the land; it breeds disease, decline, in the flesh,—debauches and consumes the heart.[103]

Community members planned to grow fields of corn, rye, barley, potatoes, squash, peas, beans, and fruits such as melons. Fruitlands was short-lived, however. By December, the experiment ended in the wake of lack of funds, conflicting opinions between Lane and the Alcotts about celibacy in marriage, a lackluster harvest, and the impending winter.

After recovering from a short-lived depression, Alcott realized that there was a lesson to be learned from the demise of Fruitlands. Changing the world had to come from within the individual and from the family, not through building communities.

Later in life, Alcott found another venue for his beliefs. In July of 1879, he founded the School of Philosophy at Concord at his home and eventually moved it to the Hillside Chapel in his backyard, a structure built especially for the school. For several consecutive summers, the School of Philosophy offered a series of lectures by prominent philosophers, writers, and other thinkers. The press gave the school and its founder plenty of coverage. Reporters remarked that the elderly Alcott was fit, energetic, and intellectually sharp. Alcott gave conversations on his favorite philosophers such as Plato and Pythagorus, and he discussed vegetarianism.

Just shy of his 82nd birthday, Alcott taught the students of his school "Man will live here until he has made this planet a garden, this orchard, with no question about the animals. Man debases himself by his use of animal food. There was no butcher in Paradise."[104]

ABOLITIONIST-VEGETARIANS

Vegetarianism was attractive to Alcott and other abolitionists. Unlike today, when social movements tend to stand apart from one another, during the Jacksonian era reformers of various causes generally were united in their views. Reformers who advocated several progressive causes, such as temperance, health, anti-tobacco, women's rights, and abolition, were called universal reformers.

Those whose principal reform was to change the nation's eating habits believed that it was the crucial first step in creating a better America—and world. Leaders in the movement, including those who were preachers of the Bible-Christian Church, held this belief.

In 1842, the Secretary of the Bible-Christian Church in Philadelphia had preached from the pulpit that for sickness, slavery, drunkenness, and violence to cease, people had to remove meat from their midst. Doing so would constitute, in his words:

> ...the first principle in the Science of Man—that principle which if put into practice would tend, more than any other to the banishment of existing evil...Abolition Societies, if they would bring down the pride and avarice of the oppressor, and raise the oppressed, must first banish from their own tables, and then teach the others to abolish from theirs the foul flesh pots. Peace societies must plead peace for animal creation—they must teach the cruelty of animal butchery in order the more effectually to reach the sin of human murder....The real interests of the whole human family are one, even as their nature is in itself the same. Possessing as we all do, physical, intellectual and moral or religious powers, it is only by judicious exercise of all that we can secure to ourselves that health and happiness for which we were designed by the great Creator. In a word, the teaching of Physiology to each is simply "Thou Art A Man." Thus was the language and the faith of Jesus and his Apostles—it is the language of Truth. Let then the Aristocrat, the Slave-holder, and the lordling, awaken to the study of Physiology, and to each it shall speak in thunder-tones, "Thou art but a Man—Thou art a Man,"—and thus uniting ALL in the bonds of a universal brotherhood, it shall lead us on in the attainment of new truths, until we reach the stature of a "perfect man"....Arouse yourselves from the death-like torpor which stupefies you, proclaim aloud the truth—that Abstinence From Murdered Animals As Food, Is THE FIRST STEP In Reform.[105]

Breaking the bonds of enslavement to sensual appetite appealed to abolitionists. That following the vegetable diet of Sylvester Graham meant there was no need for the enslavement of animals apparently also appealed to at least some abolitionists, maybe most. The early advocates of vegetarianism were motivated by morals as much as by health: abstaining from animal flesh was to them inextricable from their worldview of benevolence, empathy, and liberation for all beings.

Despite their unity on vegetarianism, the advocates were still a diverse group whose opinions varied. For example, they were not all

Christians. One of the advocates, Orson S. Murray, despised Christianity because it was a religion. An outspoken anarchist, who also protested against religion and property ownership, Murray, who hailed from Vermont, was a prominent abolitionist and publisher of *The Regenerator* newspaper. He was also a strong voice for vegetarianism and animal liberation. After reading works of Epicurus and attending lectures by Graham, Murray became a vegetarian—he believed that eating meat was as evil as slavery.

Murray, a leading slavery abolitionist and organizer of an abolitionist society, saw similarities, as did Alcott, in the way people treated slaves and the way they treated animals. For example, he was appalled that people would befriend animals on their farms, only to later slaughter them and devour their corpses. Murray stated this sentiment in the pages of his New York-based newspaper, *The Regenerator*.[106]

Horace Greeley, editor of the *New York Tribune*, described Murray and his fledgling newspaper upon the publication of its premiere edition in 1843. Wrote Greeley:

Mr. Murray commenced editing *The Telegraph*, a religious paper (Baptist), soon embarked in abolition, and thence went on until he reached the No-Church, No-Government, No-Property platform where he now stands, having "outgrown," as he says, all creeds, all idea of constraint on intelligent beings, or of worship.

He is an oddity in our city, and his long beard attracts more attention, we apprehend, than his ultra Radical doctrines will subscribers. However, if he would walk out into the rough fares and sell his paper, preaching by the way, we should have hopes of him. With all his errors and extravagance, he is a sincere, earnest, warm-hearted man, deeply intent on the extirpation of ignorance and the diminution of Human Misery, and we fear, no lasting evil from the effects of such, however ill-directed.[107]

Vegetarianism, thought Murray, would require gradual change in society. He worked towards this by publishing articles, advertisements, and even poems in support of the vegetable diet and animal liberation. Murray's *Regenerator* carried ads for the Graham House—a boarding house "excluding entirely animal foods" and offering "health, quiet and comfort" in New York City.

"Adventures of a Grahamite," a poem published in the February 19th, 1844, edition of *The Regenerator* (with no byline) provides a glimpse into the attitudes towards vegetarians at that time.

One stanza of "Adventures of a Grahamite" reads:

When I no longer use
sausage and barbecue
roasted pigs and smoking stews
    And such nauseous sights;

People marveled at the change.
How hallucinations strange
Could so fearfully derange
        Crazy Grahamites![108]

Vegetarians were ridiculed, and so were abolitionists. Like Murray, several other prominent abolitionists were Grahamites. One of these leaders in the struggle against slavery was Abby (Abigail) Kelley Foster, one of the first American women to address mixed audiences of men and women.

Yet another reformer who championed abolitionism, and many other causes meant to uplift humankind, including Grahamism, was Horace Greeley, the celebrated editor of the *New York Tribune,* the widely circulated and progressive newspaper. Greeley met his future wife, vegetarian Mary Youngs Cheney, at a Graham boarding house.

Angeline Grimke, one half of the famous abolitionist Grimke sister-team, was a Grahamite, as was her equally acclaimed abolitionist husband Theodore Weld. Abolitionist Gerritt Smith was sympathetic to Grahamism, and lent support to the cause. It is unclear if the most noted abolitionist of all, William Lloyd Garrison, publisher of *The Liberator* newspaper, was a vegetarian, but he did, like some of his associates in the cause, including fellow publisher William Goodall, dine at Graham boarding houses.

Graham Boarding Houses existed in New York City—where Asenath Hatch Nicholson had established one in 1832 in the Five Points neighborhood—in Boston, probably in Providence, and possibly in a few other urban areas. They were open to the public, and gathering places for reformers.

As Professor William S. Tyler of Amherst College noted in an 1833 letter: "The Boarders in this establishment are not only Grahamites, but Garrisonites—not only reformers in diet, but radicalists in Politics...Slavery, Colonization, Etc., constitute the unvarying monotonous theme of their conversations except that they give place to their peculiar style of living. Arthur Tappan, Goodell, & Dennison are the most prominent characters. Garrison & Leavitt are sometimes at the Graham House, & then only the presence of Mr. Thacher is wanting to complete the Editorial corps..."[109]

Advocates of vegetarianism believed meat eating brought out the beast in the human: some acts of avarice, violence, and sexual vice were linked with diet. They deduced this from the biblical book of Genesis, and from observation of carnivorous animals. "Flesh eating animals are more wild, and savage, and ungovernable than the vegetable eaters, so the flesh-eating man will partake more of the nature and character of the former, in proportion to the amount which he eats, than does the vegetable eater," stated the Bible-Christian Secretary in 1842.[110]

SOLITARY VICE

That the physical nature of the human being overpowered the intellectual, and especially the moral, when people ate animal flesh was then a conviction of the vegetarian movement. For example, Graham believed that meat eating caused one to become sexually out of control. And even obsessed.

Today, a relatively small number of Americans, including among vegetarians, know of Sylvester Graham or William Alcott. Alcott wrote dozens of books that guided readers in how to better their lives and society, ways that might seem strange or quaint to today's Americans. Graham, too, was certainly not timid about wanting to improve the nation.

When not recalled as the inventor of a cracker—that he did not invent—Graham, for his perspective on sexuality, has practically been labeled a pervert. Viewed within the context of his own time, Graham's writing and lectures on the topic of solitary vice were not perverted, nor out of place, and were commonplace for a health reformer. Historian Richard H. Shryrock noted this when he stated "it is only fair to note, however, that the reformers' exaggeration of the evils of sexual perversion reflected a similar though milder exaggeration in the medical literature of the day."[111]

Graham's efforts against the solitary vice were in keeping with his overall effort to teach the prevention of sickness, especially through vegetarian diet. What is considered exaggeration, even ludicrous, to modern Americans, was taken seriously by those of the nineteenth century. For example, the Massachusetts State Lunatic Asylum had reported in 1838 that the leading cause of insanity among men and women was masturbation.

"Humanity demands that preventives be applied.... Graham aims to apply a preventive, and in doing it, he speaks of the nature of licentious acts and their consequences.... If insanity can be prevented, the benevolence of the preventive act is greater than the application of remedies to those actually insane.... Many have thanked Mr. Graham for opening their eyes to the evils of their conduct," reported the *New Hampshire Observer* newspaper about Graham's *Lecture to Young Men*, which was later published.[112]

In his *Lecture to Young Men* (Weeden and Cory 1834), Graham began by stating that he was aware of the problems in addressing such a delicate subject as sexuality, but he believed it was necessary. Frequent sexual activity, including masturbation, irritated, and therefore debilitated, the body, making it vulnerable to disease; animal flesh in the diet led to uncontrollable sexual drive, and therefore to the disintegration of morality in society, believed Graham.[113]

Graham's stance against solitary sexual practice, he said, was because the "free use of animal food" hastens the onset of puberty. Modern science has determined that an elevated level of sex hormones—a factor in certain forms of cancer—has been linked with a diet high in fat, especially animal fat. A diet high in fat has been connected to early menarche (onset of menstruation), and early menarche has been found to be a risk factor for the development of certain forms of cancer.

The crusader lectured on the topic of sex, both to male and female audiences, but not to mixed company. His lectures to women were criticized as immoral, as was Graham himself, yet women evidently especially welcomed his talks.

When Graham scheduled a lecture in Boston exclusively for women on the subject of courtship, his opponents posted placards around the city threatening Graham if he dared lecture to them. Graham's opposition had been fueled by an accusation, published in the *Daily Herald*, that Graham had previously addressed an exclusively all-female audience (200–300 women) using very improper language.

Others declared Graham the perfect gentleman. He was an early sex educator; he taught anatomy and physiology, as well as his ideas on diet. That he sought to empower women by teaching them, despite the hostility he encountered in doing so, shows feminist sensibility. He taught that married couples should engage in sex infrequently since it depleted the body's natural store of energy; this advice, whether scientifically sound or not, must have been a boon to some wives during an era when they were expected to have several, even a great many, babies.

The *Daily Herald* reported a mob gathered outside the Boston lecture hall to stop Graham's talk to the ladies from taking place. Two hundred females climbed up the stairs to the lecture hall, followed by a mob of greater number. The mob shouted out "Graham!" Women attempted to speak in defense of Graham, but their voices were overwhelmed by shouts against him. The city marshall intervened and announced the lecture had been canceled.[114]

One woman, concerned for Graham, managed to say to the crowd, "If they are going to him, I will not move an inch!" which evoked a roar from the mob. Later Graham went to the newspaper and protested the accusations against him, which he said were not true.

It is generally not known that Graham helped break down barriers in society—and not just for the vegetarian movement.[115] He popularized the teaching of physiology and anatomy at a time when people tended towards ignorance about the human body. In teaching women about sexuality, it can be argued that he was empowering them, as a sort of early sex educator—even if his views on the subject of sexuality are today considered outdated or absurd. Some evidence suggests Graham also lectured to African American audiences on the topic of diet and health.

In 1840 Graham was still in the glare of the national spotlight. And Reverend Metcalfe found himself in the spotlight of public opinion upon the publication of his book *Bible Testimony On Abstinence From The Flesh Of*

Animals As Food: Being An Address Delivered In The Bible-Christian Church, North Third Street, West Kensington, On The Eighth of June 1840, Being The Anniversary of Said Church.

Bible-Christian Church leader Metcalfe had through the years since he had arrived in the United States been a consistent advocate of vegetarianism. Metcalfe's advocacy of the meat-free diet had not been limited to his preaching from his Philadelphia pulpit, teaching at his church school, his practice as a homeopathic physician, or to his writings in the newspapers he published. Metcalfe and his church had been holding vegetarian picnics and other social events since the early days, and inviting the public to participate. Then came the book.

In the 35-page book, Metcalfe explained that the Bible, including passages found in the Old and New Testaments, instructed human beings to be vegetarians, and to not kill animals. He began his book by acknowledging "As a religious community we have adopted a mode of life, in regulating the appetites and fulfilling the physical and organic laws of the body, altogether different from the practices of other Christian professors. We have long discontinued the very fashionable habit, of feeding on the flesh of butchered animals, and have confined ourselves wholly to vegetable productions. We have long resisted the lure of the intoxicating bow, and have been contended to slake our thirst from the limpid stream." They lived this way, stated Metcalfe, in respect of the Bible doctrine: "It is good neither to eat flesh nor to drink wine."[116]

Metcalfe's book was slight in size, but not in the attention it attracted. The words he had written were not ignored by outsiders, and, in fact, received numerous reviews. One review, titled "Flesh-Meat," published in the *Botanico Medical Recorder* on October 3, 1840, printed a few of Metcalfe's words: "As a religious community...we have long discontinued the very fashionable habit of feeding on the flesh of butchered animals, and have confined ourselves wholly to vegetable productions."[117]

The *Recorder* then noted Metcalfe's beliefs that Jesus did not eat or provide fish, and that the killing of animals is morally akin to the killing of humans. "In short," wrote the reviewer, "though some of these arguments seem to us far-fetched...we recommend to the perusal of all the champions on both sides of the question of 'meat or no meat.'"[118]

Thus, through reviews, the book itself, Metcalfe's sermons and newspapers, and the social activities of the church, people far from Pennsylvania learned of the vegetarian Christians of Philadelphia.

Metcalfe, Graham, William Alcott, and others who taught vegetarianism looked to Bible teachings on diet that they believed verified their contentions that people were designed to eat fruit, vegetables, and again, that people were forbidden by God to eat meat and kill animals.

They noted that in Genesis, the first book of the Bible, these words appear: "Behold I have given to you, even every herb bearing seed which is upon the face of the earth, and every tree, in which is the fruit of a tree yielding seed; to you it shall be for food." Another indication that God wanted people to eschew meat, advocates pointed out, is the Commandment, "Thou Shall Not Kill." Metcalfe contended in his book that this prohibits the taking of the lives of animals, as well as people. The minister stated the prophet Isaiah of the Bible spoke of the forthcoming messiah (meaning Jesus) as a man who would eat butter and honey (but not meat), and in doing so, would do good and not evil.

The Philadelphia preacher and his flock were still hard at work promoting their cause when their ally Sylvester Graham found it necessary to retire from the lecture circuit.

Early in the 1840s Graham was forced to retire; his health was failing. He might have been suffering from a severe case of arthritis. Even during his last days as a lecturer, he had attracted large audiences. Now residing in Northampton, Massachusetts, his life was beset by hardship, including the death of a child. Alienation from family members, failing health, and lack of financial support also haunted his days. Nevertheless, he continued to write, and his letters, articles, and poems were published in the local newspaper.

The sad tone of his poems provides a glimpse of Graham's emotional state. One poem, *A Transcript from the Tablets of the Heart*, began:

Ache on, old heart! ache on! ache on!
    It is thy nature to be aching:
For griefs to come, for crushed hopes gone,
    In sorrow thou are ever breaking.
In gloom, in sadness and in tears
    Thro' childhood's period thou did'st languish;
And up thro' manhood's early years,
    Thy every pulse was beat in anguish...[119]

On occasion, Graham still participated in the advocacy of his system, especially the dietary aspect. Toward the end of his life, in the same month that his "Transcript" poem was published, Graham again joined with William Alcott and William Metcalfe to support the vegetarian movement.

Dr. Alcott had not heard from Rev. Metcalfe in years, and then, in 1849, Alcott published an article about the Bible-Christians in his magazine *The Library of Health*. Contained within the article was a paragraph written some time earlier by Metcalfe on his vegetarianism. "You will, I presume, naturally and justly conclude, that as a member of that religious society (the Society of Bible Christians) I am a vegetable eater. Should I live til the approaching September, it will then be thirty years since I have so much even as tasted either fish, flesh or fowl. I have children and grand-children that have never tasted any thing of the kind; nor has animal food, at any time, been an article of diet in my family."[120]

That an entire family of three generations had thrived with no feeding upon flesh, and that there were other families doing the same—and not dying, growing feeble, or going insane—was an important fact for the vegetarian movement to announce. But such examples were largely ignored outside of the movement.

This evidently annoyed Alcott. He wrote "That redoubtable champion of flesh-eating and cigar-smoking—the editor of the Boston Medical and Surgical Journal—says that a sound state of health requires a small quantity of meat to be used. 'We have never yet seen an exclusively vegetable-eating individual,' he adds, 'who did not show the evil effects of it;' and his correspondents...echo back the same sentiments. What will they say to such facts as now lay before them? Will they continue their efforts at reproach and ridicule? Or will they consent, at length, to examine the arguments against flesh-eating, as carefully as they have those which are supposed to be in its favor?"[121]

Alcott, like Graham, believed there to be bias against vegetarianism, which was an obstacle to the growth of the movement. The bias was on the surface manifested as reproach and ridicule, but underneath, suggested Alcott, it was deliberate avoidance of evidence in favor of eschewing meat.

The bias against vegetarianism didn't affect the sales of a book by Larkin B. Coles, M.D. The book, *Philosophy of Health: Natural Principles of Health and Cure* contained health advice, including arguments for rejecting meat, arguments already identified with Graham. The book evidently had numerous readers. The 1850 edition, for example, was the 24th edition of the book. A reviewer that year writing in the *Boston Medical and Surgical Journal* noted the immense popularity of the book.

How much Coles's book contributed to the promulgation of vegetarianism is difficult to determine, just as it is hard to figure exactly how much the contributions of Graham, Alcott, and Metcalfe helped pave the way. The work of all the advocates factor in to an ever-increasing acceptance of vegetarianism today. Not only those outspoken about the practice, but those who quietly declined to eat meat and, perhaps incidentally, set an example for friends and neighbors, helping push the movement forward.

Although precise figures may be impossible to determine, Alcott and Graham, through their books and lectures, brought vegetarianism to thousands of Americans, perhaps hundreds of thousands. Word of mouth, that is, neighbor talking to neighbor, undoubtedly spread their message further.

Metcalfe and Mary Gove Nichols and others, including Bronson Alcott, Orson Murray, and Reuben Mussey planted seeds of food for thought in many minds. Yet none of this was enough to ensure that every American learned of the advocate's contention that meat was not the natural food of man. Especially not when misinformation about the plant-based diet was evidently simultaneously circulating in society.

Regardless of the intent of the writers who opposed removal of meat from the diet, their information was regarded as pernicious, as well as false, by the vegetarians.

Chapter 4

American Vegetarian Society

Storms of controversy would swirl around vegetarianism before the Civil War. The movement grew and experienced pain, as did the still-young nation. America in the late 1840s and early 1850s continued to expand westward. The California gold rush of 1849 had brought many to the coast in search of fortune. The problem of slavery, especially its expansion into the Midwest, was a source of increasingly intense dissent.

Meanwhile, vegetarianism, unlike the slavery abolition cause, lacked an official organization and publication to spread the message and answer accusations. William Metcalfe filled the void in 1850 when he organized the American Vegetarian Convention. It brought together the three greatest advocates of the nineteenth century—Mr. Graham, Dr. Alcott, and Rev. Metcalfe—even if only for a brief time. Bronson Alcott, too, was involved.

The convention was held at New York's Clinton Hall on May 15, 1850, and, "not withstanding the inclemency of the weather, there was a fair concourse assembled."[1]

People came to the convention to discuss vegetarianism, to promote it in society, and to decide if they should form a vegetarian organization.

Speakers at the historic event included William Alcott, M.D., of West Newton, Massachusetts; Sylvester Graham of Northampton, Massachusetts.; Joseph Wright of Camden, New Jersey; and Rev. William Metcalfe of Philadelphia. A letter read at the gathering from David Prince, M.D., of Saint Louis, Missouri, stated, "Animals, as food, will be substituted by the food of vegetable productions, on account of its greater cheapness and abundance, while much of the service now performed by animals will be rendered by steam and galvanism, drawing their force from the immense stores of the vegetation of former era, and from the mines of metals ready to use."[2]

Metcalfe read a letter written by Professor Reuben Dimond Mussey of the Ohio University of Cincinnati, who was unable to attend due to his duties as the new president of the American Medical Association (AMA). "It is delightful to witness the progress the vegetarian principles are making in England; Heaven grant, that in our country, a world may soon be commenced, which shall not be arrested until the whole of our vast population shall belong to the train."[3]

A letter read at the convention from Lewis S. Hough, A.M., author of *Science of Man Applied to Epidemics* (1849) and a principal of the classical Department at Germantown Academy, offered encouragement to the assembly: "The ultimate success of our cause is sure; it rests not on the caprices of the deluded multitude, but on the foundation of eternal law. The immutable laws of nature, and of nature's God, must cease to be, before the principles of a correct Vegetarian diet can be nullified. All we need, therefore, is a course of judicious efforts in this sense, to secure its ultimate and complete triumph. For such a glorius result, let us all confidently look at labor."[4]

Other notables sending letters of congratulation or attending the meeting included H.H. Hite, Esq., of Virginia; William C. Chapin, Esq., of Tiverton, Rhode Island; Isaac Jennings M.D., of Oberlin in Ohio; abolitionist Gerrit Smith of Peterboro; journalist-physician Thomas Low Nichols; and Joseph Wright, who at one point had been mayor of Memphis, Tennessee. Gerrit Smith's letter, read before the assembly, stated that he "should love" to have been there, but he was traveling on business.

Dr. Alcott, Dr. Russell T. Trall, and Dr. Nichols were elected as the committee to nominate officers. Metcalfe was made president, Rev. O.H. Wellington of Boston, Gilman Blake of Pepperrell, Massachusetts, and Joel Shew, M.D., of New York were appointed vice presidents, and Joseph Metcalfe of Philadelphia and Dr. Colin M. Dick of Long Island, New York, were appointed secretaries.

Several attendees spoke to the group about their experiences abstaining from animal flesh. Sylvester Graham and Joseph Wright conversed about vegetarianism and the allopathic medical profession:

Mr. Graham: How old were you when you commenced this mode of living?

Mr. Wright: I was between twenty-two and twenty-three...I am now in my sixty-third year....

Mr. Graham: Have you lost any children?

Mr. Wright: Yes, three. They died infants, of croup, or something like it."

Mr. Graham: Were they treated by a physician?

Mr. Wright: Yes, I called in a physician—an allopathist.

Mr. Graham: Oh, then, it is hard to tell whether the croup or the doctor killed
them. (Laughter.) So far as you have observed, what have been the
appetites and dispositions of your children?

Mr. Wright: They are healthy and of good disposition. They have, to be sure, a
portion of the infirmities of human nature; but are yet kind and affec-
tionate, and ready to do good. (Applause.)[5]

Convention attendees formulated the *Declaration of Sentiments and Resolutions,* which was read to the group later in the day by the nominating
committee.

The group was resolved that evidence shows human beings are responsible to live by "certain physical, mental, and moral laws" that will ensure
their "health and happiness." When these laws are transgressed, "misery
and evil" result. "Vegetarianism unfolds the universal law of man's
being," declared the conventioneers.

Therefore, they resolved: anatomy, physiology, and chemical analysis of
plant and animal substances showed humans are meant to eat plants; Paradise, made by God for people, was vegetarian; human beings only eat animal flesh because they are in a spiritually degraded condition since the
biblical Fall; to return to Paradise's conditions of purity, people must cease
to kill and eat animals; plants provide proper nutrition; human senses of
smell, taste, and sight prefer fruits and grains to "the mangled carcasses of
butchered animals"; flesh eating leads to other unnatural desires, whereas
vegetable eating leads to serenity and strength; the flesh eater, unlike the
vegetarian, can never enter into certain intellectual and moral delights; that
cruelty "for the mere purpose of procuring unnecessary food, or to gratify
depraved appetite, is obnoxious to the pure human soul, and repugnant to
the noblest attributes of our being"; the evidence of those such as Wesley,
Swedenborg, Franklin, Shelley, Pope, Isaac Newton, and others "testify to
the truth of vegetarianism"; promoting the vegetarian cause is an opportunity to elevate one's fellow human beings; to promote the circulating of
various publications that support vegetarianism, such as the *New York
Water Cure* and *Phrenological Journals*; to celebrate the progress of the vegetarian cause in England; and to as soon as possible organize state and local
vegetarian organizations to lecturers and diffuse facts.[6]

The convention finally resulted in the formation of the American Vegetarian Society (AVS). One among the group, P.P. Stewart of Troy, New
York, objected to the term *vegetarian.* The group worked on and adopted a
preamble and constitution, and a committee made up of John Grimes,
M.D., Dr. Nichols, and Mr. Edward Lyons appointed officers for the AVS.
Alcott was made president, Trall, recording secretary, Metcalfe, corresponding secretary, and Samuel R. Wells of New York, treasurer. Nine men
were appointed as vice presidents: Graham, Mussey, Hite, Prince, Wright,
Joel Shew, M.D., of New York, Chapin, and Joseph Metcalfe.

Shew, absent from the first meeting, offered encouragement in a letter read to conference participants. "Be not discouraged if the Convention is a small one at this season of the year.... Let us be contented even with small doings, knowing as we do the correctness and value of the principles we advocate."[7]

In an address to the group, Alcott talked about the reasons for vegetarianism, and stated that flesh should not be mixed with medicine—and most of the foods of the plant kingdom were known since antiquity to have some medicinal use. "Hence, practically, the use of animal food is a great evil; for as long as it is used, a great amount of medicine will be mingled with it, to sow the seeds of disease."[8]

Realizing the immense challenge ahead in convincing people to eschew animal flesh, Alcott encouraged the vegetarians, "A zealous, and faithful advocacy of its principles, upon every propler occasion; and endeavor to secure to the Society an increase of its members; and to their fellow-beings, the benefits which they themselves have individually derived from undeviating obedience to the dietetic principles of vegetarianism."[9]

Graham then addressed the gathering, speaking about the tradition of meat eating, and the difficult task of getting people to change their eating habits. After Graham, remarks made by a farmer from Illinois named Marquis F. Baldwin received great enthusiasm from the group.

A few months later, on September 4, 1850, Alcott and other movement leaders and supporters gathered to celebrate the First Annual meeting of the American Vegetarian Society. The meeting was held in the Lecture Room of the Chinese Museum in Philadelphia.[10] Metcalfe announced that 150 copies of a circular were mailed to individuals in various parts of the country and that replies had been received from some, including those who wrote about how they had benefited from the vegetable diet.

The assembly pledged: "I hereby declare that I have abstained from the flesh of animals for one month and upwards; and that I desire to become a member of the Vegetarian Society; and to cooperate with that Body in promulgating the knowledge of the advantages of a Vegetarian Diet."

In November of 1850 the organization published the premiere edition of its magazine, *The American Vegetarian and Health Journal*. During its brief existence, the AVS added three renown individuals as vice presidents: Orson Fowler, James Caleb Jackson, M.D., and A. Bronson Alcott.

Joel Shew, too, was a vice president of the AVS. Shew, with Russell T. Trall, another vice president, represented hydropathy (water cure)—and drugless medicine—in the organization.

WATER CURE

Dr. Shew, who was born in 1816, founded the first water cure establishment in America in 1844, after studying in Germany with the famous practitioner Vincent Priessnitz. Shew was the author of the popular book *Hydropathy, Or, The Water Cure: Its Principles, Modes of Treatment* (Wiley & Putnam, 1845).

The doctor stated, about diet: "That the 'Vegetarian Diet,' (as it is now called in England, and of which there are many followers in that country,) is destined to do yet a vast amount of good in the prevention and cure of disease, in the United States, I confidently believe. I feel myself too thankful for the great benefit I have received by adopting it for the most part during the period of nine years, to remain silent on the subject. Many in this country have indeed already found great relief and, in not a few instances a perfect cure, by the adoption of vegetable regimen."[11]

Water cure was the colloquial name for hydropathy—an ancient healing art said to have origins in Egypt. Patients were doused with water: it was continually poured over them, or applied as a douche or in a bath, and patients were typically wrapped in wet sheets when put to bed. Proponents contended water was a healing agent for a number of ailments and injuries. Evidently, a fair number of Americans agreed, since water cure establishments (water cures) became numerous, and were popular until at least the end of the nineteenth century.

Unlike modern allopathic hospitals, the water cures tended to be restful, cheerful establishments, and most were located in the countryside. Practitioners believed that such conditions encouraged healing; that is, the body healed itself once patients stopped unhealthful habits, such as wearing corsets, drinking liquor, or avoiding the outdoors, that caused their ills, and adopted a healthful regimen of rest, relaxation, fresh air, and diet.

Not all water cures offered a vegetarian diet, but those most renowned, and most recalled today, did provide it along with meat, and some of the establishments were exclusively vegetarian. Shew's water cure, located in the town of Lebanon Springs in New York, featured a vegetarian diet as an essential part of the health regimen. He also taught his patients the importance of exercise. His water cure was managed for a time by David Cambell, who published *The Graham Journal of Health and Longevity*.

It was evidently widely believed that vegetarianism might make one go insane, or grow emaciated and die; these theories were formidable barriers for the movement in those early years of advocacy of the meat-free diet.

A worse barrier was that to be a vegetarian in the nineteenth century was to suffer abuse—abuse that could correctly be labeled bigotry: blind intolerance. A vegetarian was admirable to a few, a curiosity to many, and to most an object of scorn and legitimate maltreatment. People who ate no meat were considered insane, emaciated, effeminate, and heretical.

Bias against vegetarianism was strong. It was based on ignorance, interpretation of the Bible, prejudice against farmed animals, and against people of vegetarian or near-vegetarian cultures and religions who were considered intellectually, physically, spiritually, and morally inferior to meat-eating Americans.

Vegetarians were subjected to ridicule and worse because they were a threat, as journalist–physician Thomas Low Nichols explained in *The American Vegetarian and Health Journal*. Nichols considered opposition to vegetarianism a strange perversity.

"Men get angry, and rave against Vegetarians as if they had committed some mortal offence. A man cannot make a simple natural meal, without suffering a sort of martyrdom, from all the flesh eaters around him. Men do not like to be reproved, even by the example of those who live better than themselves. To the impure, purity is a reproach. One would think, to hear some flesh eaters talk, that devouring the bodies of slaughtered beasts was the height of human virtue."[12]

Yet ironically, while vegetarians were harassed by some, they were influencing others, and their impact would eventually affect the eating habits of the nation—or at least the common thinking on what generally constituted a healthful diet.

Acknowledging that comparatively few had accepted vegetarianism, Cryus M. Burleigh, Esq., said in his speech at the First Annual Meeting of the AVS that public discussion of vegetarianism, initiated by Sylvester Graham and "his coadjutors and colleagues," had an "indirect influence" widely extended into "schools of Physiology, into Journals and Medical Works." What was more, stated Burleigh, "Throughout all classes of society, it has greatly modified, if it has not entirely controlled the habits of men. It has brought men to the knowledge and feeling that their Bodies are under control of law, and taught them their responsibilities for the use of physical as well as moral and intellectual facilities..."[13]

Another barrier to acceptance and adoption of vegetarianism was the perception by the general public that a Grahamite diet was exclusively comprised of whole wheat bread and water—a not particularly appealing menu, or enticement to reject meat eating.

Yet, vegetarians enjoyed a menu of far more than mere bread and water. One AVS vice president worked to create understanding among meat eaters that a flesh-free feast was not bland or meager, and was instead filled with appetizing foods.

An American Vegetarian Society vice president, John Grimes, M.D., who resided in Boonton, New Jersey, was already well-known in the town for his stance against slavery—as an abolitionist. He began in 1851 holding banquets for the people of the town. The first Vegetarian Festival was held on December 25, Christmas day.

The festival took place at Liberty Hall, a lecture hall in Grimes's building, located in the center of town, which also housed his medical office and apothecary, as well as his living quarters. Grimes charged no fee for admission to the banquet, and invited as many people of the town that he could accommodate at the hall. He went all out to make his neighbors welcome, and to inspire them to change their diets. Liberty Hall was decorated for the holiday with vegetarian mottoes and pictorial representations.[14] On the menu were breads, grain and vegetable dishes, fruits, and desserts.

Acceptable to some, Grimes was deemed an oddity by others of the town. An early and ardent advocate of animal liberation, which no doubt further alienated him from his neighbors, Grimes had stated during an 1850 speech before the American Vegetarian Society: "There are some who think that no animals have a right to live upon earth but man; but I think this is a great error. I think that other beasts were made as much to live and to enjoy their life, as man. The innocent birds that fly about, and sing, and chirp for us, have a right to live, and they make one source of enjoyment for us by their warblings. How unnatural and unkind for us to think we have a right to kill them for the gratification of our appetite."[15]

At the AVS's annual meeting in 1852 Dr. Alcott remarked that "The cause of Vegetarianism is that of the human race. I may be deemed arrogant but I must be permitted to call it not merely our cause, as though there were something selfish about it, but the cause—the cause of humanity. For as I may have already said, in the hearing of some, so I still say in the hearing of you all—would that I could say it to our whole race!—practical Vegetarianism lies at or near the foundation of all true reform—educational, moral, social or political. Something may indeed be done without it—something has been done—but never will our onward march in the career of human improvement be steady, regular and rapid, till the cause of Vegetarianism is triumphant."[16]

Dr. Alcott further explained that the custom of war is connected to Christian cannibalism. He said "the cruel practice of shooting down the feathered songsters and tearing from their native element the scaly tribes (fish)...steel the heart and educate for war. But these and many kindred things, though they come of wantonness, have their apology in the supposed necessities of the table. Make mankind Vegetarians for a few generations and they would pass away."[17]

During 1852 Reverend Metcalfe also commented on this aspect of vegetarianism. "But there are other and still higher reasons for distaining the use of fleshfood. Our Creator has wisely implanted in our natures a reluctance to taking life; and utter abhorence to shedding blood. The life of an animal cannot be taken without inflicting violence on our own moral feelings—without sacrificing our sympathies and filling our bosoms with remorse and compunction; nor can it be pleasant, even to those who, through long continued perverse habits, have had their sensibilities blunted, to recall to their remembrance, that the flesh they may be cutting, or tearing with their teeth, but recently quivered in agonizing torture beneath the butcher's knife."[18] In 1851 Metcalfe served as a delegate to the World's Peace Convention, representing the Pennsylvania Peace Society.

Widespread vegetarianism would usher in peace among people and between people and animals, the way life had been in Paradise before the Fall, believed advocates. Peace would reign on Earth, and so would sobriety. Vegetarian advocates of that era held that the craving for alcoholic drink was caused by meat eating, and that meat in the diet, especially prepared with mustard, pepper, and other spices, was said to stimulate (irritate) the body and resulted in such cravings. Alcott said at the annual meeting: "Flesh pots and all kindred abominations, and all high seasoned dishes induce a morbid and diseased appetite that will never, as a general thing, be satisfied with so plain a drink as water..." This intemperance in drink was a factor in the "flood of licentiousness which threatens to worse than deluge our once fair but guilty world," explained Alcott. Thus, he and others believed that vegetarianism forms the root of moral reform.[19]

Not surprisingly, articles on other reforms, including women's rights, were scattered amid the articles on diet and health in the pages of *TAVHJ*. The Committee that published *TAVHJ* explained why the periodical published such articles: "As we believe VEGETARIANISM lies at the base of every true Reform, and is, in fact, the first step in Physical and Moral Progress, so we are satisfied, that Vegetarians and their families, are generally desirous for information, if not individually interested, in the Moral and Progressive Movements of the Age. We shall, therefore, in future, devote a portion of each number, in a concise form, to Intelligence of this character, without, however, deeming ourselves the direct advocates of any other than the Vegetarian Cause."[20]

Contributing writers to the Journal provided such intelligence on how other movements related to diet reform.

FEMINISM

Anne Denton, a women's rights advocate who belonged to the AVS, writing in the December 1852 issue of the *TAVHJ*, stated: "Has not woman rights? Rights which by the foolish customs of society, she has been deprived of? Yes, custom, that venomous serpent, has coiled itself around woman and paralyzed her powers, and as long as she is passive, so long as she allows this reptile custom to coil around her, just so long will she remain in bondage."[21]

An integral step in woman's liberation from that bondage, explained Denton, was to change her diet. "Every female should be quite familiar with physiology. Hundreds die in infancy, through the ignorance of parents, who might have lived to a blessing and delight to them. To some it may appear like dragging Vegetarianism in, to introduce it here, but I do not think so. If females would study the laws of health, they would be convinced of its truth, and be themselves blessed, and their children, by the adoption of pure vegetable diet."[22]

One day, predicted Denton, women would have a voice in the ruling of nations. They would gain this power by first empowering themselves. How would woman obtain rights? "By making herself capable of using them aright; by studying and obeying the laws of nature; and lastly, by taking possession of them." Thus, women would become educated and grow strong.[23]

Denton believed that women were meant to be benevolent, and that by cooking (and eating) meat they were lowering themselves. "Woman should be something more than Fashion's doll, or a cooking-machine. Their ambition should aim at something higher than the gratification of depraved appetite. Why so much anxiety to gratify one organ, alimentiveness? Dishes of flesh form a part of almost every meal—thus are nature's laws violated, and woman, who is naturally refined and beautiful in spirit, and evidently intended to throw a benign and angel-like influence around life, is degraded to the work of cooking mangled flesh for vitiated appetites. Woman should live for something higher and nobler than cannibal tastes, good appearance, costly furniture or fine equipage," wrote Denton.[24]

The American Vegetarian and Health Journal condoned women's rights and animal rights. One of those who wrote about animal rights, and other topics, was Charles Lane, the Englishman, abolitionist, and transcendentalist who had cofounded the Fruitlands vegan community in Massachusetts with A. Bronson Alcott, and who, like the two Alcott cousins, was a leading voice for vegetarianism. Lane was the editor of *The Healthian*, a vegetarian magazine published in the UK, and published a book on the subject in 1849 titled *Dietetics: An endeavour to ascertain the law of human nutriment.*

Lane explained in the *TAVHJ* in 1852 that "the abandonment of animal substances as articles of food, has been adopted by so many individuals within the past few years that a general inquiry is now springing up for information as to the motives for such conduct. The bottle is put aside for the book—and the arts of the greasy cook are now rivaled by purer preparations, by the attractions of art, and still more by the pure intuitions of our nature."[25]

Englishman Lane explained the factors that motivated individuals to reject meat eating: "Some persons have been influenced by considerations of health, agility and strength, others by economy; more have adopted a Vegetable Diet for the intellectual benefit to be thereby acquired; still more perhaps on the ground of humanity, that is to say, of kindness toward their own feelings, and the susceptibilities of the animal world—and a few perhaps as a religious duty."[26]

Lane's assessment of the latter motivation, that is, religious reason for rejecting meat, contradicts a statement that would be made a few years later by James Caleb Jackson, M.D., an AVS vice president who contended that most vegetarians were Christians who viewed their diet as an aspect of their religion. That Lane stated concern for animals motivated an evidently substantial number of Americans to eschew meat is an indicator that the animal rights movement evolved from the vegetarian movement.

The animal liberation aspect of vegetarianism, like all the other aspects, had support from people abroad. Another book by a foreign author read and recommended by those in the American movement was *Thalysie, or the New Being* by French author Jean Antoine Gleizes, who believed that human beings were designed to be gentle creatures not predatory animals, and that the killing of animals and feeding upon them caused human deformities, disease, and shortened lifespan.[27] Gleizes believed animal liberation was a main message of Jesus to humanity.

Such ideas against meat eating would likely not have impressed every American. Surveys showed that Americans consumed more food than people of any other nation. Americans were also said to have eaten faster. "It is common enough for men in active business habits to make an onslaught upon a well furnished table about five or ten minutes, during which time they swallow, with fearful rapidity, parts of half a dozen dishes, and then rush out to their posts of business, as one would suppose from their haste, and immediately scat themselves with their feet thrown up and their heads back and leisurely puff their cigars—without the least possible sign of hurry or care."[28]

Many arguments presented in favor of the rejection of meat nearly mirror modern arguments. James Caleb Jackson writing in the *Water Cure*, presented a few of the arguments of his day, including that human anatomy was that of a fruit-eater not a carnivore, and that butchering of animals to satisfy one's appetite for their flesh caused people to become coarse and brutal, destroying their finer sensibilities.

Jackson believed that since man was given dominion over the other beings on the Earth, "he can therefore afford to spare life...to kill a lamb to eat it—is it not horrible? Its dying bleat and the flavor of its flesh do not harmonize well in the sphere of associations." The doctor also protested the use of meat because it was stimulating to the nervous system and "injurious as alcohol."[29]

Meat, stated Jackson, "must be habitually used, or abstinence will create the same very unpleasant effects that arise from its excess in its first use. That is, "flesh, eaten largely by one who had eaten none, disturbs digestion—creates acute dyspepsia and an entire disrelish of all other food." Vegetarians can withstand longer periods of abstinence from all food than can those who are not abstainers, said Jackson." Conversely, Jackson claimed, vegetarians have a greater power of mental endurance. When children eat flesh it leads to "nervous and arterial excitement, to undue development of the passions, and to premature puberty."[30]

DEATH OF SYLVESTER GRAHAM

The American vegetarian movement experienced triumph and tragedy in the 1850s. The AVS was born in 1850 and Sylvester Graham died in 1851. Sylvester Graham did not live a long life. His death was grist for the rumor mill. His early demise had shaken the foundations of the vegetarian movement, at least in the perception of a few journalists and an unknown number of other people.

If, after all, the promulgator of the system of health of abstaining from meat was dead before his time, what did that demonstrate about the system? Like today's headline-hunting reporters eager for the sensational story, reporters of yesteryear wanted all the details on the death of Graham. They sought William Alcott for the dirt on his deceased associate in the vegetarian movement.

Alcott noted this in an article published in *TAVHJ*; in it he quoted reporters: "Will Dr. Alcott inform the public how it could possibly come to pass that Mr. Graham, living in a perfect way,—in such a way, according to his own saying, as would enable a man to live til he was about a hundred years old (and wrong to die any sooner) could run down in one year, and at last die while living in accordance with his own system of Physiology, Dietetics, etc., so that upon a post mortem examination no traces of disease could be discovered sufficient to justify death? We want, in fact, all the particulars of his last days and hours; and we wish also to know whether he died in the true faith of the gospel."[31]

Seth Hunt, a peace movement leader and Grahamite leader, as well as friend of Graham's, and renowned resident of Northampton, addressed the matter of his friend's death in Horace Greeley's *New York Tribune* newspaper. Wrote Hunt:

Mr. Graham was in his 58th year, at the time of his decease; not, as has been stated in the papers, about 50. 2. He had, by inheritance, a feeble constitution. His father, an inhabitant of Suffield, Connecticut, was, as I have always understood, nearly 70 years older than he, and besides, he was nearly or quite the youngest of a large family of children. 3. He did not become a "Grahamite" until he was well nigh 40 years of age—till his constitution had been much impaired by the influence of wrong habits. 4. He was of a constitution and temperament which naturally rendered him mentally precocious, and predisposed him to nervous and scrofulous maladies. Few, if any, public men with such a temperament, have been so healthy, or lived as long as he. 5. He was not sustained in his supposed office of reforming the world, by that cooperation which might have been expected in the domestic relation. Those who know this part of his history, will not be surprised that he ran down soon. The wonder is that he held out as long as he did. 6. It does not appear that he was always true to his own system—in all its particulars—as it is said he often confessed. But that his dietetic errors were not considerable, would appear probable from the sound condition of his digestive system, as shown by a post mortem examination. It is not quite clear that his medical management was judicious; or if judicious, that he faithfully followed it. 7. But he did not run down in one year. He has been running down, both mentally and physically for many years. A constitution like that of Hercules would have been used up by the treatment to which he subjected his, in his public life, as many of his friends well know.[32]

Sylvester Graham died relatively young. Whether or not vegetarianism prolonged his life, or if he was worn down and finally broken by the pressure he endured might never be known, The exact cause of Graham's death is a mystery: an autopsy found no organic disease.

The rumors flew about the end of Graham's life, but Russell Trall, M.D., was ready for combat. Dr. Trall, the drugless doctor who visited Graham at Northampton a few times during the last days of the vegetarian crusader's life, explained that the doctor treating Graham was an allopath. The doctor and Graham's wife, against Graham's wishes, demanded that he drink wine, eat meat, and take opium for pain. It was said by Trall, Seth Hunt, and others who knew the family that Graham's wife was not supportive of his ideas, and that she ate meat and drank wine.

Trall, writing in *TAVHJ*, claimed that Graham did:

maintain, both in theory and practice, his Vegetarian creed, to the last, so far as his own volition was concerned. It is true he had eaten flesh, in two or three instances, on compulsion, as he informed me; his friends and physicians insisting upon it as a condition upon which he was to have their attention. But as Mr. G. assured me that he only used it a short time to satisfy his friends by the only evidence they could appreciate that his own views of diet were correct, I did not consider this yielding to necessity or importunity, as recreancy to his own teachings. Moreover, he suspected that, in his last moments, some scheme would be devised by those around him, who were personally at variance with, and bitter opposers of his system, to extort or distort from him a renunciation of his Vegetarian doctrine, or at least a confession that in his works, it had been carried too far. I am fully satisfied that such an attempt was made, but that it did not succeed...[33]

The late crusader's associate in the cause Dr. Trall told the story of Graham's last weeks in the pages of the *Water Cure Journal* (republished in same as above pp. 217–218). In August of 1951, Trall had received a letter from Graham's daughter with a request from her father for Trall to come to Northamptom to treat the ailing crusader. Graham had wanted to go to the water cure at Lebanon Springs for treatment, but had become too weak.

Trall went to Northamptom and talked with Graham, as well as with his wife, and his physician, an allopath named Dr. Thomas. Trall learned that despite Graham's wish to go to the water cure, and his disapproval of meat eating and use of drugs and liquor, even as medicine, he was forced to comply with his doctor's and his wife's orders, or receive no treatment at all. Thus, Trall explained, Dr. Thomas "gave the patient opium enema, to allay pain and procure sleep; cherry wine and quinine to support the strength, and insisted on flesh food, or what he called tonic diet."[34]

Dr. Trall wrote of Graham: "that he was honestly of the opinion that it did him no good, was evinced by his conduct; for, at the time I visited him, he had peremptorily refused to eat any more flesh, and was confining himself to a very strict allowance of rice. Moreover, he declared to me, before Heaven, that he considered himself fully aware of the kind of treatment he ought to have had, but could not get; that the most of his troubles—gastric irritation and sciatica—were the consequences of over-distention of the stomach, from eating too much and too great a variety; and that he fully and verily believed in the theory of vegetable diet as explained in his works."[35]

Graham had confidently proclaimed that one day people would visit his house to see where he had lived, and to see the monument he assumed would be built to honor him. His prediction was not entirely wrong. In 2003, his Northampton, Massachusetts, home was a restaurant named Sylvester's, which served some vegetarian food, but also meat and some white flour-based foods, as well as tea, coffee, and alcoholic beverages. No monument to Graham has yet been erected.

GRAHAM'S LEGACY

Graham the man is virtually unheard of today, even in the vegetarian world. Journalists and scholars who have mentioned his name have tended to disparage him as a Victorian quack or crank. What is widely known is the Graham cracker that bears his name, if not his principle of whole, unadulterated wheat flour and no animal ingredients. He did not invent a cracker or start a food company. As Graham said, he had nothing to sell. The term *Graham cracker* was not used until years past the crusader's death. Some speculate the cracker he supposedly invented was just the recipe he gave for bread, which he thought should be several hours old before fit to eat.

But his contribution to public health, nutrition, and the vegetarian movement lives on. The seeds of vegetarianism—of Grahamism—had been planted into the fertile soil of the American consciousness, and would eventually sprout and bear fruit as the Great Crusader himself had predicted. "(Yet) when the core elements of his credo are examined critically (exercise, avoidance of alcohol, tobacco and stimulants, a prudent meat-free diet and daily bathing), we encounter a secular formula warmly advocated by modern medicine," wrote Stanley M. Aronson, M.D., dean of medicine emeritus, Brown University, in an editorial.[36]

Richard Harrison Shryrock, historian of medicine, did not disparage Graham. "A century after Graham first made his appeal, his preachments have begun to be practiced, and today at least part of the population apparently eat less and select their food with greater care than did their fathers. People nowadays are seekers after roughage and the whole grain in cereals. They worship fresh air and sun-tan, and the bath room has become the very symbol of American civilization. Verily, Americans have been 'physiologically reformed.' "

The medical community dispenses large doses of Grahamite advice, and the American public has largely adopted Graham's teachings. However, most doctors are not yet prescribing the vegetable diet, and the nation has not recognized Graham's contributions. Reformers who aided a particular class or sex "appear on a pedestal" while Graham's "is still relegated to the grocery store," wrote Shryrock.[37]

FRONT PAGE HEADLINES

Vegetarians were still struggling against the tide in the 1850s, but that didn't stop them from sailing ahead. They rode the waves of vacillating attitudes: sometimes up towards acceptance and more often back down to rejection. Publicity was one life raft which kept the movement from drowning.

One of the vegetarians' gatherings made the front page of the *New York Daily Times*. The year was 1853 and approximately 300 to 350 people attended the Vegetarian Festival, which was held at New York City's Metropolitan Hall on a Saturday night in September.[38]

Dr. Trall was there, and attendees included Horace Greeley and Frances Dana Gage, a well-known figure in the antislavery, women's rights, and temperance movements. Also at the festival were women's rights advocates Lucy Stone, Susan B. Anthony, and Emilia Bloomer.

The evening's speakers didn't hold anything back when it came to espousing vegetarianism. Greeley, whose *New York Tribune* was a favorite newspaper of reformers, began by telling the gathering that the world would be "wiser and stronger and richer than it is now were we to discontinue the use of animal food altogether." He went on to say that he wished that an "enterprising man would favor us by starting a Vegetarian Hotel in New York, and a Vegetarian eating-house." Great applause followed. "When we shall have a good vegetable product, it will be found that men will gradually disuse and reject animal food altogether," Greeley predicted.[39]

The festival featured a menu that might be judged unusual by today's culinary standards, as it was deemed by some nonvegetarians who had joined in the feasting. The Bill of Fare: Vegetable soup, tomato soup, rice soup, farinacea, Graham bread, mixed-fruit cake, fruitbread, apple biscuit, wheat-meal cakes, moulded rice, corn blanc mange, moulded wheaten grits, vegetables, baked sweet potatoes, stewed cream squash, pastry, mixed-fruit pie, pumpkin pie, fruits, melons, apples, peaches, pears, grapes, pineapples, cooked fruits including plum jelly and baked apples, relishes consisting of coconut custard and fruited ice cream, and a beverage of pure cold water.

Once the meal was over and speakers like Grahamite Greeley had taken to the podium, the audience became rowdy. Amid the 500 spectators and passerbys who gathered in the gallery, hecklers shouted their preference for eating meat.

One of their targets was the famous Dr. James Caleb Jackson. His statement that animals are placed in the "most unhealthy conditions possible, in order to secure to them such a state of body, organization or condition as will justify us in eating them" evoked strong reaction from the gallery.

A woman interrupted Jackson by yelling out "Put me down as a meat eater!" and another spectator shouted something similar as roars of laughter echoed throughout the gallery.

Jackson diffused the heckling by firing back that meat eating was "extremely injurious to children." Some nonvegetarians eventually joined the meat-free feast, where women outnumbered men two to one.

The feast didn't lack for entertainment, as a singing group called the Amphions serenaded the audience with their tune, "Song of Grace." The words are as follows:

Thankful all, His praise repeat.
Every herb and each tree yielding,
Seed and fruit, shall be our meat.
Nature's banquet, pure and peaceful,
Is a "feast of reason" too;
Every healthful sense delighting,
Ever changing, ever new.

The American Vegetarian Society nourished affiliate organizations. The New York Vegetarian Society had been established in 1852. Dr. Trall served as president.[40] The vegetarian movement grew, but not without experiencing pains. By 1854, the American Vegetarian Society was on unstable ground. Sylvester Graham and William Alcott were dead, and William Metcalfe had moved back to England, as had Thomas Low Nichols and Mary Gove Nichols. The Society was sustained for a few more years, but funds for *The American Vegetarian and Health Journal* dried up and it was discontinued in October.

However, largely through the efforts of Henry Steven Clubb, who had been involved with the AVS, information about vegetarianism continued to flow to the public. He arranged for *The Water Cure Journal*, a popular magazine, published by Fowler and Wells, for which he was a reporter, to regularly print a section about vegetarianism. Fowler and Wells was the

primary publishing house on reform subjects, including books on vegetarianism, and the books seem to have sold in substantial numbers.

One of the founders of the house, Orson Fowler, the famous phrenologist, advocated vegetarianism and served as a vice president of the AVS
in 1852. Meat, believed Fowler, was bad for the brain because it over-
stimulated that part which controlled physical urges, as well as emotions.

In his 1847 book, *Physiology, Animal and Mental: Applied to the preserva-
tion and restoration of health of body, and power of mind* (Fowler and Wells),
Fowler included information about the importance of the plant-based diet
for health, and why foods of the plant kingdom were the natural diet for
human beings.

Even earlier, in 1844, Fowler had addressed the subjects of vegetarianism and animal liberation in his book *Religion; Natural and Revealed: Or The
Natural Theology and Moral Bearings of Phrenology and Physiology*. In the
chapter titled "Benevolence—Its Analysis, and the Truths Taught Thereby,"
Fowler quoted from a lecture given by his brother:

Were a flesh diet productive of no other evil consequence than lowering down and
hardening benevolence, that alone should forever annihilate so barbarous a practice.... The cruelties practiced upon our animals that are slaughtered for the meat
market, are sickening and incredible. See the poor calves, sheep, &c., tumbled
together in the smallest possible space; their limbs tied; unfed, bellowing continually, and in a most piteous tone, their eyes rolled up in agony, taken to the slaughterhouse, and whipped, or rather pelted by the hour with a most torturing
instrument, and then strung up by the hind legs, a vein opened, and they dying by
inches from the gradual loss of blood, the unnatural suspension, and cruel pelt-
ing—and all to make their meat white and tender.[41]

Fowler's benevolence—vegetarian diet and animal liberation—was
part of the phrenology for which he was widely acclaimed. The phrenologist also defended the rights of other animals; for example, in his book
Fowler presented an argument against shooting birds, a popular pastime
of the era.

Phrenologist Fowler published a magazine favorable to vegetarianism:
The American Phrenolological Journal and Miscellany. His books, periodicals,
and lectures, along with articles about diet in *The Water Cure Journal*, were
among the factors that helped carry the vegetarian movement forward.

The *American Vegetarian and Health Journal* was no longer published, but
the work of Graham, Alcott, Mr. and Mrs. Nichols, and others, such as
Mussey, Grimes, and Bronson Alcott, had not failed. The nation was not
vegetarian, but the message of food reform, that less meat was good and
none best, reached deep into America. That it was printed in *The Water
Cure Journal*, a publication read by tens of thousands, was one sign of the
depth it had reached. Another was that crusaders for other causes, like
Fowler, included vegetarianism on their list of reforms.

One of these crusaders was a Quaker named Jeremiah Hacker who published the *Portland Pleasure Boat,* a small reform newspaper. In the pages of the Portland, New Hampshire-based paper, Hacker championed a number of related causes including peace, environmentalism, animal rights, and vegetarianism.

Hacker was proud of a story that he published in his newspaper on vegetarianism and temperance and stated "it is worth the price of several thousand years' subscriptions." The article by Nelson Newland of South Alden, New York, outlined Grahamite arguments against meat eating. "To slay animals, and feed on their flesh, is repugnant to nature, and in violation of her most sacred ordinances.... On a natural system of diet, which consists of bread, fruit, berries, beans, and pure water...and the practice of due moderation and prudence, debility is converted into strength; disease into healthfulness; ungovernable passions into calmness; fretfulness and ill-nature into serenity of temper; in a word, we should in the fullest sense of the term, enjoy life..."[42]

The mainstream press was on occasion covering vegetarianism. A short story about a Grahamite was published in *The Ladies' Repository* in 1853. The story, titled *Portliness Illustrated,* by William T. Coggeshall, depicted a conflict between an overweight uncle who believed what he ate and drank had no relation to health and a young woman and his nephew who tried to get him to change his health habits. The uncle considers the young lady and his nephew nuisances: "This world is coming to a great pass. We shall all be fools one of these days, and feed on air. Temperance societies would take a man's drink away, Grahamites would take his food, some other ites want his land, and next you know some new ism will be after his soul." Ignoring the young people, the portly uncle, who loved meat and port, succumbs to an attack, and then another, this time a fatal attack of apoplexy.[43]

People like those who wrote such stories, and like Portland publisher Jeremiah Hacker, were not leading the vegetarian movement, but they helped cultivate its growth.

One reason vegetarianism was taking root at this time was the overall interest in eating habits. Journalist Thomas Low Nichols, M.D., a leader of the vegetarian movement, would years later, in his 1864 book, attribute, to some extent, the public's interest in vegetarianism to a "reaction against excesses and abuses" in eating habits.

"But," stated Nichols, "some thousands of Americans abandoned the use of flesh entirely, and many never returned to it. These believe that most of the diseases and evils of life are caused by eating flesh, and that with its disuse would come health, purity, and happiness."[44]

The nurturing the movement received during those early decades created firm ground that was needed for its survival when its greatest challenge came: the Civil War.

Chapter 5

The Water Cures, Seventh-Day Adventists, and the Civil War

America was not yet fertile ground for the unimpeded growth of vegetarianism. Advocates had rocks to remove and soil to fertilize. Several dynamic leaders met the challenge. The vegetarian movement experienced no dry spells in the late 1850s. Then came the Civil War. The people of the nation were preoccupied. War was taking American lives by the thousands. Soldiers either died on the battlefield, or, more often, they died due to the treatments administered by the allopathic doctors, according to at least one medical authority. One wounded soldier who survived would eventually revive the vegetarian movement. His name was Henry Stephen Clubb and he was a Bible-Christian.

An official of the American Vegetarian Society, Henry Stephen Clubb had emigrated to the United States from England in 1853. As a youngster, he attended the school at Greaves's Alcott House. As an adult he moved to Philadelphia in 1853 and found work as a journalist for Greeley's *New York Tribune.* Clubb, an abolitionist and a pacifist, lectured against slavery. He was evidently convincing to audiences, since at one point a reward was offered by slavery proponents for the capture of Clubb.

Clubb in 1855 drafted grandiose plans to build a vegetarian city in Kansas (Kanzas in those days) on the banks of the Neosho River the following spring. He founded the Vegetarian Settlement Company, which was similar to other organizations formed to entice settlers to homestead in the plains, such as the New England Emigrant Aid Company. Clubb altered his colonization plan to include a second settlement on the opposite bank of the Neosho to accommodate the strong interest among non-vegetarians, and formed the Octagon Settlement Company to carry it out.

Henry S. Clubb: Vegetarian advocate for several
decades.

More colonists, more money, and more of a chance of success, believed
Clubb.[1]

The city would be about 16 square miles with an Octagon-shaped park
of 640 acres at the center, complete with a hydropathic institution, an agricultural college and a scientific institute, and a museum of curiosities and
mechanical arts.

The company would purchase the land from the government at $1.25 an
acre, and resell it to vegetarian members at $5 a share. Colonists could
purchase an acre of land with one share, or with labor. Under the plan, the
proceeds from land sales would be set aside to pay for infrastructure proj-
ects such as roads and schools.

Colonists would make their living working in industries such as timber,
agricultural tools and machinery, and farming and mining. They would
export agricultural products such as Graham flour, Graham crackers,
cracked wheat, and ripe and dried fruits all over the United States—
"enterprise worthy the exertions of young and enterprising vegetarians,"
wrote Clubb.[2]

Before the colonists were scheduled to begin arriving in May, Clubb sent settlers in advance to construct a central building to house the incoming settlers and to build mills. The idea was to help emigrants settle rapidly and immediately earn livings.

However, the settlers who arrived in the spring of 1856 were in for a surprise. They found no saw mills, or mills of any kind, and just a 16 by 16 foot log cabin with a dirt floor. Mariam Davis Colt, who arrived that May with her family, summed up the shock of the experience in her book, *Went to Kanzas:* "Can anyone imagine our disappointment this morning, on learning from this and that member, that no mills have been built..."[3]

Matters worsened for the small band of settlers. Although they successfully raised corn, melons, and other crops, they had to live in primitive, makeshift cabins that did little to keep out rain, swarms of mosquitoes, or poisonous snakes. The colonists also had to deal with hostile Indians who stole some of their crops, and faced the threat from outlaws or border ruffians who preyed on settlers.

The settlement never really got off the ground. The only reminder of the doomed pilgrimage is a creek in the area named Vegetarian Creek.

Clubb's dream did not come true, but another man's did, at least for a time. Dr. James E. Spencer in 1857 established the Harmonial Vegetarian Society, a small community in Benton County, Arkansas. And it was likely that the locals wanted the community to stay small.

Not all Southerners, or Americans, approved of vegetarianism—or vegetarians. "The numerical majority, as public opinion, produces the multitude of 'false doctrines, heresies, and schisms,' the growing infidelity, the Grahamites and Fourierites, the Mormonism and Millerism, and all those wild vagaries of fanaticism to which the people of the free States are so prone, but which cannot live beneath the southern sun," announced a writer in the magazine *Debow's Review, Agricultural, Commercial, Industrial Progress and Resources.*[4]

Like the country, the Harmonial Vegetarian Society community came undone with the onset of the Civil War. It ceased to exist in 1861 when Spencer left and the other members of the commune were arrested by the Confederate army.

After Octagon City failed to become a reality, journalist Clubb in 1857 moved from Kansas to Grand Haven, Michigan, where he founded the Clarion newspaper featuring Republican politics and literary topics.

THE WATER CURES, SEVENTH-DAY ADVENTISM, AND TO THE CIVIL WAR

Clubb's dream had vanished, Sylvester Graham was gone, but several other advocates kept the fires of the cause burning. Vegetarianism had taken root. Like the roots of a mighty oak, vegetarianism was spreading

James Caleb Jackson: Founded Our Home on the
Hillside. Courtesy of William Dailey Collection.

far and wide into society, both in slowly growing acceptance, and in geographic range. The vegetarian diet was still talked about, even if skeptically, and now the plant-based diet was incorporated into the regimen of many of the water cures across America. One of the most renowned of these establishments was located east of "Kanzas" and owned by James Caleb Jackson, M.D.—who had served as a vice president of the American Vegetarian Society.

Jackson was acclaimed, perhaps internationally renowned, as a drugless doctor. As a young man he had enjoyed good health until he grew worn out from working at his profession of traveling slavery abolitionist.

Activists who lectured on the eradication of slavery had some supporters, but they were often hissed at, pelted with rotten fruit, shouted down, and violently attacked by people who disagreed. Jackson was a lecturer and he edited several abolitionist newspapers. He was instrumental in the founding of the abolitionist Liberty League political party.

By the age of 37 Jackson was exhausted, sick, and unable to continue his travels and lecturing on the antislavery cause. His career came to a halt in 1847, and he checked in at Dr. Silas O. Gleason's Water Cure establishment in upstate New York, a health institution that would inspire in him a new calling. Jackson eventually recovered and then opened a water cure in

New York's Cayuga County with Gleason. During this time Jackson also attended medical school.

Jackson, who was born in 1811 in Manlius, Onondago County, New York, became a medical doctor and then the sole owner of Glen Haven water cure. It was a widely acclaimed health establishment, particularly among abolitionists and other reformers, including women's rights leaders Amelia Bloomer and Elizabeth Cady Stanton. Glen Haven was a haven for the reformers; they flocked there to discuss politics and social change while building up their bodies or overcoming health woes. Dr. Jackson, like a number of his comrades in the war against slavery, didn't separate that crusade from other causes. He was also in favor of women's rights, temperance—and vegetarianism.

Until the age of 36, Jackson's eating habits, and other daily health habits, were the same as those of his contemporaries. Jackson's health had not broken suddenly; it was a process that took years. He had been a sickly child. His physician-father administered medicines in attempt to help his son. But the son's health grew worse over time. Jackson was diagnosed as suffering from organic heart disease and other maladies. He was expected not to live long.

He survived, but for years he suffered constant pain and near-invalidism. Over those years, 200 doctors, including some of the most respected names in medicine, examined the suffering young man, diagnosing a variety of ailments, and administering medicines in vain attempt to heal him, according to Jackson. The soon-to-be crusader for vegetarianism reported that none of the doctors, including his father, whom he deemed a typical old-school physician, thought to tell Jackson he could take steps to help himself back to health, including changing his eating habits.

Then, in the winter of his 36th year, his health worsened and he became totally incapacitated. One physician remarked that Jackson would never regain his health. Jackson was confined to bed until spring, when, without much faith in its restorative power, he decided to try the then relatively new water cure treatment.

That was when he went to Gleason's hydropathic institute. Jackson heard the same diagnosis: he was incurable. He nevertheless convinced the doctor, an allopath Jackson deemed as unfamiliar with "the laws of life and health as any physician of his day," to let him stay at the water cure.

Then Jackson had a revelation: "I came to the conclusion that if I could live, it must be through a very radical change in foods and drink; that I at least, needed food which was nutritious, but non-stimulating rather than its opposite."[5] Jackson stated that he had not set out to be a vegetarian; only after he had more than once experienced the revitalizing power of the vegetable diet did he finally decide to permanently reject flesh foods. He became a leading advocate of abstinence from meat eating.

OUR HOME ON THE HILLSIDE

One day in 1796 in the town of Dansville, New York, a spring burst from out of a hillside, sending rocks and dirt spraying into the air and uprooting trees. The townspeople called it All Healing Spring. A water cure establishment was built at the spring in 1853. It lasted just a few years.

Then in 1858, Dr. Jackson decided to locate his new health institution on the spot. It was named the Jackson Sanatorium, but it was better known as Our Home on the Hillside, set amid panoramic views of the Finger Lakes region.

The Graham system with requisite vegetable diet was part of Our Home. Health, thought Jackson was a matter of following the laws of health, which were the laws of God. Humans had grown depraved by straying from God's laws of health, and that was why so many Americans suffered with sickness, reasoned Jackson. He had expanded upon Graham's work, and that of Russell T. Trall, M.D., and created a system of holistic health—perhaps the first in the nation.

Jackson's reputation as a healer who treated his patients effectively and with kindness, grew along with business. He used no drugs, which he considered the "popular delusion of the nineteenth century." Rather than medicate his guests, as they were called, Jackson treated the sick the natural way with a regimen of diet, exercise, rest, hydropathy, massage therapy, and use of newly invented electrical stimulating devices that were supposed to help the body heal.

Ninety-five percent of the patients, Dr. Jackson would later state, "have been (so) helped during the time they stayed with me, or have been thoroughly cured while under my care.... "

The doctor employed what he called Psycho-hygienic methods—treating the mind as well as the body. Our Home guests were encouraged to go outside in good weather and relax. On the lawns they were seen swinging in hammocks, lying on blankets and cots, and sitting beneath shady trees. In winter, Jackson's guests went on sleigh rides in the snow-covered hills.

As part of his patients' therapy, Jackson provided concerts and poetry readings. Giles E. Jackson, who was the doctor's son, designed and built Liberty Hall adjacent to the main building, where his father held lectures and, according to Dansville historian Wilfred Rauper, some of the nation's most outstanding persons came to lecture.

Dr. Jackson encouraged his guests to cast off conventional rules of "artificial, fashionable and false methods of living." Women, he believed, should not wear constricting corsets and heavy skirts—clothing not exactly conducive to walking through the woods, or to regaining robust health.

Dr. Harriet N. Austin, Jackson's adopted daughter whom he had first worked with at Glen Haven, was a women's rights advocate. She developed the American Costume. The costume was a matching tunic and pants designed for comfort and freedom of movement. Women at Our Home on the Hillside were urged to wear the radical pantsuit.

The sanatorium enjoyed phenomenal growth in its early years and in 1864 was ready to expand. More than 20,000 people were treated at Our Home. It was one of the largest institutions of its kind in the world and had a national reputation as a top health establishment.

Jackson encouraged guests of the Our Home health establishment to eat the vegetarian food, and he provided plenty of food for thought against the eating of meat. He called for vegetarianism as a Christian duty essential for purity and physical perfection.

His vegetarian message spread beyond the sanitarium. Many people who never visited Our Home learned of Jackson's work—and about the vegetarian diet—from his books and from his magazine *Laws of Life,* which he edited with daughter Harriet Austin. Jackson was a prolific writer who also contributed regularly to *The Water Cure Journal and Herald of Reforms, Devoted to Physiology, Hydropathy.* As a writer and lecturer, Jackson did not sugarcoat his words.

In "To Allopathic Physicians," the title of a series of articles by Jackson published in *The Water Cure,* Jackson scolded the regular (allopathic) doctors and explained the prevailing opinion of meat eating and vegetarianism held by most of the allopaths. He made his position of opposing the use of drugs and medicine very clear:

You are advocates for flesh-eating. And you range over the whole domain of vertebrate life for your constituents. You except horse-flesh; but as civilization advances, of which flesh-eating men are the type, this animal also will come to be included in your list of food-furnishing animals. The French gourmands who have tasted it speak of its deliciousness in extravagant terms.

But setting it aside, the ox, the sheep, the swine, the bear, the deer, the raccoon, the squirrel, the musk-rat, and the hedge-hog are proper aliment for man. More than this. You deemed them essential for human health. You laugh at vegetarianism. You ridicule it. You speak of it contemptuously. I might, with much pertinence, ask you to what extent you have knowledge of what you laugh at and ridicule? Have you tried to live without animal food yourselves? Have you experimented upon your patients? Are you sure that in endeavoring to keep the people from discontinuing the use of flesh-meat, you are not inducing them to employ you? Will you stake your reputations on the fact that if every family whom you visit were to abstain from meat and other such articles of food as are only eaten in connection with flesh, for one year, that your practice as drug-doctors would not diminish very perceptibly? I am sure it would; for I am sure that of those diseases peculiar to the United States, one third of them all is owing to the food-eater, aggravated, of course, by the manner in which it is prepared. And I am morally certain that were the people to abstain from flesh-eating, and its cognates, they would diminish in the use of drugs and medicine to that degree that another third of the prevalent diseases would disappear, and so the health of the masses by this simple process be improved at least 60 percent.

Many persons dine on scrofulous beefsteak, or bacon, to die of consumption years afterward, then and there induced. Many children die, poisoned at their mother's breast, because their mothers would eat pastry enriched by scrofulous hogs' lard. Many girls and boys die before blossoming, because they are stuffed with grease and gravies, urged into them by wiseacres of your school, traveling about as "Peripatetic Physiologers."[6]

The Peripatetic Physiologers were a problem. Jackson and others contended that these drug doctors made deliberate attempts to crush the spread of vegetarianism. Graham was dead, and apparently some in society also wanted his message to die.

For example, a year later, in 1859, *The Water Cure* carried a brief item titled "Grahamism" by correspondent J.C.B. of Marion, New York, which read: "Sylvester Graham did not, at any time, renounce his theory of vegetarian diet; nor did he ever confess that his teachings were in any respect wrong; nor that his opinions had undergone any change—all the false and ridiculous stories to the contrary notwithstanding. It seems to be the policy of many 'drug-doctors and beef-eaters' to circulate all manner of false statements about those who advocate such habits of living as would deprive them of a lucrative business."[7]

That one of the founders of the vegetarian movement in America died that year probably did not help the status of vegetarianism. William Alcott died on March 29, while still a relatively young man just short of 60. These were tumultuous times for vegetarians; the negative stereotypes lingered and would remain well into the twenty-first century.

Jackson, in his book *Flesh as Food for Man in Dyspepsia and Its Treatment*, told of the status of vegetarianism during the mid-nineteenth century. "There is no class of persons more misapprehended than vegetarians, or those who abstain from the use of animal food. They are regarded as 'odd,' 'eccentric,' 'half-crazed' persons, who are dyspeptic, ill-tempered, ill-bred, sour-visaged, lank and lean in body, and fit only in mind to traverse all higher rules of social culture. They are supposed to be 'Skeptics,' 'Come Outers,' 'Infidels,' 'Radicals,' and 'Revolutionaries.' All such ideas of them are mistaken; for, as a great fact, exactly the reverse is true. The larger share of them in the United States and Europe are Christian men and women, who eat no meat because they think without it they will better adorn the doctrine of Christ their Saviour by holy lives and godly conversation."[8]

Most vegetarians of that era were Christians, as were most Americans. But the movement was not exclusively for Christians. Some vegetarians were interested in the teachings of other religions, and a few might have been members of those religions. Occasional references were made to the

"Hindoo" in the pages of *TAVHJ*; and to the sacred scripture, Bhagavad-Gita, which instructed believers to respect animals and to revere all life—traits that the American vegetarians found in the words of the Christian Bible, especially in the life and teachings of Jesus Christ.

SEVENTH-DAY ADVENTISTS

Guests of Jackson's original health establishment, Glen Haven, included a young woman named Ellen G. White and her husband, James White; the latter treated by Jackson. "Sister White" later became world renowned after she and her spouse founded a new Christian religion—the Seventh-Day Adventist Church, which encouraged its members to become vegetarians.

The Seventh-Day Adventist Church and its leaders were an important new ally in the vegetarian movement. The church in the decades ahead would become a leading teacher of vegetarianism in the United States, and eventually the world.

The Adventist Church originated with the Millerites, named for William Miller, a Baptist preacher with apocalyptic views. Miller calculated that the Advent, or the end of the world, would occur on October 22, 1844. His followers, the Millerites, were convinced. One of the signs that they believed heralded the return of Jesus and the end time was a comet that appeared in the winter of 1843. But October 22 came and went without incident, a day known to historians as the Great Disappointment.

The sect was disillusioned, but some members were galvanized by a teenager named Ellen G. White, who held prayer meetings and talks after October 22. People were also entranced by White's visions, which were occurring with increased frequency and sometimes occurred in public. Before long, White had her own flock. She refined the Millerite creed—there was no mention of an Advent date, just an assurance that its occurrence was imminent. The prophetess, as she was called, mandated Saturday, or the Seventh Day, as the Sabbath.

Ellen Gould Harmon was born in 1827 in Gorham, Maine, the youngest of eight children. Her childhood was marred by an incident that occurred when she was nine years old. Ellen Harmon was struck by a rock thrown by a schoolmate and the youngster's face was permanently disfigured, and she dropped out of school.

As a teenager, White, who was raised as a Methodist, began to have religious dreams and visions. Physicians and other witnesses present at her visions said that she would slip into a trance-like state, her heartbeat and respiratory functions would slow down dangerously, and that her limbs were virtually unmovable.

Harmon married James Springer White in 1846, and the couple traveled to preach their Adventist beliefs and published *Present Truth*, a compila-

Ellen G. White: Adventist founder and leader. Courtesy of Loma Linda University.

tion of their teachings. After living in Connecticut and later New York, the
Whites moved to Battle Creek, Michigan in 1855. The couple officially
formed the Seventh-Day Adventists in 1863.

That same year, White said that visions from God in 1863 instructed her
to urge people to abstain from flesh eating. At the time she was preaching
Grahamite health practices such as cleanliness and abstinence from stimulants such as coffee, tea, tobacco, and alcohol.

White, however, wouldn't become a vegetarian until later in life.
Although she might have infrequently eaten meat when other foods were
not available, especially when she traveled, it was not until much later
that she abandoned meat eating. Nevertheless, she was consistent in
advocacy of vegetarianism. "God gave our first parents the food. He
designed that the race should eat. It was contrary to His plan to have the
life of any creature taken. There was to be no death in Eden. The fruit of

the trees in the garden, was the food man's wants required," White wrote in 1864.

"God has bountifully provided for the sustenance and happiness of all His creatures; if His laws were never violated, if all acted in harmony with the divine will, health, peace, and happiness, instead of misery and continual evil, would be the result," White wrote in an 1866 issue of the *Health Reformer,* an Adventist publication.

That year, White and her husband founded the Western Health Reform Institute in Battle Creek, Michigan, which would many years later become a world-famous health institution. Under her guidance, the church over the next few decades founded a network of sanitariums and institutions in the United States and abroad.

Ellen G. White instructed physicians at these institutions not to give their patients meat. "The physician who uses and prescribes meat...leads the patient by his own example to indulge perverted appetite," wrote White, in one of countless passages that she wrote on the topic of diet. "In grains, fruits, vegetables, and nuts are to be found all the food elements that we need."[9]

Sister White's church soon expanded throughout the world. The Seventh-Day Adventist church helped to keep vegetarianism alive in America, and ever expanding.

The founder of the SDA religion, and Jackson's daughter, feminist Harriet Austin, would not be the only women associated with Dr. Jackson still spoken of today.

Among the many guests at Our Home was a woman known to the world as the Angel of the Battlefield. Clara Barton earned that distinction by nursing wounded soldiers during the Civil War. She was at the front lines to aid soldiers as they fell—the first woman allowed to do so by the federal government. Barton was already highly esteemed for her courage before her war duties; for example, she had worked as a clerk in the U.S. Patent Office, enduring harassment from male coworkers.

In 1872, at the age of 61, Barton founded the Red Cross in the United States. The organization was started in Europe as a confederation of relief societies to aid wounded soldiers and victims of disasters and other calamities.

But a year later Barton's health failed. She suffered from nervous prostration, and was unable to read, write, or stand, according to Isabel Ross, Barton's biographer. She went to Jackson's Our Home, where she regained her health under the doctor's vegetarian, drug-free, spiritually uplifting regime.

Barton's food preferences caused difficulty when she traveled to other countries and stayed at hotels that offered no vegetarian meals. That's a likely reason why, years later, she would allow her name to appear in promotions for vegetarian food products (Bromose and nut butter, products of Dr. John Harvey Kellogg's food company, foods that must have been a boon to vegetarian travelers).

DRUGLESS MEDICINE

Russell Thacher Trall, M.D., was another physician who, like Jackson, served the American Vegetarian Society as a vice president and was making waves. Trall, in 1854, said: "The Vegetarian question involves the relations of food to health, and, indeed, the theory of progress, improvement, and destiny of the human race."[10]

Vegetarianism was "scripturally and scientifically true," said the doctor. He was aware that the medical establishment objected to leaving meat off the plate. Trall publicly challenged them to provide a single scientific argument or fact favoring the eating of animal flesh.[11]

Trall was no dreamer. He was a pragmatist. On the prospect of widespread acceptance and practice of vegetarianism in the United States, he contended it was a "subject so radical in relation to prevailing opinions, so subversive of established interests and occupations, and so revolutionary with regard to the habits, customs, education, and appetences of society, it can not be expected to be seriously agitated without encountering much opposition; nor can it be expected to become immediately popular."[12]

"The greatest truths that were ever known were, when first announced, the most unpopular subjects heard of," said Dr. Trall.[13] Trall was used to swimming upstream. His entire career was a challenge to the regulars in medicine. He was a leading practitioner and proponent of hydropathy, and hygienic medicine; that is, Graham-inspired medicine that relied on vegetable diet and other natural methods of helping the body heal itself.

The doctor's version of hygienic medicine was Graham's system made more sophisticated and into a science sometimes called drugless medicine, which included water cure, vegetarian diet, and absolutely no medicine, whether drugs, herbs, or homeopathic remedies. Today's practitioners call it natural hygiene. It is not alternative medicine and is, in fact, no medicine if medicine means the use of drugs or herbs.

Trall, a vegan, said in a lecture, "The Problems of Medical Science," delivered before the 1863–1864 class of his New York Hygeio-Therapeutic College (Hydropathic and Physiological School):

WE ARE NOT reformers; we are Revolutionists. Medical reform—the world has had quite enough of that. Reforming the drug system by substituting one set of drugs for another is a ridiculous farce. It may, to be sure, substitute a lesser for a greater evil, in many cases, but it is like reforming big lies with little falsehoods. It is like...promoting temperance by substituting cider and lager for rum, brandy, gin, wine, or flesh eating by substituting milk, butter, cheese, for animal food.

Russell T. Trall: Vegetarian and holistic health crusader. Courtesy of William Dailey Collection.

The goal of the hygiene movement was no less than "to rid the world of disease, drugs, doctors, and unnatural death," according to *The Water Cure Journal* in 1858. By that year, the journal estimated that there were thousands of individuals and families who through study and practice of hygienic living "have realized an almost entire immunity from disease, and for whom doctors and drug shops might as well have no existence."[14]

Drugless Doctor Trall wrote on the difficulty of convincing people to change their habits. He gave the example of one patient, treated by a Dr. Gorton, who disbelieved that diet was the cause of his distress, and instead wanted a prescription "that would cure (him) without a meddling with his eating habits at all."

Diet, believed Trall, "is, in fact, the greatest error our system has to contend with in society. Unwholesome food, and erroneous habits of eating, stand at the very head of the list of the causes of disease. Wrong eating expresses more of the origin of disease in the human family than any other two words that can be found in the English language…"[15]

In 1846 Trall established the New York Hygienic Institute with Joel Shew. Four years later, Trall founded the Hydropathic and Physiological

School in New York City, a medical college that admitted men and women on an equal basis, a rarity in those days. Students were taught medicine without use of drugs, bleeding, burning, and other standard treatments, and they were taught the vegetable diet.

Trall, like Shew, helped popularize hydropathy. He was well-known as an author of more than a dozen health books for the layperson, including *Popular Physiology, Digestion and Dyspepsia, The Hydropathic Cookbook,* and *The Hydropathic Encyclopedia.*

Hydropathic institutes like Trall's acquired a reputation in society for bringing people back to health. Lost in antiquity, water cure had been revived in the early eighteenth century in Germany. The best water cure establishments provided a relaxing atmosphere, with elements intended to stimulate the intellect and elevate the spirit, all to help the body heal itself. One of the lecturers hired by Trall to work on the spirit was Bronson Alcott, who gave a series of Conversations, including two on the subject of vegetarianism. In 1856 Alcott conversed with patients, pupils, and professors. He had titled his Conversations "Health and Temperance" and "Health and Virtue."

Health establishments like Trall's were the antithesis of today's hospitals and more like simple health spas or retreats. Patients, who received treatment, instruction on lifestyle changes, and plenty of encouragement from the physicians and staff were largely responsible for their own recovery.

Trall, who had seen Graham just before the great crusader's death, would for years to come continue to include articles about Grahamism and related topics in *The Health Journal,* which he published for more than 25 years. The Journal also published ongoing arguments between drugless medicine and the allopaths, which grew stronger with the years. The drugless group claimed certain allopaths were deliberately attempting to confuse the public, and turn them away from studying the laws of life, and practicing prevention against disease.

O.W. May, M.D., of the Madison (Wisconsin) Water Cure, in a letter to *Water Cure,* called a remark by Dr. Henry Glasspool, printed in the *Western Water Cure Journal,* a falsehood. Glasspool had claimed that "water and vegetable diet comprise the whole material medica" of the drugless doctors. The public, or at least a healthy percentage of it, during this time seems to have been swaying towards drugless medicine. However, conflict between the schools of medicine must have caused confusion in society over which was the best type of medicine.[16]

On the drugless side of the controversy was Dr. May, who replied in *The Water Cure Journal* to Glasspool's remark: "Let the writer attend one course of lectures at our Hygeio-Therapeutic Medical College, and he will learn that his representations are not only untrue, but evince a kind of meanness unbecoming the truthful gentleman any one should be, who assumes to hold the honorable position of a true physician."[17]

James Caleb Jackson believed that Dr. Trall's drugless college was doing good by "teaching its graduates, and through them the people, that 'drugs and medicines' do not cure sick persons...;" that the "graduates will show the people how to keep well;" and that the college gave advantages to women "to become intelligent on the subject of health." Jackson also added: "We can not readily get through your College a class of graduates less fit to illustrate right ideas on health-questions than the other medical schools vomit forth—tobacco chewers and smokers, lager-beer and rum and brandy drinkers—mint-julep suckers, 'tea and coffee guzzlers,' pork eaters, poison givers—men whose flesh is foul, whose breath is fetid, whose language is unchaste, whose lives are a burlesque on the profession they have chosen..."[18]

Not only were their eating and drinking habits unhealthful, the regular physicians had misled the public regarding what was best to eat and drink, claimed Trall. "The doctors have given their heads a round-about twist; told them they had carnivorous teeth," explained Trall. With the physicians' encouragement "the whole world has gone to hunting and fishing, and fattening and butchering, and salting and pickling, and smoking and broiling,...until they have become filled with (morbid humours) scrofula, canker, erysipelas, gout, rheumatism, biliousness, and putrid fevers," wrote Trall. Trall did not exactly win popularity with the regulars. "I regard the medical profession, taken in the aggregate, as the most ignorant class in (the) community on the whole subject of diet...they have been miseducated—led away from truth by false theories."[19]

By the 1860s the Civil War had come, taking at least one advocate out of the vegetarian movement, at least for a few years. In 1862 Henry Stephen Clubb fought in the Civil War. He refused to carry a weapon. A man of peace, he was wounded in Corinth, Mississippi. He would serve his adopted country as a captain and assistant quartermaster in the 17th U.S. Army Corps from 1862 to 1866. The military did not accommodate his vegetarian diet, and, at times, when no other food was provided, he had to eat flesh. This was not something that pleased the soldier, who had been a vegetarian since his youth.

The health of the soldiers was very much on Russell Trall's mind. He believed that not only war, but allopathic medicine used to treat injured soldiers, was a cause of the slaughter of the soldiers—and that he could save them. Trall made this announcement in 1862 during his speech before an audience of influential men at the Smithsonian Institution in Washington, D.C. "The soldiers of our camps and hospitals were dying off fast of typhoid fever, pneumonia, measles, dysentery, etc..., and quite unnecessarily. I knew that the application of our system of hygienic medication would save most of their lives," said Trall during his two-hour lecture, "The True Healing Art: Hygienic vs. Drug Medication."

Trall, who was born in 1812, explained why the system of drugging the sick to make them well was wrong, and he called drugs, in any form, poison. He said that humans were driven to early graves, and the cause of death was not bodily ills but medication. Drugs did not act on the body, the body acted on the drugs, stated Trall. Contrary to what people believed, he explained that the stomach ejected the emetic, the bowel expelled the purgative, and the kidney got rid of the diuretic, and not the reverse.

America's expert on drugless medicine had, as a boy in Vernon, Tolland County, Connecticut, battled sickness and experienced the effects of typical treatments of the day. Trall believed that he was made worse by the medical treatments of his doctors. He was dissatisfied with their explanations for his sickness. Eventually, he regained his health, and decided that he would help others to do the same. After Trall had attended lectures on drugless healing, perhaps presented by Graham, he enrolled in medical school.

However, Trall came to realize, and publicly announced, that vegetarianism—more than water cure—helped people to rebuild health. He came to this realization both through his own experience in treating patients and after receiving thousands of letters from people who had read one or more of his books and had told him that their health had improved once they had changed their eating habits.

Trall totally opposed the use of drugs; he did not differentiate between the medical systems of the day, which included allopathic, homeopathic, and eclectic Physio-medicine. Each system was the same to the natural hygienist—they were all wrong.

Newspapers of the day, said Trall, were filled with lying advertisements for hundreds of quack nostrums from charlatans intent on robbing the sick. In the next century, a similar charge would be made against drugless healers: that they were quacks. Most of them prescribed vegetarianism.

Natural hygiene was associated with vegetarianism in Trall's era, as it is today, to a much lesser degree. Some natural hygienists even oppose vegetarianism. Trall explained at a September 1860 meeting of the American Vegetarian Society, held at the Bible-Christian Church in Philadelphia, that health was not the only reason flesh foods were to be eschewed. He described the motivations of the meat-free people of his day:

- Some persons are Bible vegetarians. They think that this book inculcates this doctrine.
- Some are Scientific vegetarians. They think that nature teaches it.
- ...Vegetarians from Benevolence—they regard it cruel to kill animals for food. They can see no "peace on Earth and good-will to men" while cruelty, even to animals, prevails.
- ...Esthetic vegetarians—they see the sublime and the beautiful in human nature, only in circumstances which dispense with slaughterhouses, fowl-pens and piggeries.

- ... Economical vegetarians—they perceive a vast saving in soil and territory, and in the wear and tear of human machinery.

- ... Vegetarians from experience—they have in some way learned that others have subsisted very well, and perhaps improved, on a vegetable diet, and so they try it as an experiment, sometimes just to see if it will agree with their constitutions.

- ... Vegetarians from necessity—this is altogether the most numerous class. They are mostly invalids, and are quite numerous at some of the Water-Cures, which, by the way, are quite often Diet-Cures as Water-Cures.[20]

The drugless doctor was, like other abstainers from animal flesh, a vegetarian for several reasons. Although Trall's main goal was teaching what he deemed the true theory of health, he had other motivations for avoiding meat. Trall expressed empathy for animals. He denounced water cures that served meat, and those that provided opportunities for patients to hunt and fish at the establishments. "We are sorry to know that some who seek health at the 'Water-Cures' have no better idea of a true life, and no higher conceptions of Hygiene medication than to imagine that fishing and hunting are among the legitimate auxiliary remedies ... Hunting and fishing go naturally and almost necessarily with liquor, tobacco, and the flesh-pots," he wrote.[21]

Trall was concerned about the degrading influence of these activities on the mind, and especially on the young. "They imbue the mind with the spirit of sensuality and cruelty, grossness and selfishness. Hunting and fishing may be very refined amusements, because they are practiced by those who claim to move in fashionable circles; but the spirit of the thing is precisely the same as that which impels the rowdy and the bully in his cruelty to his horse or in assault on a fellow being." Like other advocates of vegetarianism, Trall directly linked violence towards animals with violence toward people. This link would be acknowledged by psychologists in the later twentieth century.

For many reasons, vegetarianism was moving forward and gaining adherents, if not great acceptance in America. Trall seems to have been optimistic about the future. He announced in the first number of the 38th volume of *The Herald of Health*, "it is now a quarter of a century since Medical Reform was born. It is but little more than a dozen years since its principles were established. Now its believers and advocates may be numbered by hundreds of thousands." Likely a large percentage, if not all of these thousands, was vegetarians, since refraining from meat eating was a principle of the hygiene system as initiated by Sylvester Graham and continued by Trall.[22]

The *Herald of Health* was one vehicle used by Trall to promote vegetarianism, but it might not have been his most important. He urged readers of his numerous books to consider the diet question. Doctors trained at

Trall's New York Hygeio-Therapeutic College went out into the nation like missionaries, carrying the message of health and diet to the masses. Trall warned them they would not make a good income. He explained that since hygienic doctors teach patients to get well and to prevent illness, after that they might not be needed at all.

Students at Trall's school wrote papers on pertinent topics; for example, the graduate theses of the class of 1864 included that of N.D. Thompson, of St. Louis, Missouri, titled "Vegetable Diet"; Miss Nancy M. Haynes, of Peru, Vermont, wrote on "Dyspepsia"; and Mrs. Nancy E. Miller, of West Manchester, Ohio, on "Digestion."[23]

Trall helped vegetarianism in yet another way. Foods, including Graham bread, so named for the coarse whole wheat flour advocated by the crusader, and likely Graham crackers, were prepared and sold at Trall's water cure establishment. One of the visitors to Trall's medical establishment was a young man named John Harvey Kellogg, who visited Trall with his brother M.G. Kellogg. John Harvey Kellogg would soon become an acclaimed medical man, and later, a manufacturer and inventor of vegetarian food products, as well as one of the movement's greatest leaders.

The growth of vegetarianism was continuing, even if it had been stalled some by the Civil War. Then, a blow struck the movement. In the same year Trall lectured before the Smithsonian, Rev. William Metcalfe died at the age of 74. The American Vegetarian Society ceased to exist.

The heyday of the water cure establishment was waning. Numerous cultural changes in society precipitated the change. Advocacy of abstinence from animal food also changed; some aspects of its advocacy were retained and others added. After the storm of the Civil War, a springtime began to blossom for vegetarianism, but it would take decades of cultivation to mature.

Chapter 6

The Civil War to the End of the Century

The Civil War ended in 1865, and the nation entered the period known as Reconstruction. The vegetarian movement, initially centered in the Northeast, spread westward. Whether vegetarians in places like California and Chicago—areas far from Boston, New York, and Philadelphia—were inspired by the works of the earlier advocates, such as Graham and William Alcott, is difficult to determine for certain. However, the new generation of advocates absorbed the teachings of the trailblazers. More people now talked and wrote about eating less food, simpler food, and omitting meat from the menu, and a minority actually followed these Grahamite rules.

Shortly after the war ended in 1866, Dr. Mussey died at the age of 86. His death came four years after his book, *Health, Its Friends and Foes*, was published. He used anecdotes and other evidence to prove his point that man was not meant to eat meat.

Mussey wrote on the vegetarianism of the Roman Catholic Trappist monks who lived in Kentucky. Their wholesome lifestyle, together with their plain vegetable diet, prevented disease, even during the cholera epidemic, according to the testimony of a doctor who examined them, Mussey explained in *Health*.

The *Journal of the American Medical Association* paid tribute to his stellar career in 1896. In it, he was referred to as a great surgeon, "one of those who made his mark in the history of medical literature: one who as much as any other helped to develop higher medical education in this Western country." This was said by John B. Hamilton, M.D., in his tribute to Mussey before a graduating class of the Ohio Medical University.[1]

As they had since the start of the American vegetarian movement, some physicians and ministers continued promoting meat-free diets. Reverend Miles Grant, of Boston, Massachusetts, editor of *The World's Crisis*, preached that "sickness is to a great extent the result of violated law, and that what a man eats, and drinks, and breathes; how he thinks, and acts, and works; how he uses all the organs of his body, and faculties of his mind, is what makes him a Christian or an infidel," according to the *Herald of Health*.[2]

Similarly, Rev. Henry Ward Beecher, an anti-slavery lecturer, advocated against meat eating. Beecher, brother of Harriet Beecher Stowe, author of *Uncle Tom's Cabin*, observed that men with uncontrollable tempers could bring them under control once they stopped eating meat. The famous reformer-minister had said in a lecture before the New York Medical Students' Christian Union (February 3, 1867, Plymouth Church, Brooklyn, New York) that when a man came to him depressed and sickly, and seeking prayers, that the man was ignorant of the physical means of helping himself. "Why should I stand before men that are puffed and bloated and wheezing from over-abundant eating, and attempt to lift them up to heaven, when there are vast herds of beef lying between them and heaven?"[3]

Beecher, like Trall and others, attributed sickness and untimely death to injurious health habits, especially eating habits. If diet did not kill, then doctors did, they warned the public. At times natural hygienists like Trall wrote matter-of-factly on this topic of the deadliness of doctors; sometimes they wrote as passionate preachers, and on occasion they used humor.[4]

One example of witticism is this poem, published in 1867 in *The Herald of Health*.

Dr. Drake, the Quack, and His Victim

A duck who had got such a habit of stuffing,
That all the day long she was panting and puffing,
And by every creature who did her great crop see,
Was thought to be galloping fast for a dropsy...

I feel so distended with wind, and oppressed
So squeamish and faint, such a load at my chest;...

By the feel of your pulse, your complaint I've been thinking,
Must surely be owing to eating and drinking...
Oh! No, sir, I believe me, the lady replied
(Alarmed for her stomach as well as her pride),
I'm sure it arises from nothing I eat,
But I rather suspect I got wet in my feet.

I've only been raking a bit in the gutter,
Where cook has been pouring some cold melted butter,
And a slice of green cabbage, and scraps of cold meat,
Just a trifle or two, that I could eat.

Then grave Dr. Drake, in his business proceeding,
Us'd cathartics, emetics, blisters and bleeding;
While his patient suddenly rolled on her side,
Gave a terrible quack, then a struggle, a died![5]

Vegetarianism was still alive in the post-Civil War era, but it lacked a national organization. Henry Clubb would fill the void by forming one years later. But in the 1860s and 1870s, he was busy promoting fruit growing. Clubb, who moved to Michigan and founded *The Grand Haven Herald* newspaper, wanted fruit trees planted along city streets, making fruits available to all who dwelled in the city. Orson Fowler had earlier proposed a similar idea.

Clubb established the State Pomological Society in Michigan, and he wrote legislation that funded the society and its fruit fairs, which attracted thousands of people. After becoming a Republican state senator in 1871, he helped enlarge the fruit-growing business in Michigan.

Michigan and the nation were not vegetarian, but people across America were increasingly questioning the habit of meat eating. The press was publishing articles on the subject now and then, but not always from a favorable angle.

The writer of an 1869 article titled "Popular Fallacies Concerning Hygiene" claimed the writings of William Alcott, Sylvester Graham, and others were responsible for errors Americans made regarding diet. George M. Bearid, M.D., the writer, claimed that they were "all sincere, honest men, but thoroughly at fault on nearly all their ideas of hygiene," and that they "exercised a powerful influence in their day, and the evil effects of their teachings still remain, and work terrible mischief." Vegetarianism was one of the widely accepted dietary fallacies Bearid blamed on the reformers.[6]

"Comparative anatomy, physiology, experience, our natural appetites, and the history of the world, all show us that man should have a mixed diet—flesh, fish, fruit, and vegetables. The contrary doctrine is one of the most monstrous errors that ever infested society. It has carried hundreds and thousands to early graves. The popularity of this error, at one time, was partly the result of the popularity of the men who advocated it," believed Bearid.[7]

The good doctor believed that Americans loved extremes "and roll them as sweet morsels under our tongues. Vegetarianism is an extreme, and therefore Americans cherished it. At the present time it is not practically advocated by any large or influential number; but there are very many who theoretically believe in the heresy and who think that they do wrong when they eat flesh or fish. Thus they go on all their lives violating their consciences."[8]

The doctor also employed a typical argument against vegetarianism. Vegetables and legumes such as potatoes, turnips, and carrots, he claimed, were less nutritious and less digestible than fresh beef and mutton. Although he agreed that humans need fruit, vegetables, and bread, he also cautioned that more "acute diseases—far more—arise from fruit and vegetables than from flesh and fish."[9]

After Graham's death, Americans were still debating his ideas. An article appearing in *Appletons' Journal* addressed the subject of the Graham diet. "Sylvester Graham, a few years ago, undertook to reform the world dietetically. He ascribed the chief evils of society to eating meat, and maintained that human nature can never be perfected until it adopts a vegetarian diet," stated the writer. But the writer condemns Graham for opposing nature, or the fact that humans are physiologically designed to eat a mixed diet.

Talk about vegetarianism, and also about problems with meat, was not uncommon. One article, published in the *New York Times,* and later reprinted in *The Health Reformer,* discussed the high price of meat, the non-simplistic manner in which it was usually cooked, and the large quantity eaten by Americans.[10]

The article also stated: "Whether this meat-eating is beneficial seems to be more than doubtful. Are our men or our women stronger, healthier, larger-limbed, ruddier, and fairer, than Europeans of corresponding occupations and habits of life?" The writer gave an example of "the Irish girls" who arrive in America and go into domestic service with "rosy cheeks and full figures," and who probably eat meat no more often than once a month, but then undergo a change.

Once here, they rush ravenously at the joints, the steaks, and the chops, which are to them luxuries and the great signs of luxurious living. The result is almost invariably that they lose the figures, and the rosy cheeks, and the health, that they brought with them, and that came with, if not of, a diet of potatoes and buttermilk. The more observant of them have already begun to notice this themselves. And in the second generation, the change is very manifest. There is rarely a paler and thinner creature than your Irish girl of the second generation.[11]

The writer, taking a page from DeToqueville, summarized his beliefs:

In brief we eat too much meat—too much for our health, probably, and certainly too much for the well-being of our pockets. Great, brawny Scotchmen live month after month on oatmeal and buttermilk, and a healthier, hard-working class of men, it would be difficult to find....Among our more comfortably-situated classes, it is safe to say that they eat meat twice a day. There is no need of this; and

John Harvey Kellogg: Great vegetarian advocate and top surgeon. Courtesy of Loma Linda University.

more, it is not wholesome. Women, who are not hard-workers, and children are much more healthy upon a lighter and less concentrated diet. Children, until they reach their teens, do not really need meat at all, and are better in health and in looks for not having it…. There is nothing more certain in regard to this subject than that our consumption of meat, particularly by women and children, is needless and unwholesome.[12]

The story was reprinted in *The Health Reformer,* the magazine published by The Western Health Reform Institute—the hygienic water cure institution established by the Whites and the Seventh-Day Adventist church in 1866. It was in Battle Creek, Michigan, which would decades later become the breakfast cereal capital of the world.

In 1872 the Whites had hired John Harvey Kellogg, M.D., a man who would build the little water cure into a legendary institution. The Whites knew talent when they saw it, and it paid off. Kellogg was largely responsible for building the foundation for a breakfast cereal industry, and for taking the vegetarian movement to an all-time high level. He was a surgeon, as well as a health and nutrition authority and food expert.

Although the name John Harvey Kellogg has become associated with the mythological buffoon created by an acclaimed novelist whose novel was made into a Hollywood movie, he was no fool. Kellogg's ideas on health and diet, and the food products he invented, made meatless meals more appealing, and the doctor world famous. He would soon become one of the greatest surgeons in the world.

Further west, vegetarians were banding into their own communities. Fruitlands and Octagon City were not in existence, but vegetarians did form some successful colonies. Isaac Rumford and his wife Susan founded Joyful News, a community in the California town of Joyful. Members pledged to live the Edenic Life, based upon following the laws of nature, as did the Bible's Adam and Eve before the Fall. Therefore, use of meat, alcohol, and other stimulants, along with activities such as gambling and the use of vulgar words, were not tolerated. Members followed the Edenic diet of grains, nuts, fruits, and vegetables—in their natural state untouched by fire. Joyful News residents also worked for dress reform for ladies and published a newspaper, *Joyful News Co-operator*.[13]

A newspaper, *Woman's Herald of Industry and Social Science Cooperator*, published by a group of women in San Francisco, supported the commune's way of life. "It is with feelings of intense delight that we throw open our doors to the Edenic Life.... This life will eventuate in pure continence and until it is adapted the flesh pots of Egypt will continually astray." The Edenic Life, stated the newspaper, "is rapidly gaining in numbers, and enthusiasm."[14]

Another woman who published a newspaper was Victoria Woodhull, who caused an uproar in society with her outrageous ideas and boldness in stating them. The women's and workers' rights crusader ran for president of the United States in 1872, decades before women were granted the right to vote. Her platform was women's suffrage, dress reform, free love, and Grahamite principles, including vegetarianism, specificially the eating of living food. The same year she ran for president she began the six-year run of her newspaper *Woodhull & Claflin's Weekly*, which on occasion published articles about diet reform, including vegetarianism. Woodhull's husband, Captain Blood, was a vegetarian, and Woodhull was an advocate. Evidence suggests that she also abstained from meat.

PHILADELPHIA AND CHICAGO

The vegetarian movement in the 1880s was stagnant and unorganized. But Clubb breathed new life into vegetarian advocacy by founding the Vegetarian Society of America in 1886. A decade earlier, Clubb was ordained a minister in the Bible-Christian Church after connecting with members while reporting on the Centennial Exposition in Philadelphia, where the church had an exhibit promoting vegetarianism.

The activities of the Philadelphia-based VSA included public dinners, lectures, trips, and the publication of literature to further the cause. The VSA published a cookbook, sold dozens of other books on various aspects of vegetarianism, and sold foods from Kellogg's Battle Creek and Sanitas food companies.

In June of 1886, the society celebrated with a picnic in Philadelphia's Alnwick Park. About 125 people gathered at a pavilion to choose among beet sandwiches, rice fritters, green pea pot pie, omelet sandwiches, lettuce and beet salads, cherry pie, tea biscuits, corn starch pudding, oranges, bananas, blanc mange, graham gems, date gems, strawberry, sponge cake, jelly cake, and lemonade. The society also held some events at the Hygeia restaurant in that city, which served vegetarian food.

In 1889 Clubb launched the Vegetarian Society of America's magazine *Food, Home and Garden*. The magazine featured first-hand accounts of new vegetarians, scientific facts, recipes, and even the latest methods for cultivating fruits, vegetables, and flowers. In two years *Food, Home and Garden* had increased in size from a monthly, 8-page leaflet to 20 pages printed on superfine paper and adorned with cover artwork in the art nouveau style. Clubb said that several printers who told him that a weekly newspaper was needed for the topic of food reform had encouraged him.

The Vegetarian Society of America maintained strong ties with the Chicago Vegetarian Society. The officials and members of the latter society hoped that their city would become the national center of vegetarianism, and invited Clubb and the VSA to move there. However, Clubb explained that finances were an issue and he had to decline.

Rev. Clubb and the Bible-Christians were not alone as Christians in the country advocating abstinence from animal flesh. Articles about other Christians, excerpts from their sermons, and articles written by them were on occasion published in *Food, Home and Garden*.

For example, Rev. A. T. De Learsey of Stamford, New York, stated: "...what were cattle created for?...They were no more made to be eaten than dogs, cats or worms.... For almost seventeen centuries—from Creation to the Deluge—man was vegetarian.... When everything was very good, there was no blood shed!...Let the Vegetarians put forth all their efforts in order to propagate this divine truth and much happiness and peace will be introduced into many a home."[15]

Vegetarian advocates often stated that practicing nonviolence to animals would lead to peace among humans. That this was taught by preachers associated with the Bible-Christians, by some Christians unaffiliated with that church, and by some lay individuals involved in the peace movement is a fact largely unreported in the history of the peace movement in the United States.

Minister Clubb was prominent in the peace movement. The VSA promoted peace, and Clubb was involved with organizations exclusively devoted to peace. He served as vice president of the Universal Peace Union, and was editor for three years of *Peacemaker*.

Despite the prominent presence of Christian writers in the pages of vegetarian publications, by the late 1800s the character of the movement was changing. Vegetarianism in America now encompassed a broader base of faiths and philosophies. As it grew, the vegetarian movement was also expanded by individuals involved in Hinduism, Theosophy, New Thought, and other religions and philosophies increasingly of interest in the United States.

For example: Annie Besant, a British woman and leader of the Theosophists, lectured in the States on spiritual and related subjects such as vegetarianism and animal liberation. Newspapers reported on her arrival at the 1893 World's Columbian Exposition at Chicago, where Besant lectured about slaughterhouse conditions, particularly about the men who worked in them. She said the workers "become coarsened, hardened, brutalized, less men as men because they are slaughterers of animals. And everyone who eats flesh meat has part in that brutalization; everyone who uses what they provide is guilty of this degradation of his fellow-men..." Besant was said to have felt the bad karma that had accumulated at the famous Chicago stockyards.[16]

Little known today, the New Thought movement, based upon Christian principles of positive thinking and action, had a large following, and its leaders tended to be people who espoused vegetarianism. Two of these leaders, Charles and Myrtle Fillmore, established the Unity School of Christianity in Missouri. The Fillmores never required Unity members to reject meat, but strongly recommended vegetarianism for spiritual growth. During the twentieth century, Unity Village of Missouri and its no-meat restaurant would become world renowned.

Other New Thought leaders recommended vegetarianism. Ralph Waldo Trine was a minister and popular author and lecturer. His book *In Tune With the Infinite* still sells today, but it was in one of his others, *Every Living Creature*, a book calling for kindness to animals and people, that he espoused animal liberation and vegetarianism. In this book Trine quoted Henry Salt, Annie Bessant, and a Hindu leader (name not provided). American advocates of vegetarianism looked to the Hindu nations as a spiritual example of benevolence toward animals.

THE WORLD'S FAIR AND TRAVELING ENGLISHMEN

The United States in 1893 was thrust into a depression, which caused several hundred banks to fail and railroads to go broke. Meanwhile, the state of Colorado enacted voting rights for women, and the westward expansion continued as over 100,000 white settlers journeyed to the Oklahoma Territory to stake claims.

That year the steamship *Alaska* left England and churned through the turbulent waters of the Atlantic en route to the United States. On board were several British vegetarians, who took their meat-free meals at a vegetarian table set aside by the ship's staff.

The other passengers noticed that the people at this table were livelier than normal, and found out they were not shy about espousing the benefits of a meatless diet. But the Victorian vegetarians were apparently well received—the English men and women reported that they made at least two converts to the meat-free diet on their trip.

These vegetarian travelers did not travel to the states just to see the sights. They were on their way to the Chicago World Exposition, arguably the greatest exposition of all time. They were led by William Axon, who was secretary of the Vegetarian Federal Union—an English organization that would become the International Vegetarian Union 15 years later. Their account of their travels, which appeared in the *Vegetarian Messenger*, an English magazine that was already decades old at the time, gives insight into the state of vegetarianism in America at the time.[17]

After landing in New York, Axon and his group embarked on many adventures. In Washington, the Brits seemed to be a hit on the party circuit. They socialized with officials at the U.S. Department of Agriculture and reported that they almost made vegetarians out of the ladies who worked there, and went to a party at a women's club where they met a family of life-long vegetarians. The visiting vegetarians left a legacy by helping to form a vegetarian society in Washington, D.C.

For most of the trip, they had no problem getting vegetarian food, and they dined on fruit, fried potatoes, salad, waffles, pies, and cracked wheat. Many people today seem confused about what a vegetarian eats, and people in the 1890s were apparently not so different. At one point, reported the *Messenger*, they had trouble convincing people that "vegetarians would have nothing to do with flesh meat." On a train bound for Niagara, they had to convince the steward that beans could be served without the pork.

The traveling Englishmen also went to the world-famous Chicago Stockyards. It is no surprise that they didn't have a good time. *The Vegetarian*, another English magazine, recounted that the "shrieks and deafening din of each of the doomed porkers are heart-rending." An employee told the group that cancer is sometimes scooped out of the carcasses, giving more weight to the long-held contention by vegetarians that most of the meat on the market is infested with disease.[18]

At the World's Fair, they joined their American counterparts in the Liberal Arts Building for a series of lectures on vegetarianism. The lectures featured well-known vegetarians; Dr. Suzanne Way Dodds delivered a lecture on "Vegetarianism, Meat Eating," Tokology author Alice Stockham, M.D., talked on "Food of the Orient," Dr. James Caleb Jackson's son,

James Henry, spoke on "Vegetarianism for Convalescents," and Dr. John Harvey Kellogg presided over an evening session and gave a talk titled "Vegetarianism and Surgery."

It was a major coup for vegetarians to participate in the event: Over 27.5 million people, many of them exhausting their life savings to make the trip, attended the fair, which ran from May to October. There were 65,000 exhibitions on anything from agriculture and anthropology to machinery and accomplishments by women. Many new inventions were unveiled, including the world's first Ferris Wheel and a crude fax-like device. The first all-electric kitchen, complete with range and broiler, was displayed. So it is likely that a good number of men in top hats and frock coats and women adorned with felt hats and tailored jackets were exposed to vegetarianism.

During the course of the events, Axon and his wife were invited to a gathering of black clergyman, lawyers, doctors, and other professionals. The group included former slave Frederick Douglass, then 77 years old, and Francis Ellen Watkins Harper, a well-known black author and poet who spoke out for abolition and women's rights. Axon, who was asked to discuss how vegetarianism could help improve race relations, said vegetarianism helps to "break down distinctions between rich and poor, and promoted friendship and brotherhood between all classes." He drew applause after urging the group to "go forward in the name of education, of righteousness, of temperance, of abstinence, and of justice."[19]

Axon and his group believed that vegetarianism would advance like a tidal wave and wash away meat from plates as far away as Europe. The *Messenger* stated that the World Vegetarian Congress "was successful beyond any previous gathering of the kind, the attendance was good, the interest deep and continuous...The Chicago Congress will, we hope and believe, form the starting point for an earnest and active forward movement, and lead to a wide diffusion of vegetarianism alike in the Old and in the New World."[20]

The English travelers were correct. The Columbian Exposition gave vegetarian advocacy additional momentum, and put woman advocates like Stockham into the spotlight.

Alice Stockham, M.D., who was an obstetrician/gynecologist and popular author on health, sociology, and other topics, did not believe that meat was an unhealthful food. However, she stated, "from the aesthetic point of view, I can not believe it is either physically clean or morally right." The doctor was the author of *Toxology*, a health book for women that recommended vegetarianism.[21]

The moral aspect of meat eating was gaining attention, as Americans were apparently thinking about ethics and spirituality. So much was this on some of their minds that attending talks and reading books on these subjects was a trend of the times. Some individuals such as Stockham extended their ethical consideration to animals. In Dr. Stockham's view this inclusion of animals was an ecological and spiritual wholeness—animals must be included because they shared with humanity divine creative force.

Like other leaders of vegetarianism, Stockham was aware that for people to change their eating habits the change had to be easy. She, along with experts on food like John Harvey Kellogg, thought that nuts should replace meat in the diet. "I should recommend that they constitute one of the chief staples of diet.... I prepare nuts in soups, in croquettes, in salads and hash. All of these preparations can be made very delicious, more so than if they were prepared from flesh, and are really more nourishing."

Economy, too, was a factor that advocates addressed in their attempts to convince the country to eschew meat. Stockham addressed the issue: "We should aim to simplify the preparations for the table. One of the growing failings of the nation is the complexity of diet. In the study of sociology it comes to me very strongly that one great point that should be made is furnishing a diet that requires less labor, to say nothing of expense."

In her lecture "Food of the Orient" before the Vegetarian Congress at the World's Fair (June 8, 1893), Stockham recalled her experience traveling in the East, where she observed that Brahmins and Hindus true to their religion never used animal food. "However, so far as I could observe, their greatest and most potent reason for adhering to a vegetable diet is their great abhorrence to dead animal matter. As soon as life leaves any created thing, that thing to them is polluting, and no power except fire is great enough to eradicate that pollution.... The hair, the skin, the hoofs, the feathers, the fat, are simply obnoxious to the Hindu," she observed. "You can not imagine the disgust with which he looks upon the western lady who wears gloves made from the skin of a dead animal."

Stockham also observed that they loathe soap made from animal fat, and feathers used for beds. "Can we wonder that he calls the meat-eating and soap-washing people of the western world, 'filthy barbarians?'... You can not imagine what barbarians we Westerners are considered, we who are devoted to flesh-pots and beer-mugs, and who can not travel without bath-tubs and sponges, and in preparation for days of hunting and sight-seeing do not even forget finger-bowls, tea-baskets or air beds."

Westerners, said Stockham, define progress as "science applied to the physical world" and view this world as material and not spiritual. But if someone does recognize "the power and dominion of the spirit," they would choose fruits and grains for food and "not wish conscious life to be taken for their sustenance."

The popular author and lecturer added: "Let us remember that there is spiritual law, and if we understood it, if we are trained to become acquainted with its workings, to let it have dominion over us, the needs of our bodies will not dominate us." Stockham also pointed out that the "inconsistency of the man who one day exhibits fondness, indeed almost adoration, for a pet animal, and the next day becomes a butcher of this life, or a similar one, to subserve his unnatural appetite, must cease," stated Stockham.

Another vegetarian advocate who lectured at the fair, Susanna Way Dodds, M.D., was the fourth woman in the nation to become a physician. She attended Russell Trall's New York Hygeia-Therapeutic College, graduating in 1864. Her sister Mary also became a physician, and the two established Hygienic College of Medicine and Surgery of St. Louis, Missouri. The sisters were strong advocates of women's rights; Dr. Dodds was also a leader in the fight for women's right to wear pants.

Dr. Dodds wrote articles and books, among them the two-volume *Health in the Household or Hygienic Cookery*, and the 1,700-page *Drugless Medicine*. In the latter she wrote: "With all her wealth of resources, Nature never intended that we should prey upon our fellow creatures below us for sustenance."

The eating of the flesh of animals was neither healthful nor aesthetically pleasing, believed the doctor. "Nor is it enough that we devour the several parts of the animal, even to his liver and kidneys; we strip the intestines of their fat, melt it down, and use it in the form of lard! This latter is the very quintessence of the swine; it is the diseased product of all his filthy feeding; and it is the article that forms a staple in almost every American family. It shortens the biscuits, the plain cakes, and the doughnuts, the Saratoga potatoes, and all the other 'fried things,' or nearly all. In short, there is neither breakfast, dinner, nor supper without it, in some form or other. Do the people wonder that they are afflicted with scrofula; and that it crops out, full-fledged, in a single generation?"[22] Americans, through the efforts of well-known people like Stockham and Dodds, were increasingly weighing what was commonly known as the food question and the vegetarian question.

Health reformer and vegetarian Martin Luther Holbrook, M.D., knew this well. "In no period of the world's history has there ever been so deep an interest in the subject of foods as at the present.... It would almost seem as if the time had nearly arrived when mankind would eat to live, would feed themselves so as to nourish their bodies most perfectly and render themselves capable of the most labor, and least liable to disease."[23]

Among the questions people were pondering was "should we eat meat?" One answer was published in the popular woman's publication, *The Home Magazine*. "It is an open question, whether meat is really necessary to the proper nourishment of the body. Were we to listen to the disciples of Graham, the anaemic condition of our butcher's bill would be most gratifying; but till the advocates of a purely vegetable diet can show biceps and calves as well-developed as their theories, they will make few proselytes from the ranks of this carnivorous people."[24]

Like Dodds, Dr. Holbrook advocated abstinence from animal flesh in the late nineteenth century and lectured at the World's Fair Congress on vegetarianism and agriculture. He believed the rejection of meat for plant-based meals was progress for humanity, much as the use of electricity instead of candles was an improvement.

One of three partners in the Laight Street Sanitarium, Holbrook was also a partner in and, for more than 25 years, editor of Russell Trall's *The Herald of Health* magazine. A native of Ohio, Holbrook practiced and wrote about medicine in New York City. Holbrook knew quite a few vegetarians, and wrote: "I have never known one to be a lover of alcoholic drinks or tobacco, and they suffer less from disease than flesh-eaters." Although Holbrook wrote and lectured on vegetarianism as beneficial, he was not consistent on the subject; for example, he once stated that oysters were a beneficial food.

Nevertheless, Holbrook wrote several books, some featuring sections on diet. The doctor had translated *Fruit and Bread,* a book advocating fruitarianism that originally was written in German by Gustav Schlickeysen. *Fruit and Bread* presented arguments for an uncooked diet of fruits, grains, and nuts. Schlickeysen pointed out an argument against drinking cow's milk still employed today: only humans suckle beyond infancy, and, at that, from another species.[25]

The American vegetarians kept branching out to the like-minded of other nations. The movement was part of an international web that included some of the most influential vegetarians, especially Count Leo Tolstoy, the great Russian novelist and philosopher, and Irish playwright George Bernard Shaw, who was frequently quoted in the U.S. press.

Early ties with England remained as Americans embraced works and lectures by Britain's leading advocates, and the British accorded their United States counterparts the same respect. For example, British advocates read books by authors Sylvester Graham, Mary Gove Nichols, and Thomas L. Nichols. In the States, books by Anna Kingsford, M.D., and Henry Salt found an audience. Dr. Kingsford's doctoral dissertation and later book titled *The Perfect Way In Diet* provided plenty of facts in support of eschewing meat. She and her friend Edward Maitland were leaders of the vegetarian and antivivisection movements in England. Coauthors of several books, they also addressed the spiritual dimension of vegetarianism. Another writer influential in America was Henry Salt, who wrote several books about vegetarianism and animal liberation.

Clearly, vegetarian advocacy of the nineteenth century was deeply rooted in Christianity. But towards the end of the century, a growing number of Americans were exploring other religions and beliefs. Vegetarians were no exception. The movement evolved with the times, placing deeper emphasis on science as a test of the legitimacy of a diet without meat.

Chicago's J. Howard Moore, then the leading proponent of ethical vegetarianism, was an author, philosopher, and a science teacher who

believed that vegetarianism was "the expansion of ethics to suit the biological revelations of Charles Darwin." Moore believed that if man
evolved from primates, then it was natural for man to eat from plant
foods. "I am a vegetarian because anything else is hideous and unnatural," he said.[26]

Moore, who was born 1862 on a farm in Missouri, denounced religions
for not extending their teachings of mercy to cover animals that "do not
come into existence endowed with the right to life and happiness simply to
be torn to pieces and crunched." He also disliked members of humane societies who ate meat. They protect certain animals and "massacre and swallow" others "without compunction," he wrote in *The Universal Kinship*.[27]

Arguments against abstaining were all too familiar to advocates. Yet
advocates had replies to every reason given by meat eaters. The Chicago
Vegetarian Society's magazine, *The Chicago Vegetarian*, featured a debate
between Moore and Lawrence Grunland, an opponent of vegetarianism,
that covered the arguments.

Grunland presented the following arguments:

- …many forms of flesh of animals are far more nutritious and more easily
  digested than the corresponding nitrogenous productions of the vegetable kingdom and these are the nourishing products, and further, are those for which
  man's internal organs are admirable adapted.
- All the great intellects of the world in ancient and modern times have been produced by flesh-eating nations.
- The consumer of flesh and fish may feel a perfect conscientious pleasure in eating them. Death is inevitable termination of life in every instance in man or animal. A violent, instantaneous death is probably the most desirable mode for
  all—including man.… But the life, enjoyed by all animals, reared for food,
  whether in the poultry yard or in the field, is undoubtedly a very happy one,
  happier as a rule than for man. For no other animal is existence so easy or may
  death be so swift and painless.
- The breeding of animals for food confers life on millions of beings, possessing
  considerable capacity for enjoyment in their own way on the best conditions
  attainable—superior in point of comfort, freedom from pain and accidents, to
  those of the wild breeds.
- Another reason for opposing the rejection of meat eating was it was not desirable for a collectivist to differ from other people and be deemed one of the peculiar people.[28]

J. Howard Moore, a prominent member of the *Chicago Vegetarian Society*,
dismissed all of these arguments as incorrect. Moore, a writer and teacher,
rebuked people who proudly proclaimed they were not vegetarians. To
Laurence Grunland he replied that, to rapacious animals, including meat-
eating human beings, "Every meal is a murder." Moore also believed that

"To tell why one is 'not a vegetarian' is to give justification, or to attempt to give justification, for being a predatory animal."[29]

- "If there is one fact thoroughly known to modern biologists it is that man is physiologically a vegetarian.... Admirably adapted to the use of flesh, indeed! About as admirably adapted as a broomstick is for flying.

- "Is murder stripped of its blackness by becoming a fine art? All assassination is practically instantaneous and painless, the assassination of men as well as that of birds and quadrupeds. What would the author of such nonsense think if the assassin of his brother or mother blandly attempted to relieve himself of all guilt by means of the assurance that his victim had experienced no suffering? The crime of extermination does not consist in the creation of pain, but in the destruction of that precious and mysterious essence called life."[30]

That Grunland, like Moore, a collectivist, would refuse to stop eating meat because he did not want to be different, seemed childish to Moore. "Such reasoning universalized would convert the race into a set of exclusive and hopelessly fossilized camps, each desiring the regeneration of the others and each refusing absolutely to live up to his ideal.... The consistent individual is the individual who, so far as his defective nature allows him, lives up to the highest light that comes to him. The consistent life is the grandest life and is the most influential."[31]

So-called progressives that didn't embrace vegetarianism could be likened to "our forefathers relentlessly advancing the proposition that all mankind are endowed with inalienable rights, and never once suspecting that mankind included women and blacks," believed Moore. It was time to extend mankind's compassion and respect, if not membership in his race, to animals, implied Moore, who also included women's rights on his agenda for improving America.[32]

The intertwining of the rejection of meat with causes such as feminism would remain a theme of the movement into the twentieth century. Not participating in the slaughter of animals by refusing to eat them, and instead showing them respect as sentient beings, was integral to the progress of humanity, Moore believed, as had advocates who had come before him.

While Moore expounded on ethical arguments for vegetarianism, other advocates were mainly concerned with propagating the plant-based diet into the practice of medicine and for staples. One of them was Henry Perky, a vegetarian who invented and manufactured shredded wheat, a product hailed by some in the movement as the perfect replacement for meat, and a superior food at that. In advertisements, and through his New Era Cooking School, located in Worcester, Massachusetts, Perky promoted wheat.[33]

In between addressing audiences, or publishing movement magazines, and other advocacy activities, vegetarians participated in purely pleasurable events. One of the earliest gatherings of vegetarians to celebrate Thanksgiving occurred in 1895 at the University of Chicago. Vegetarians in the Chicago area who were members of The Vegetarian Eating Club attended the feast, which featured a menu that included chestnut soup with pasta D'Italia, mushroom rissoles, spanish olives, red french beans, creamed potato with pea dressing, date and whole wheat bread, grand pâté au jordan, and desserts ranging from pumpkin pie and fruit cake to pineapple sherbert and angel food cake.[34]

In July of 1898 Chicago vegetarian members enjoyed an excursion from the city to St. Joseph, Michigan on the steamship named City of Milwaukee. On the steamer the adventurers were treated to a concert by Miss Mabelle Lewis, a piano solo by Miss Blanche Irwin, several lectures by various individuals, and humor by Dr. J. R. Price. The members of the society dined on cheese sandwiches (for the nonvegans), hygienic cake, peaches, bananas, shredded wheat biscuits with fruit, berries and cream, fig mince pie, and other dishes.[35]

THE ANIMAL QUESTION

Vegetarian advocates such as Moore were now placing more emphasis on animal rights as reason to leave off eating meat. Criticism of animal protection organizations and leaders who did not advocate vegetarianism was sharp. Vegetarians noted that *Our Dumb Animals,* the magazine published by the Massachusetts Society for the Prevention of Cruelty to Animals, the organization headed by the renowned veterinarian Dr. Angell, failed to include the slaughter of animals for food as an issue of concern, and that this was an inconsistency.[36]

That animals suffered so that people could dine on their flesh became more prominent a theme. This message could be found in vegetarian publications, and in others such as *The Animals' Defender,* which was the magazine of New England Anti-Vivisection Society. Likewise, vegetarian publications published articles in support of the antivivisection movement.

Clubb spoke out on animal rights. "The movement for the prevention of cruelty to animals is one of the most promising efforts for the promotion of humane sentiments... that in the United States of America, there are no fewer than 233 local societies for the prevention of cruelty to animals," Clubb said at the start of the twentieth century. In a 1913 Thanksgiving day sermon delivered from his Philadelphia pulpit, Clubb summarized his and other advocates' feelings on the link between animal rights and vegetarianism.

We have made one of the largest of our domestic birds serve as our supply of our most delightful food; we see the turkey extolled and pictured. But it is seldom we hear any pity expressed for the poor bird we have made the victim of our absurd custom. Shortly after the war I was traveling over the Texas plains with an escort of soldiers. We happened to arouse a brood of young wild turkeys. One of the men jumped off his horse and picked up a little member of the family. The mother turkey, at the risk of her life, followed us, making loud cries for her little one. Her cries were so piteous, that we halted the command and asked the soldier to return the young bird to its mother. He did it without hesitation. When we think of all that maternal devotion and eager self-sacrifice on the part of the mother bird of that young flock, how can we justify the slaughter of those creatures in celebration of our Thanksgiving to One whose mercy to all His creatures endureth for ever?[37]

The move towards humane sentiment, or animal welfare as it would be called in the future, was growing. But Americans would first have to change their eating habits before animals could be liberated, believed vegetarian advocates.[38]

And this was a problem that Holbrook acknowledged in a paper he read before the New York Teachers' Cooking Association on May 9th, 1896. Holbrook said that he believed primitive human beings became flesh eaters out of necessity because they had no agriculture and lived as animals. He said man and woman had advanced considerably, and must no longer eat meat. Extended agriculture, and the large variety of foods from the vegetable kingdom made it no longer necessary to eat meat.[39]

The meat-eating habit, Holbrook explained, was an obstacle to the widespread adoption of vegetarianism. "We can hardly tolerate one who does not do in the main as everybody else does. Useful as habits are, they at last are spectres and hold the race back in progress."[40]

Despite the difficulty of overcoming habits, vegetarians had hope. A report in *The Animals' Defender* stated that meat was losing favor. "The butchers even are taking up the supply of fruit and vegetables in the large cities. The sale of meat has decreased immensely since the prices advanced. The manufacture of vegetarian or health foods is rapidly increasing. In the little city of Battle Creek there are over 30 large factories devoted to various kinds of health foods, and the demand for them is increasing all the time."[41]

But progress was not manifesting fast enough for some. At the turn of the century, many vegetarians who felt estranged from society yearned to form colonies with their comrades.

In a 1901 issue of *The Vegetarian*, a writer from Missouri informs readers that a community of 40 or 50 families, all vegetarians and Catholic, was doing well in the town of Old Orchard. The older members arrived there from Germany, and there were many "young ladies between fifteen and twenty-one years old, highly accomplished, well educated, that have not tasted flesh-meat in all their lives."[42]

Maine also featured a colony in the town of Hodgden, made up of 22 families of all religious and political backgrounds. An issue of *The Vegetar-*

ian and Our Fellow Creatures in 1901 claimed the colony was 11 years old, and that members, despite using horses and oxen, avoided such animal products as milk, butter, and wool. They used cotton and linen for clothing, and barberry fruit instead of tallow to make candles. The magazine noted that no member of the community ever contracted consumption.

The century was concluding. Ground nurtured earlier in the 1800s by Reverend Metcalfe, Doctor Alcott, Crusader Graham, and the rest brought forth fruit. Reverend Clubb and the Seventh-Day Adventists carried the movement through the later years, and would continue to do so for several more decades. Ideas on eating they had presented to the country found some fertile ground, enough to keep the vegetarian movement alive through tumultuous times. Ridicule, misrepresentation, and reputation assault, as weeds in the garden, had sprouted during the century and temporarily interfered with vegetarianism's growth. These, and more noxious weeds would nearly strangle the movement in the next century.

But before that would occur, the forgoing of meat would first enter a period of popularity—the Golden Age of vegetarianism. Soon meat eating would be a relic of the past. Or so it must have seemed to some during the period of American history known as the Progressive Era.

Chapter 7

The Progressive Era

Life in the United States was changing rapidly at the dawn of the twentieth century. An increasing number of families were installing telephones, lighting their homes with electricity, and driving automobiles. It was a time when many people were leaving their rural homes to seek the American dream in cities dotted with smokestacks. Europeans, with visions of streets paved with gold, were coming to America in record numbers.

The sun was setting on the Victorian Era and the new Progressive Era was rising. It was a time when social activists were vigorously calling for improvements in American daily life. Enacting child labor laws, cutting the tremendous powers of monopolistic corporations, giving women the right to vote, conserving land, and protecting the food supply were just a few of the goals of reformers. Their leaders included *The Jungle* author Upton Sinclair, Jane Addams of the Settlement movement, and feminist Charlotte Perkins Gilman. Some politicians, such as Senator Robert LaFolette, who was a vegetarian, were reform leaders in Congress fighting for workers' rights and wilderness protection.

Vegetarianism was entering a golden age, helped in part by the efforts of such reformers. Other activists worked for causes such as temperance, anti-vivisection, and reproductive rights. In fact, some feminist gatherings featured vegetarian food and vegetarian leaders. At the February 1903 meeting of the National Women Suffrage Association in Chicago, animal rights and vegetarianism were discussed. The treasurer of the club, Harriet Taylor Upton, answering a request by an attendee that suffrage women should include animal rights in their agenda, said if club members did not support it, then "Nobody who will eat a chicken or a cow or a fish has any right to say a word when anybody else kills a parrot or a fox or a seal." Upton urged members to expand their beliefs beyond just the right to vote. Another delegate in agreement stated: "Why do we make one reform topic a hobby and forget about the others? Mercy, Prohibition, Vegetarianism, Woman's Suffrage, and Peace would make Old Earth a paradise, and yet the majority advocate but one, if any, of these."[1]

But innovations in a wide array of fields also played a significant role in helping vegetarianism increase in popularity. On the food front, the Western world was pulling out of the nutritional stone age with the discovery of vitamins by scientists such as Casimir Funk. Vegetarians had long contended that fruits and vegetables were the healthiest of foods, but now some nutritionists were beginning to agree. Simultaneously, however, junk food was showing up on grocery shelves. Americans were now guzzling Coca-Cola, Pepsi, Dr. Pepper and snacking on new products such as the Hershey Bar and Jell-O.

Meanwhile, a few maverick scientists were presenting strong evidence that the American diet contained far too much protein and that meat was not a necessity. One of them was Professor W.H. Wiley, chief chemist of the U.S. Department of Agriculture. "It is well known that men nourished extensively on cereals are capable of the hardest and most enduring manual labor," he told the press. "Meats are quickly digested and furnish an abundance of energy soon after consumption, but it is not retained in the digestive organism long enough to sustain permanent muscular exertion. Cereal Foods, on the other hand, are more slowly digested and furnish the energy necessary to digestion and the vital functions in a more uniform manner. They are thus better adapted to sustain hard manual labor for a long period of time," explained Wiley.[2]

Innovations in technology were also making it easier for people to cut beef, pork, fowl, and fish from the diet. Refrigerated train and truck cargoes were transporting fruits and vegetables thousands of miles. It was now possible in the middle of January for a Connecticut family to top their cereal with strawberries from California, and for a mother in Philadelphia to serve peas and potatoes picked just a few days before from farms in the West.

Vegetarians in this time period had food choices not available to their counterparts of the past. Between 1895 and 1905, about 100 health foods, including breakfast cereals and containing no meat, were developed at the Battle Creek Sanitarium under the guidance of its superintendent, Dr. John Harvey Kellogg. One of the new foods was Protose, which Kellogg called an ideal meat substitute that mimicked the taste of chicken or beef. A vegetarian restaurant in 1901 located in New York City listed Protose on the menu at a price of 15 cents.[3] Kellogg had developed Protose in 1899 at the request of the U.S. Department of Agriculture.

Charles Dabney, assistant secretary of the department, and former president of the University of Tennessee, was seeking a protein alternative to

Turn-of-the-century vegetarian restaurant.

meat, which was expensive in those days. Dabney was also concerned about the wasteful economics of feeding grains to animals raised for food when it made more sense to feed these grains directly to the world's proliferating population. Dabney had suggested navy beans (soybeans were then used mainly for animal feed) as the protein substitute, but Kellogg chose peanuts as the base of his new food product.[4]

Dabney also believed that meat eating was not necessary, and that Protose was the ideal replacement. "I believe that the craving of meat is an artificial one, like the taste for alcohol, resulting from the education of the taste to like its peculiar flavors, and of the nerves to enjoy its slight stimulation. Besides furnishing proteins, fat, carbohydrates, lime, etc. in a better form and free from bacteria and urea and uric acid, Protose is doing

Battle Creek Sanitarium.

a noble work as a satisfactory substitute for meat in teaching people how to form better dietaries."[5]

Kellogg was the leading promoter of vegetarianism of the era. His invention of flaked and ready-to-eat cereals in 1894 did much to break the breakfast habits of Americans. At the time, it was not unusual to start the day with a heaping portion of meat such as sausage and then wash it down with a shot of booze.

In the late 1870s, the doctor established the Battle Creek Sanitarium Health Food Company to produce granola, whole-grain cereals, and graham and other types of crackers, along with Caramel Cereal Coffee, a coffee substitute. A decade earlier James Caleb Jackson had developed Granola, the first breakfast cereal; it was a success, but it had to be soaked overnight before eating. After developing additional meat substitutes, Kellogg formed the Sanitas Nut Food Company in 1889. In the early years, Sanitas sold most of its products by mail to former patients of the Battle Creek Sanitarium, including the flaked cereal products developed by Kellogg.

Several of the Sanitas products were nut-based substitutes for meat, including Nuttose. They were generically called vegetable or nut meats. Nuttose was largely made from nuts, and it had the consistency of cream cheese. The food, according to company literature, "exhibited none of the objectionable qualities of flesh meat" with "no toxins." Nuttelene, another nut-based food, was billed as a "delicate white meat as dainty and juicy as the breast of a spring chicken."[6] Demand grew in the 1890s and the company began shipping its products to health food stores and restaurants.

Kellogg explained his motives for creating new foods: "In dropping meats from the dietary it was difficult at first to find a satisfactory substitute because for so many generations meals had been built around meats and to most people a meal without meat as its center was unthinkable.... In biologic living we left out the meat, left out all the condiments, coffee and tea, and what was finally left was very plain and tasteless for those who were accustomed to high flavors."[7]

John Harvey Kellogg was born in 1852 and was raised by his parents, who were converted to the Adventist faith and moved to Battle Creek when John was a child. His reputation as a bright boy caught the attention of Ellen White and her husband James. They offered him a position in the Seventh-Day Adventist print shop, and helped finance his way through medical school. Kellogg began to read the works of Sylvester Graham and cut meat from his diet. "It became a ruling passion with me—the belief that there was in everything one best way, nature's way," recalled Kellogg later in life. While attending Bellevue Medical College in New York City, he lived mostly on apples and crackers made from Graham flour, an occasional potato that he would bake over a fire while he was working, and oatmeal gruel and coconut once a week.[8]

In 1883, Kellogg journeyed to Europe to study with the best surgeons and physicians on the continent, including Dr. Lawson Tait, a renowned English surgeon. Kellogg, using techniques learned from Tait, performed a record 162 surgical operations without a single death. The doctor also learned about the new science of plastic surgery and abdominal surgery techniques, and visited cold water cures in Germany and massage therapy institutions in Sweden.

Considered by many to be one of the finest, if not the best, surgeon in America, Kellogg over the course of his 67-year career performed more than 22,000 operations with an extremely low mortality rate. The doctor invented new surgery techniques and stitches. He never took a fee for his operations, opting instead to plow the money back into the Sanitarium. Kellogg promoted vegetarianism as an integral measure to prevent and even reverse numerous maladies such as heart disease and gastrointestinal disorders. Unlike other vegetarian advocates of the era, Kellogg was well respected within the medical community. He was a member in good standing with professional organizations, including the American Association for the Advancement of Science, American Public Health Association, and the American College of Surgeons.

For decades, the doctor lectured about vegetarianism. The more influential the audience, the better. At the 1907 Lake Placid Conference on Home Economics, an annual gathering of scientists, professors, teachers, dietitians, and other decision makers, Kellogg warned his audience that meat contains toxins and was unessential in the diet. Back at the Sanitarium, his staff of scientists compiled additional evidence on the health ben-

efits of fruits and vegetables and Kellogg published the results in his popular *Good Health* magazine, a publication that he edited for over 60 years.

At its height, Kellogg's Battle Creek Sanitarium was receiving over
7,000 guests a year and employed a staff of more than 1,000, including
nurses, physicians, and technicians. During Kellogg's reign, the Sanitarium attracted rich and influential people, including Henry Ford, J.C.
Penny, S.S. Kresge, Montgomery Ward, Harvey Firestone, and others who
founded companies that carried their name. Others who stayed at the Sanitarium included polar explorer Vilhjalmur Stefansson, aviator Amelia
Earhart, actress Sarah Bernhardt, Thomas Edison, president William
Howard Taft, and actor and athlete Johnny Weismuller.

In the early decades of the Sanitarium, the bill of fare was mostly vegetarian, but some meat was served to patients who insisted on having
some. Kellogg instructed the staff to strongly discourage it, and eventually
meat was dropped entirely from the bill of fare. On occasion, Kellogg liked
to remind his guests of the animals that they spared by eating vegetarian
fare. At one Thanksgiving dinner, the doctor stated "Let us be thankful,
not only that we are alive, but that everything else is alive."

The Sanitarium owed some of its success to Kellogg's wife, Ella Eaton
Kellogg. Mrs. Kellogg was in charge of the facility's kitchens, where she
oversaw the preparation of hundreds of meals each week and, more than
that, tested foods and recipes.[9] A Battle Creek newspaper stated that she
"was the greatest single factor in developing the Sanitarium dietary." She
was also the author of *Science in the Kitchen* (Good Health Publishing Company, 1892). Another driving force behind the Sanitarium's success was
Lena Francis Cooper, who was the director of dietetics. Cooper co-founded
the American Dietetic Association in 1917.

HEADLINES

Thanks to Kellogg and other promoters of the meat-free bill of fare, vegetarianism gained much-needed exposure in the early years of the twentieth century. Growth was stagnant during the last quarter of the nineteenth
century, yet at the start of the new era popular newspaper and magazines
featured many vegetarian stories. The meat-free message popped up in the
pages of *Good Housekeeping, American Literary Digest, Harper's Bazaar,* the
New York Times, and many other widely circulated periodicals of the day.

In 1909 *The Ladies Home Journal* ran a vegetarian-friendly article entitled
"The Mistake of Eating Meat." "Substantial Meals Without Meat: A Vegetarian Diet Which Has Proved Acceptable to Many," was a headline that
year in the magazine *Good Housekeeping.*[10] The author, Mary Sanderson,
M.D., said she has "avoided the use of flesh foods because I believe them
to be nonessential and in many cases injurious." Sanderson also explains
that "primitive man was a vegetarian" and links disease with meat eating.

There's no doubt that vegetarianism as a topic, and as a practice, was gaining in ground in those days. The May 1913 *Literary Digest* reported that "vegetarianism is gaining many recruits, and what speaks well for it is the fact that many great brain-workers of national and international prominence not only get along well without meat, but make it part of their business to urge others to adhere to a vegetable diet."[11]

About the same time, the *New York Sun* reported that the "popularity of vegetarianism is rapidly increasing the World over, particularly in England and in the United States.... Health, religion, desire of beauty, taste and artistic feelings are among the various excuses."[12]

Some newspapers and magazines of the day covered the never-ending debate among meat eaters and vegetarians over many issues, including whether carnivorous or non-flesh-eating animals were superior. Vegetarians often heralded animals such as elephants and gorillas as an example of strong and majestic herbivores, while meat-eating proponents pointed out that the king of the jungle—the lion—was a carnivore.

The early 1900s was also a time when vegetarians and meat proponents weren't shy about putting their spin on news events to further their points of view—even if the facts they provided were wrong. For example, vegetarians liked to point out that a vegetarian Japanese army defeated a meat-eating Russian army in the 1904 war between the two powers. Vegetarians wrote letters to the *New York Times* and other newspapers pointing this out as one more piece of evidence for the superiority of a vegetarian diet.

However, the Japanese army wasn't vegetarian, according to E.V. McCollum, one of the era's most prominent nutritionists and an esteemed professor of biochemistry. Takaki, a top Japanese Naval official, was said to be impressed by the superior health of British naval personnel, and studied the nutrition of his navy when a beriberi scourge hit the Japanese Navy in the late 1870's, affecting about one-third of all the men, wrote McCollum in his *A History of Nutrition*. Takaki attributed the difference to the fact that the British sailors had more protein in their diets. He introduced evaporated milk and meat into the Naval diet, which had been mainly polished rice and fish. The beriberi plague was wiped out, but McCollum believed that Takaki, because of the nutrition ignorance of the times, incorrectly attributed the benefits of the new diet to higher protein intake.[13]

The champions of meat eating also pushed some dubious propaganda, particularly in publicizing the eating habits of famous explorers. Hall, Peary and other Polar explorers in the early twentieth century were apparently doing well on an all-meat Eskimo diet—an assertion that was publicized well into the century. But Kellogg noted in his book, *Natural Diet of Man*, that many of them died prematurely of apoplexy and cardiovascular disease.

However, not all of the explorers died prematurely. Vilhjalmur Steffanson, who was said to be healthy even after a year of eating strictly meat, became a trophy for the meat industry. Steffanson gave his reasons why Eskimos age rapidly and die young to a 1936 Kansas City gathering of chemists. "Because of the heat in their homes—heat so terrific that they walk about naked and sweating," he said, according to the *New York Times*. But Steffanson also said that man could live "the Biblical three score and ten" on either an all-meat or vegetarian diet.[14]

Sometimes the arguments were absurd. The *Times* in 1912 reported how a Frenchman upset vegetarian theory with a dietary experiment using ducks. Edmond Perrier took some ducks and separated them into several groups: some ducks were fed meat, some fish, others just insects, and a group of ducks were fed a diet of strictly vegetables, maize, and bread. At the end of two-and-a-half months, the meat-eating ducks weighed on the average 1,500 grams, the insect eating group tipped the scales at 1,100, the fish eaters were at 900, and the vegetarian ducks registered at 600. The *Times* writer said that the experiment proved a "serious blow to the vegetarian cult."[15]

Some of the stories of the era showed that vegetarians were not without humor. A first-person account by journalist Elsie McCormick in a 1928 issue of the *Literary Digest* summed up the feelings of vegetarians of the early twentieth century. She wrote that being a vegetarian was no "gold-tinted situation. Whenever I go into a restaurant, I must look anxiously down the menu for something which my tabu will let me eat. I often end up with a vegetable plate. During the past two years I have cavorted among hundreds of pale, languorous carrots, fraternized with pecks of weepy boiled beets, and eaten at least a silo full of various greens and grasses." McCormick called the "greatest trial" of being a vegetarian is the fact that other vegetarians "rush up and call you brother."[16]

Magazines and newspapers frequently featured articles about famous vegetarians, including literary giant George Bernard Shaw, who was vocal about his preference for a plant-based diet. Playwright Shaw, renowned for his keen wit, when asked why he was a vegetarian replied, "Oh, come! The boot is on the other leg. Why should you ask me to account for eating decently? If I battened on the scorched corpses of animals, you might well ask me why I did that." Shaw was a favorite with the public, and a favorite celebrity vegetarian. Vegetarian advocates and magazines often quoted the sage. Shaw was a role model. That a man could be intelligent and successful yet never eat meat was a boon to vegetarians, and especially to vegetarian men, since for decades males who did not eat flesh food had been labeled by some in society as emasculated.

Women who abstained from eating chicken and cow had role models, too. One of the most popular actresses in the pre–World War I days was Sarah Bernhardt, a vegan who ate dried and fresh fruits, nuts, cereals, and vegetables and drank spring water. Bernhardt, according to *The Literary Digest*, became a vegan to lose weight and regain her figure. The *Digest* reported that "her figure has greatly improved so that she is enabled at nearly 70 and as a great-grandmother to act the role of Joan of Arc in tights and to reveal an agile, graceful figure."[17]

While Bernhardt was in the twilight of her career, the Salvation Army, a Christian charity organization that was founded in England and soon branched out into the United States, advocated vegetarianism. Its founder, General William Booth, said in a 1914 interview that he tried vegetarianism but gave it up. "I tried a vegetarian diet, but gave it up owing to the difficulties I experienced in my wandering life, especially as it seemed to involve those about me in extra labour, a little vexation, and always an amount of unprofitable controversy." But Booth believed the multitudes would gain wisdom, health, happiness, and holiness by rejecting meat. He asked that people try it for one month.

Booth's son Bramwell, however, was a vegetarian. Among General Bramwell Booth's 19 reasons for rejecting meat, which was published: "I have myself tried a vegetarian diet with the greatest benefit, having been for more than ten years at one time a strict vegetarian. Because according to the Bible, God originally intended the food of man to be vegetarian. Because a vegetarian diet is favorable to purity, chastity, and to perfect control of the appetites and passions, which are often a source of great temptation, especially to the young. Because a vegetarian diet is favorable to robust health and strength. Because tens of thousands of our poor people, who have now the greatest difficulty to make ends meet after buying flesh food, would, by the substitution of fruits and vegetables and other economical food, be able to get along in comfort, and have more money to spare for the poor and for the work of God. Because a vegetarian diet of wheat, oatmeal and other grains, lentils, peas, beans, nuts and similar food is more than ten times as economical as a flesh diet. Meat contains half its weight in water, which has to be paid for as though it were meat! A vegetable diet, even if we allow cheese, butter and milk, will only cost about a quarter as much as a mixed diet of flesh and vegetable. Because a vegetarian diet would stop the enormous waste of all kinds of animal food which is now consumed with scarcely any advantages to those who take it."[18]

The London Vegetarian Society noted that some Salvation Army homes established that diet had an effect on moral character. The Army established that placing an alcoholic on a non-flesh diet led to a quick cure—an idea that harks back to Sylvester Graham's teachings of the 1830s.

ATHLETES AND SHOWMEN

In the early years of the twentieth century, vegetarians looked to athletes to prove to the world that vegetarians were not emaciated or unmanly. Eustace Miles, who was a trainer for members of the fashionable

Tuxedo Club of New York and an amateur tennis champ in England in 1899, wrote about the effects that meat had on his game. "After returning to the old foods, even to a single helping of meat alone, my game of rackets has been wont to go down between three to five points."[19]

One of the most prominent vegetarian athletes was Karl Mann, whose walking and cycling feats were reported widely in the vegetarian community and in the mainstream press. Mann, who was from Germany, won a 70-mile European walking race in 1898 and told the press that during the walk he ate fresh fruit, lettuce, bread, and milk. Other athletic feats performed by vegetarians, particularly those participating in bicycle races, were widely reported in the early years of the twentieth century.[20]

The question of whether meat in the diet of athletes was injurious was debated in the early twentieth century. In 1914 the captain of the Harvard football team missed nearly the whole season because of appendicitis. Dr. Richard Newton, president of the New Jersey State Board of Health, blamed meat eating and outlined his arguments in the *Harvard Alumni Bulletin*, which was printed in a 1915 *Literary Digest* story. Newton used Kellogg's observation that populations who abstain from meat were healthier than meat eating populations, and suffered no appendicitis. Newton called for a massive study of vegetarian and meat-eating athletes and nonathletes.[21]

Perhaps the most popular showman of the times was Bernarr MacFadden, who built a vast publishing empire based on a foundation of physical culture. He advocated exercise, fasting, vegetarian diets, and pure food laws. He was a patriot who believed that a physically fit America would be strong and prosperous. "We need stronger, more capable men; healthier superior women...Why not throb with superior vitality!" wrote Mac-Fadden in *Vitality Supreme*.[22]

In 1899 MacFadden published the first issue of *Physical Culture* magazine, a publication that slammed the medical establishment and patent medicines, fought prudery, covered vegetarian issues, and heavily advocated fasting, exercise, and muscular development for both sexes. *Physical Culture* gave vegetarians a forum for their views, particularly in the publication's early years. It covered athletic events where vegetarians bested meat eaters, mainly in bicycle races in the United States and Europe.

The September 1902 issue reported that a vegetarian cyclist finished first in a European race 8 hours ahead of the best meat-eating competitor. "A few more examples like this, and even the veriest numbskull will begin to think that there is a possibility of there being some truth in the claims of the vegetarian," concluded the story. The magazine also included recipes for vegetarian mock turkey and mock pheasant, and often ran stories on the evils of white bread and the harmful effects of excessive meat eating.[23]

Physical Culture, which often featured a tastefully nude MacFadden on the cover, eventually reached a circulation of 500,000. MacFadden was not

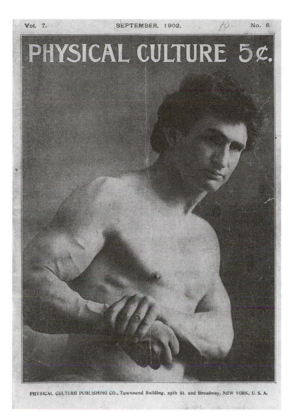

Vol. 7.   SEPTEMBER, 1902.   No. 6.

PHYSICAL CULTURE 5¢.

PHYSICAL CULTURE PUBLISHING CO., Townsend Building, 25th St. and Broadway, NEW YORK, U. S. A.

Physical Culture magazine with Bernarr MacFadden on the cover.

satisfied. In 1919 he introduced *True Story,* a sensational magazine that featured articles on love and romance, followed by *True Romances, True Ghost Stories, True Detective,* and *Midnight.* MacFadden also launched several newspapers, including the *New York Evening Graphic* in 1924. Often called the "Evening Pornographic," it used sensationalism, sex, and composite photos while promoting vegetarianism, hygiene, and exercise. Two of his columnists were Walter Winchell and Ed Sullivan, two men who would become household names. By the 1930s, the combined circulation of his magazines and newspapers reached into the tens of millions—even topping that of Luce and Hearst.

The physical culture king also established a chain of vegetarian restaurants. The first Physical Culture restaurant opened in New York City, close to the Bowery. Customers, for just one cent, could buy a bowl of hot vegetarian soup at the basement counter or a slice of whole wheat bread. For five cents, customers could go upstairs and choose from a more varied menu, which featured a beef substitute made from chopped nuts and vegetables, and "gave the illusion of eating good bloody beef, without the danger." By 1911 there were 20 Physical Culture restaurants throughout the country, but the chain declined when MacFadden turned the management over to someone else.

Although he was not always a vegetarian himself, he advocated a lacto-ovo vegetarian diet of mostly raw fruits and vegetables during the first few decades of the twentieth century. "There is absolutely no question as to the superiority of this plan over a regimen that includes meat.... A vegetarian diet will usually make a better quality of tissue; you will have more endurance, and there is but little doubt that a healthy vegetarian will outlive a meat eater," he said.

Born on a farm in Missouri in 1868, MacFadden traveled to England in 1912 and met his second wife, Mary Williamson, a champion swimmer. The physical culture king held a contest in 1913 to find the most perfect specimen of English womanhood. Williamson won, and MacFadden married her. He converted his new wife to vegetarianism and gave lectures and demonstrations on the wisdom of physical culture. The newlyweds traveled and put on physical culture stunts, which usually ended with Mary climbing to the top of a ladder taller than she and jumping onto her husband's stomach.

THE EVIDENCE IN FAVOR OF VEGETARIANISM

Vegetarians needed to rely on role models like Mann and MacFadden, especially when the scientific evidence proving the power of plants in the diet to prevent disease had not yet been established. Not that there wasn't plentiful anecdotal evidence, but until the twentieth century, scientific evidence for the health benefits of vegetarianism was rare. Sylvester Graham and other vegetarian advocates in the previous century had used anecdotal evidence, observation, anthropological evidence, ancient philosophy, and the Bible to prove the benefits of meals that did not include meat. One example, as noted in a previous chapter, was when Graham observed that vegetarians seemed less likely to contract cholera during epidemics of that disease. However, the prevailing allopathic medical profession of the era didn't perform controlled studies to isolate diet as a preventive measure against cholera, even when other physicians, including those who practiced drugless hygienic medicine, had accumulated tremendous success in helping people back to health by changing their diet to one that contained no meats.

Vegetarians had long proclaimed the value of foods from the plant kingdom, and at the turn of the century, the scientific community began to scrutinize the role of diet in health and fitness. Much was written and said about vegetarianism during the era, and science could not ignore the fact that a significant percent of Americans were not eating meat, or at least thinking about eliminating it from their diets. Another major concern pushing people towards vegetarianism was the cost of food, and much was written on inexpensive sources of protein such as nuts. University of California nutrition professor M.E. Jaffa, working with the Department of Agriculture's California Agricultural Experiment Station, conducted experiments to determine the dietary value of fruits and nuts and the economics of including such foods in the diet.[24]

At the time, meat was expensive. These were the days before mechanized factory farms replaced family farms as chief sources of meat. In fact, high prices, coupled with the growing awareness of vegetarianism, fueled a several-pounds-a-year decline in per-capita meat consumption that lasted into the 1920s. Scientists such as Dabney and Jaffa, none of them vegetarians, were looking into cheaper sources of protein and nutrition.

Jaffa studied a family of fruitarians, which are vegetarians who eat mainly uncooked fruits and nuts, and found them to be healthy and strong. Strange as it might seem to people today, fruitarianism had a following during the Progressive era, and perhaps as large or larger a following as it has today. Jaffa and the experimental station studied other California fruitarians, some of them life-long vegetarians, and found them all to be healthy and spending less on food than the average American. The subjects ate the foods of a fresh fruit-and-nut lover's dream: plenty of nut varieties and loads of luscious tomatoes, cantaloupe, watermelon, oranges, bananas, strawberries, and grapes.

Perhaps the most significant scientific work in favor of vegetarianism was the weakening of the protein myth. At the time, it was widely believed that people needed anywhere from 118 to 145 grams of protein per day, depending on physical activity. The generally accepted belief was that meat was essential for strength—if a man wanted strong muscles, he would eat plenty of protein-rich pork or beef. These recommendations came from field studies of men and their diets. But McCollum pointed out that the proponents of these high-protein intakes erroneously believed that the protein consumed by people represented actual need.

Russell H. Chittenden, a Yale University professor of Physiological Chemistry, proved that an intake of about 35 to 40 grams of protein daily was not only adequate, but much healthier. Around 1900 the professor, who was suffering from headaches and rheumatic knee pain, put himself on a low-protein, low-calorie diet for several months. His health problems went away. Chittenden knew that he was on to something. He put students and athletes on low-protein diets consisting mainly of fruits and vegetables and little or no meat. The health of the subjects improved over the months, and the athletes generally performed better under the low-protein diet.[25]

Chittenden, along with Professor Irving Fisher, also ran a series of endurance tests at Yale that pitted vegetarians against meat eaters. Like the Chittenden protein trials, these experiments were widely reported in the press.

One of the tests was a contest where participants held out their arms until they tired and had to drop them. The average time posted by the 15 meat eaters was 10 minutes, but the average time for the vegetarians was 89 minutes, or nine times as long. None of the meat eaters held out their arms for more than a half hour, but 15 of the vegetarians surpassed that mark. Nine of them lasted over an hour and four of them exceeded two hours.

The two groups squared off again for deep-knee bends. Few of the meat eaters were able to squat more than 300 or 400 times and it was nearly impossible for them to walk down the gymnasium stairs after the test without falling. However, one Yale student who had been a vegetarian for over two years did 1,800 squats without exhaustion. He even ran around the track and walked several miles afterwards. One vegetarian nurse borrowed from the Battle Creek Sanitarium did 5,000 deep-knee bends.

About a decade later, an experiment involving millions of people hit the headlines. During the First World War, Denmark was faced with the possibility of food shortages resulting from an allied blockade. The government sought Dr. Mikkel Hindhede, a vegetarian, to solve the problem. Hindhede recommended that the government ban the feeding grain, such as barley, to livestock and instead give it to the people directly.[26] Danish livestock was sold to Germany, and the people began eating mostly vegetables and grain products such as bran and rye-based bread, along with some milk. It was a widely publicized experiment in lacto-ovo vegetarianism that yielded good news: the death rate from disease plummeted about 35 percent from October 1917 to October 1918 to the lowest rate ever recorded for any country.

The Inter-Allied Scientific Food Commission, a group of researchers from Allied countries, met during the First World War to discuss the high price and scarcity of food, particularly meat. The body, which Kellogg called the "most authoritative body which ever met to consider the subject of nutrition," gave a ringing endorsement to vegetarianism.

The commission decided that it was unnecessary to go ahead with a minimum meat ration "in view of the fact that no absolute physiologic need exists for meat, since the proteins of meat can be replaced by other proteins of animal origin such as those contained in milk...as well as by proteins of vegetable origin."

Vegetarians used these studies to support their claims that cutting meat from the diet was beneficial to the body. Kellogg publicized such studies in *Good Health* magazine. Other editors published the scientific findings in vegetarian publications, as did numerous authors of vegetarian cookbooks.

Nicola Tesla, a well-known genius of the era whose work with alternating current led to widespread electricity, believed that the scientific evi-

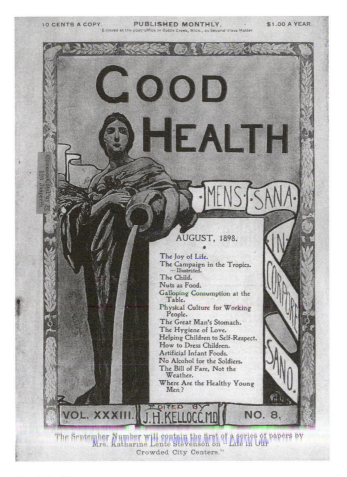

10 CENTS A COPY.   PUBLISHED MONTHLY. $1.00 A YEAR.
Entered at the post-office in Battle Creek, Mich., as Second-class Matter.

GOOD HEALTH

MENS · SANA ·

AUGUST, 1898.

The Joy of Life.
The Campaign in the Tropics.
    —Illustrated.
The Child.
Nuts as Food.
Galloping Consumption at the
    Table.
Physical Culture for Working
    People.
The Great Man's Stomach.
The Hygiene of Love.
Helping Children to Self-Respect.
How to Dress Children.
Artificial Infant Foods.
No Alcohol for the Soldiers.
The Bill of Fare, Not the
    Weather.
Where Are the Healthy Young
    Men?

· IN · CORPORE · SANO ·

VOL. XXXIII.   EDITED BY J. H. KELLOGG, M.D.   NO. 8.

The September Number will contain the first of a series of papers by
Mrs. Katharine Lente Stevenson on "Life in Our
Crowded City Centers."

Good Health magazine.

dence was in support of vegetarianism. "On general principles the raising of cattle as a means of providing food is objectionable.... I think that Vegetarianism is a commendable departure from the established barbarous habit." Tesla, considered by many one of the most brilliant scientists who ever lived, believed that the evidence of the healthfulness of a plant-based diet was firmly established. "That we can subsist on plant food and perform our work even to advantage is not a theory, but a well-demonstrated fact."[27]

Tesla stated that "every effort should be made to stop the wanton and cruel slaughter of animals which must be destructive to our morals." At the time, there were a few members of the nutritional establishment who endorsed vegetarianism. McCollum was the most prominent. In a 1923 lecture delivered at the Battle Creek Sanitarium, he stated: "All the evidence from both animal and human experience supports in a manner which can never be broken down the viewpoint that meat is not necessary in the human diet. I am convinced that any one who eats the average amount of meat consumed in this country will improve rather than suffer by cutting it all out of his diet. Meat greatly increases intestinal putrefaction."[28]

On the other hand, McCollum was reluctant to state such beliefs in mainstream and scientific publications. The medical establishment frowned upon vegetarianism, and McCollum knew it. In a letter to a friend, he wrote:

I will only say that the lacto-vegetarian diet is a highly satisfactory regimen, if the food is properly selected. Meat eating is entirely unnecessary and indulgence in it is due to its palatability. In fact we should all be better off, if we had no meat, although I never made so strong a statement for publication and should prefer not to do so.[29]

The nutritionist knew he would be discredited if he openly advocated vegetarianism. "Dr. Kellogg is...right in most of his tenets, but is more extreme than I care to be along certain lines because I do not regard it as politic for me considering the kinds of people I have to work with. In other words, he is willing to be known as a food faddist and to express extreme views, whereas I, as an investigator must take a more judicial attitude, and speak only on the basis of our experimental data, and in such language as will not brand me as an extremist...in order to avoid the antagonism of the medical profession and many others, I must not be justly accusable as being a faddist, but must rather be looked upon as the most unprejudiced authority, and the best informed investigator."[30]

During the Chittenden and Jaffa studies, vegetarianism was gaining reinforcement on another front: fiction.

THE MAN AND THE JUNGLE

A newly famous novelist had unwittingly mobilized many among the masses toward a meat-free diet with his novel *The Jungle*. The world-famous novel, written by Upton Sinclair and published in 1905, was a fictional account of Lithuanian immigrant Jurgis Rukus and his family as they struggled with illness, poverty, and Jurgis's job at an unsanitary packing plant. *The Jungle*, often called the *Uncle Tom's Cabin* of salary slavery, also depicted filthy slaughterhouses and a graphic description on how animals are slaughtered.

One scene described how hogs met their fate. They had chains which they fastened about the leg of the nearest hog, and the other end of the chain they hooked into one of the rings upon the wheel. So, as the wheel turned, a hog was suddenly jerked off his feet and borne aloft. "Sinclair then describes the shrieks of these doomed hogs, and the reactions from the horrified visitors watching from the gallery while the workers went about their jobs as if they were robots. "There were high squeals and low squeals, grunts, and wails of agony; there would come a momentary lull, and then a fresh outburst, louder than ever, surging up to a deafening climax...neither squeals of hogs nor tears of visitors made any difference to them; one by one they hooked up the hogs, and one by one with a swift stroke they slit their throats.

Concern over the unsanitary food and the political power of the meat packers had been growing for years. Passages such as the one above shocked many readers, and the popularity of *The Jungle* was said to be the spark that resulted in the passage of the 1906 Pure Food Act and the Meat Inspection Act.

The legislation was an attempt by Congress to keep food pure and disease free, and to clean up unsanitary conditions in the food processing industry. Sinclair, who wrote the book to depict the plight of workers, said: "I aimed at America's heart and hit their stomach."

Sinclair's *Jungle* did much for vegetarianism. "*The Jungle* made many converts to vegetarianism," said University of Pennsylvania Physiology and Chemistry Professor Alonzo Taylor in an article he wrote for *Popular Science* in 1911. Taylor also said that "a proper vegetarian diet is in every way a normal and competent diet."[31]

Sinclair was well-known for his dietary experiments in fasting and vegetarianism, which he outlined in "Starving for Health's Sake" in the May 1909 issue of *Cosmopolitan*. The magazine, in August of that year, reported that Sinclair's article created a country-wide sensation.... Men and women in every walk of life recognized in Mr. Sinclair's plain narrative of his restoration to perfect health, through long periods of abstinence from meats and other heavy foods, the open sesame to their physical betterment."[32]

Sinclair also made enemies. One of them, J. Ogden Armour, the powerful meat tycoon who was shaken when Sinclair openly attacked his company by charging that it sells meat tainted with diseases such as tuberculosis and gangrene while coloring canned and potted meats. Armour ran advertisements claiming that his meat was disease free and articles appeared in the *Saturday Evening Post*, signed by Armour, defending the meat industry.

In a letter to the *New York Times* dated May 4, 1906, Sinclair challenged Armour to take legal action. "If the things which I have charged are false, why has Mr. Armour not sued me for libel?" wrote Sinclair. The novelist implied that Armour had plenty to hide. "One hundredth part of what I have charged ought, if it is true, to be enough to send the guilty man to the gallows," he wrote.[33]

Other letters by and about Sinclair on the topic of pure food, vegetarianism, and other issues appeared in newspapers frequently in the months and years to follow.

Vegetarianism had friends and foes. But most people—the meat-eating majority—fell into neither category: they were either uninterested in vegetarianism or unconvinced of the potential health, economic, and ethical benefits. Therefore they did not even consider a change in diet. Apathy was a factor that put the brakes on vegetarianism's rapid growth. Sometimes that apathy eventually became suspicion when it was fueled by hostility arising from a few potent and persuasively unfriendly forces.

The battle for America's dinner plates took place in lecture halls and on college campuses, and in the pages of newspapers and magazines. In a 1909 letter to the *New York Times*, Hereward Carrington, author of *Vitality, Fasting and Nutrition*, addressed the then-common argument that people must eat animal flesh because it more closely resembles the human body in composition than food from plants.

Carrington, perhaps sarcastically, yet taking the argument to its logical resolution, contended that meat eaters should feed upon human flesh, since it most closely resembled the protein constituents of the body. "If the human race were consistent it should be of either cannibals or vegetarians. The vegetable kingdom can easily supply the body with all the proteid it needs—that fact is acknowledged by all competent authorities in diet— and if it be urged that vegetable proteid is not suited for the body, then why is animal proteid of an entirely different constituency...," wrote Carrington. "The anti-vegetarians have never succeeded in answering this question successfully."[34]

The antivegetarians, as Carrington called them, did not have an answer, but they had plenty to say against vegetarianism—and vegetarians. The arguments varied. J.E. Fries, responding to Carrington's letter, wrote that it was natural for man to feed upon animals and that animal suffering serves a divine purpose.[35]

Critics used another popular argument that vegetarians are ascetics and weaklings. That is, the critics classified all non-meat eaters as like-minded, self-depriving neurotics—images that have taken decades for vegetarians to shed, but that still persist in the minds of some unaware of the variety of vegetarians.

One *Atlantic Monthly* writer picked up on the ascetic and weakling themes in an article published in 1905. "It would be absurd to deny that among the confirmed Vegetarians there are no good men, though meagre," he began. Calling vegetarianism a cult, the writer grouped all vegetarians as people who dislike eating and only do it out of necessity.

He then went further and pointed an accusatory finger at vegetarians: "Persons who are insensible to the delights of a rich and varied menu may well be suspected of surreptitious methods of propagating their peculiar

doctrines," the writer warned, using language to shed suspicion on people who did not eat meat.

The *Atlantic Monthly* journalist, like other antivegetarians, even picked
on people who were not vegetarians, but who stated facts favorable to the
no-meat diet. When a high-ranking USDA official published a nutrition
booklet for the agency that mentioned that even men who worked at
heavy labor occupations could thrive on a diet consisting primarily of
grains and vegetables, the journalist seemed to take up arms and come
gunning for the official, at least symbolically:

"The head of the department does not look like a man who would quail before a
beefsteak, or like one who regards eating as a mere duty. It is incredible that he
would suggest a dietary of 'corn-bread, wheat bread, rye, oats, and rice,' with the
assurance that 'men who feed on these exclusively are capable of enduring hardest manual labor,' " the journalist argued. "The insidious hand of the vegetarian
missionary may be detected in publications of the very government itself, the purpose being to popularize the idea that meats are not necessary to man, but injurious and immoral; and, also, that to find pleasure in eating is low."[36]

The writer was on the attack. But there was a kernel of truth in what was
written because vegetarianism had champions in socialism, feminism,
and pacifism—beliefs that were considered out of as well as among the
mainstream.

The *Atlantic Monthly* writer had also mentioned a comment by Ernest H.
Crosby, a progressive leader who labeled meat as "the dead bodies of the
slaughtered." This bold description of meat, that most other people called
beef, veal, or bacon, elicited sharp criticism from some nonvegetarians,
who then labeled vegetarians as rude and their words as emotional outburst.

Crosby, then president of the New York Vegetarian Society, also came
under fire in January of 1906 for a letter that he wrote to the *Times*. "Meat
is an altogether unnecessary article of food, and it is the simplest thing in
the world to get on without," and the meat-laden diet was "unclean, barbarous, and cruel," wrote Crosby, who also noted that the scandal surrounding the filthy conditions of the meat packing houses was a good
thing because more people would be disgusted with flesh foods and turn
to vegetarianism. However, a *Times* editorial writer later labeled Crosby's
remarks "an outburst highly characteristic of vegetarianism."[37]

The *Times* writer also countered with an often-used argument against
vegetarianism: the supposed superiority of the meat-eating peoples of the
world. The attitude of the era was that populations who weren't techno-
logically oriented and differed culturally from the populations of the
United States and Europe were inferior. "Everyone of the vegetarian races
has been and is such from dire necessity and they all turn gladly to the

stronger food at the first opportunity. If Mr. Crosby will look around the world and observe the physical and mental development of the peoples who eat little or no meat, he will be—or ought to be—deeply grateful that he comes of forebears of another kind..."[38]

"A MODERN AMERICAN IDEALIST"

Other publications praised Ernest Crosby, and the activism of the era. "The old apostolic spirit is again abroad among us," a journalist wrote for *The Arena* magazine during the Progressive Era. "To-day throughout the Republic—in cities, towns, villages, hamlets—there are young men and women stepping out of the ranks of slothful conventionalism and devoting all that is best and finest in their natures to the service of progress."

The Gilded Age was giving way to a new era, one that continued to make fortunes for industrialists, but raised protests against the inequalities in the promised land of democracy. Voices rang out for the downtrodden, for children forced to work in factories, and for numerous other social problems.

Conditions in the country, pertaining to the level of activism, resembled that of the Jacksonian Era, and the Civil War era. The journalist declared: "I doubt if in the last forty years there has been a time when anything like the same number of young Americans have been silently and unostentatiously, but intelligently, seeking to further the principle of the Golden Rule as are at the present... they are laboring for social righteousness, and are ready to make great sacrifices to hasten the day of better things, (and that) promises well for the future."

Vegetarians, young and old, were included in this mix of those devoted to creating a better society. The rhetoric of vegetarianism had evolved and expanded: secularists and religion devotees, feminists and pacifists, and socialists and capitalists concerned about the ethics of killing animals for human use contributed to this change. But beneath the words and the philosophies, the main ethical meaning of vegetarianism, in its many dimensions, had not changed since the advent of the national vegetarian movement in the mid-nineteenth century. It still stood for nonviolence toward animals, and therefore, was considered by some as a step in the right direction for a human being to become his or her best self.

The progressive vegetarians, like the more conservative vegetarians of the previous century, had role models. One of them was Crosby, who was initially well-known as a socialite, and later as a social activist. One popular magazine of the day dubbed Crosby as a "modern American idealist" and a modern moral leader who "in the name of justice and freedom dares to break lance with Church, State, and society, when they stand for intolerance, injustice, greed, and aught else that tends to corrupt manhood or work injury to the weak."[39]

> *The N. Y. Vegetarian Society will hold its regular monthly meeting on March 27th, 1895, at 8 P. M., at*
>
> ### 240 West 23d Street.
>
> *Subject: "Perfect Food," by Prof. Hart, from England. Discussion, Alex Gustafsen, Dr. M. L. Holbrook, and others. Yourself and friends are cordially invited.*
>
> J. W. SCOTT, President,
> *40 John Street.*
>
> ---
>
> *It is requested that members and friends who can make it convenient, will dine on the 27th inst. at the Vegetarian Restaurant No. 1, 240 West 23d Street, L. Volkmann, Manager.*
> *Dinner served from 5 to 7.30 p. m. Price 40c. Souvenir presented.*

N.Y. Vegetarian Society announcement.

Crosby was born in 1856 into a family of wealth and position. He practiced law and was a member of the New York legislature from 1887–1889, replacing family friend Theodore Roosevelt. Crosby had a fallout with the future president over the issue of war. As a legislator, Crosby wrote the High License Bills, which would have restricted the sale of alcoholic beverages, but the bills were vetoed by the governor. In 1889 President Harrison and the Khedive appointed Crosby a judge of the Mixed Tribunals of Egypt at Alexandria. Crosby served five years of the lifetime appointment.

It was during his time as a judge that Crosby experienced a transformation in his life. He had money and power, yet felt an emptiness in his life. In 1894, Crosby, after searching his soul and reading the writings of the great Russian novelist and philosopher Leo Tolstoy, began to make dramatic changes in his way of life. Possessing all the material goods wealth could provide and status that society afforded to people of his class, Crosby, like Tolstoy who had also been born an aristocrat, chose by 1897 to reject meat eating, militarism, and materialism.[40]

The result: Crosby supported numerous social reforms, such as workers' rights, the single tax, pacifism, and vegetarianism. He founded the Social Reform Club and the Anti-Imperialistic League, became involved with the New York Vegetarian Society, and served as the organization's president for a number of years. He also worked on legislative campaigns, and he gave galvanizing lectures.[41]

"War is hell, as General Sherman long ago told us; but he did not go on to tell us why," Crosby explained to the audience gathered for the Episcopal Church Congress held in Providence, Rhode Island, in November. "There is only one possible reason. Hell is not a geographic term; it is merely the expression of the spiritual condition of its inhabitants. War is hell because it transforms men into devils...War is hate. Christianity is love. On which side should the Church be ranged?"[42]

Crosby talked to audiences, and he also wrote poems, essays, articles, and books to forward his ideals. One of Crosby's books, *Tolstoy and His Message*, helped introduce the great philosopher's Christian-based ideas into America. Tolstoy, an influential vegetarian, had written in 1892:

The vegetarian movement ought to fill with gladness the souls of those who have at heart the realization of God's kingdom upon Earth, not because vegetarianism itself is such an important step towards the realization of this kingdom (all real steps are equally important and unimportant), but because it serves as a criterion by which we know that the pursuit of moral perfection on the part of man is genuine and sincere.[43]

Like his mentor Tolstoy, Crosby wrote much about vegetarianism. When Upton Sinclair raised the curtain that had enshrouded the packing house industry in mystery, and the public responded in outrage at what they saw, New York Vegetarian Society president Crosby used the opportunity to advance the meat-free way. When he wrote to the *New York Times* in 1905, he announced that he had eaten no meat in eight years, and that since the valuable ingredient in flesh food was the "proteid," people could instead easily obtain it in "cereals, whole-wheat bread, eggs, cheese, peas and beans."

That same year Crosby published *The Meat Fetish*, a slim volume containing his essay on vegetarianism. The essay is one of the most powerful on the topic of vegetarianism published by an American during the twentieth century. Crosby's combination of smooth prose and passion with earnestness and erudition has had few peers.

The essayist's use of imagery, for example, could today still compel some nonvegetarian readers to reconsider their diet. Crosby asked artists in Venice about the agonizing sights, terrifying sounds, and foul smells of the slaughterhouse: "Where are our artists, that they can enjoy and edify themselves in their doges' palaces and academies of belle arti, with such a background to it all, and discuss beauty and colour over a table d'hote dinner fresh from the shambles? Are they really so much more dainty than the old doges themselves, who used to feast while the rats gnawed at their living captives?"[44]

Crosby's essay was not addressed only to artists, but to the whole of humanity that was nonvegetarian. "The essential idea of butchery is cruel, and you cannot be cruel humanely," wrote Crosby. He then recounted how a horrified official of the Society for the Prevention of Cruelty to Animals inspected a packing house and then asked the slaughterer how he could select such a business. The humane officer had no reply when he was told, "We're only doing your dirty work, sir."

The socialite also wrote "The Shadow on the Farm," a poem that was popular with vegetarian and animal rights advocates for years to come.

The Shadow on the Farm

Over the peaceful barnyard yonder where the calves
are waiting for the tardy pail and the chickens are scratching for their
supper...
Over it all I see the dull, inevitable shadow of the butcher's knife...
Death is natural, I own, and without it this world would be cursed with life, but when it comes at the edge of the cold and sharpened steel, at the behest of man's perverted appetite and cruel will, and strikes the young and lusty and vigorous,—when death is made the chief end of life, and life becomes the hand-maid of death, and nature is prostituted to the express manufacture of fattened corpses, then is death hideous indeed.

American vegetarians in the Progressive Era more openly expressed their belief in animal liberation than it had been in the past. Crosby had not been alone in teaching that nonviolence toward animals was linked to peace among humans. When he died in 1907, others, whether they knew of his efforts or not, carried on with the work of vegetarianism. Crosby was a radical who represented many causes, but another soon-to-be prominent vegetarian, while sharing some of his views, including opposition to war, was squarely centered in capitalism, at least in her fabulous wealthy lifestyle.

THE GLAMOROUS VEGETARIAN

Several hundred miles north of Crosby's stately home in Rhineback, New York, a woman was making waves for vegetarianism. Like Crosby, she was a socialite and an ardent antivivisectionist; she was the author of *The Golden Rule Cookbook,* which contained philosophy and practical advice for eliminating meat from the menu. Mrs. Maud R. L. Sharpe was about to become one of the leading advocates of vegetarianism in America, and she would hold that position for decades to come.

A Boston newspaper reporter informed readers in February of 1914 about this unusual woman's venture that would transform her celebrated Chestnut Hill estate into a beacon of meat-free living:

A vegetarian temple where adherents of the herbivorous diet will congregate to listen to doctrines practiced by true vegetarians, and where lecture hall, reading room, bakeshop, restaurant and motion picture play will provide physical and mental entertainment, is to be Boston's latest and most novel contribution to twentieth century living, through the activity of the Millennium Guild founder and leader, Mrs. Maud R.L. Sharpe...[45]

Mrs. Sharpe, who made a point of dressing in luxurious fake fur coats and hats, and who was not the stereotypical lady of the time who politely refrained from expressing her opinions, told the press: "We wish to convert the world to our cause."[46] The cause was more than just vegetarianism: the Millennium Guild was named for that prophesized day when humankind and animals would enjoy perpetual peace on Earth. Therefore, the organization advocated nonviolence and opposed vivisection, fur and feather fashions, and war, as well as meat eating. Yet the focus of the Guild was not the *anti* stance, but rather on positive action people could take instead of participating, however indirectly, in violence against animals.

One way Sharpe and Guild members promoted vegetarianism was to offer tantalizing food options. Victorian vegetarians had happily proclaimed the health-promoting value and heartiness of their cuisine, which was often depicted by foes as being limited to brown bread and water. But compared with Sharpe's high society standards of dining, the foods of the nineteenth century were not glamorous. Mrs. Sharpe brought a much-needed element of the gourmet, and of glamour, to the food and the image of the vegetarian movement.

Born Maud Russell Lorraine Hammer in West Virginia in 1866 (and later known as Mrs. Sharpe, then M.R.L. Freshel after she married Curtis Freshel in 1917), she grew up in Chicago, Illinois, and graduated from Organtz College. She lived and traveled in Europe, primarily in England, where she studied art and literature. An ardent antivivisectionist, Sharpe didn't stop eating meat until meeting some influential vegetarians. She met Dharmapala, the Buddhist leader who lectured before the World Parliament of Religions on nonviolence, in Chicago at the 1893 Columbian Exposition (World's Fair). Sharpe, according to news accounts, went to the World's Fair representing the Christian Science church.

Later Sharpe visited writer and philosopher Count Leo Tolstoy in Russia, a vegetarian who was disappointed to learn that the Christian Science church did not espouse vegetarianism. She also visited Germany and met Frau Cosima Wagner, wife of Richard Wagner, and discovered that the composer had been a vegetarian as well as antivivisectionist. Sharpe then befriended another famous vegetarian: playwright George Bernard Shaw, then a very popular public figure in America. Shaw told her that he found it absurd that she should fight laboratory-based vivisection while tolerating barnyard vivisection. Shaw also gave her the nickname "Emeral," based upon her first three initials. Ralph Waldo Trine, a Christian minister, was the fourth famous vegetarian to influence Freshel. The New Thought leader's best-selling book *Every Living Creature* convinced her to finally renounce her carnivorous ways. She published the *Golden Rule Cookbook* in 1906, which contained her philosophy of vegetarianism as well as recipes.[47] The socialite founded the Millennium Guild in 1912.

The organization held well-publicized Thanksgiving dinners at the posh and newly constructed Copley-Plaza Hotel, which was situated in the heart of Boston. Mrs. Sharpe's celebrity status as a much-admired, beautiful, intelligent, and charming woman of wealth certainly did not hurt her ability to attract the attention of reporters who, it seems, treated her and her cause more fairly than other reporters had treated vegetarian advocates of earlier eras.

Sharpe and her unusual activities were the subject of numerous articles in newspapers published in various parts of the nation, and her Thanksgiving dinner was reported in the same style of writing used to describe any high society event. The most prominent guests at the dinner were mentioned (Professor William O. Crosby, artist Emily Selinger, poet Sidney Lanier, and Lotta Crabtree), as was the menu.

Described as making a mark in the culinary arts, the meal included: mushroom cocktail, Vegex (vegetable extract) consommé, coeur de palmier (heart of palm—"piping hot and tasting like chicken"), cranberry punch, Golden Rule roast, and crepes bordelaise (a plant-based dish that tasted like mushrooms).[48]

The menus featured the renowned Saint Rupert hunting scene, which depicts a deer with a Christian cross on its head, and the motto of the day was "No turkey need feel the slightest alarm, our members will feast on the heart of the palm."

Famous and popular poet Ella Wheeler Wilcox was expected to attend the feast, but instead she sent a poem written for the occasion, entitled "Morning Prayer": "Let me today do something that shall strike a little sadness from the world's vast store. . . . Let me tonight look back across the span 'twixt dawn and dark, and to my conscience say—because of some good act to beast or man, The world is better that I lived today."

Another progressive woman connected oppression of women and animals. Charlotte Perkins Gilman, whose book *Women and Economics* was widely read, was a leading spokesperson for women's liberation. In *Herland*, Gilman's utopian and ecofeminist novel, women knew no oppression or violence and ate no meat, unlike the male visitors who, "civilized," are brutal meat eaters. Gilman, likely not a vegetarian, wrote the poem "Cattle Train," which was strongly animal liberation and seemingly pro-vegetarian.

Hot, fevered, frightened, trampled, bruised, and torn,
Frozen to death before the ax descends,
We kill these weary creatures, sore and worn.
And eat them—with our friends.[49]

THE ROARING BACKLASH

While Freshel and the Millennium Guild were practicing their brand of advocacy, the American Medical Association moved against the growing interest in vegetarianism, natural health, and the like. The organization and the entire medical establishment was under attack by advocates of alternative medicine, most notably Bernarr Macfadden, particularly when Macfadden spent most of his life battling conventional medicine, a fact that wasn't lost on the readers of *Physical Culture* and his newspapers. Over the years, he had many harsh words for the American Medical Association. The physical culturist once wrote that the AMA punished doctors with expulsion if they failed to obey the mandates of the organization. "This obnoxious and monopolistic power held over individual doctors by the American Medial Association is a menace to the life and health of the citizens of this country," he said. The feelings were mutual and the two opponents fought each other for decades.

Natural Hygienists, naturopaths and other unconventional health practitioners were frequently arrested, usually charged with practicing medicine without a license. They argued that they were not practicing medicine, but natural healing through methods such as diet without medicine or drugs.

Benedict Lust, a German-born naturopath who strongly advocated vegetarianism around the country and at his Florida retreat, was a favorite target of health authorities. Lust believed that the germ theory of Pasteur was a scientific fallacy; therefore, he was opposed to the allopathy of the AMA. He was also an outspoken opponent of vaccinations and vivisection—all the more reason why the medical establishment loathed him.

Born in Germany in 1872, Lust was one of many naturopaths who arrived in the United States from that country in the late 1800s. Upon his arrival in America in 1892, Lust attended the New York Preparatory College, and then enrolled at Universal Osteopathic College, where he graduated in 1897. A year earlier, he had founded a health food store and center in New York City, and the American School of Naturopathy and the American School of Chiropractic. He founded two health cure resorts in the early 1900s, one in Butler, New Jersey (Yungborn Nature-Cure Resort), and one in Tangerine, Florida (nature Cure resort Qui-si-sana). The resorts offered guests vegetarian, fruitarian, and raw food diets; sun and light baths, massage, hydrotherapy, bathing, fasting, outdoor sports, and swimming.

Morris Fishbein, M.D., editor of the *Journal of the American Medical Association*, wrote in his 1927 book, *The New Medical Follies*, that Lust's system of "exercise, health resorts, magnetic healing, mud packs, vegetarian and fruitarian diets and what not" was a "capitalization for the purposes of financial gain." Fishbein would in the years that followed be known by opponents as the "Medical Mussolini."

M.R.L. Freshel.

The powerful editor stated: "One finds him promoting actively the interests of the manipulative cults, including chiropractic and osteopathy...colonic flushing and vegetable diet...antivaccinationists and antivivisectionists...," wrote Fishbein.[50]

Fishbein pointed a finger of blame at Macfadden. "The outlet for such faddists is the publishing plant of Bernarr Macfadden," he stated.

KELLOGG BATTLES THE MEAT INDUSTRY

Meanwhile, John Harvey Kellogg had his own battle to fight. To say that Kellogg was a thorn in the meat industry's side would be understatement akin to saying that sticking your hand in a beehive would be an inconvenience. The Battle Creek doctor posed the most formidable threat to the meat industry in the early decades of the twentieth century.

One of Kellogg's toughest actions against meat occurred when the industry circulated "And He Ate Meat," a jingle to persuade people that their product was safe and healthful.

Methuselah ate what he found on his plate,
   And never, as people do now,
Did he note the amounts of the calorie count,
   He ate it because it was chow,
He wasn't disturbed as at dinner he sat,
   Destroying a roast or a pie,
To think it was lacking in granular fat,
   Or a couple of vitamins shy.
He cheerfully chewed every species of food,
   Untroubled by worries or fear,
Lest his health might be hurt by some fancy dessert,
   And he lived over nine hundred years.

Kellogg was not going to let the meat packers' propaganda go unanswered. He circulated his own jingle, "Methuselah's Meat."

What Methuselah ate
   Was not on a plate....
   For paradise meat
   Was delicious to eat,
And kept him in finest condition.
   And 'twas hung on trees,
   And not made to please
The deadly Live Stock Commission.
   No fish was he fed,
   No blood did he shed,
And he knew when he had eaten enough.
   And so it is plain
   He'd no cause to complain
Of steaks that were measly or tough.
   Or bearded beef grimy,
   Green, moldy, and slimy,
Of cold-storage turkeys and putrid beefsteaks,
   With millions of colon germs,
   Hams full of trichina worms,
And sausages writhing with rheumatic-aches.
   Old Methuselah... [51]

Kellogg and the meat industry squared off again a few years later when the meat packers circulated a poster, prepared with help from the USDA, that urged consumers to eat more meat. The posters were put in post offices. John Harvey fought back, decrying the industry for misusing tax dollars. Kellogg dug into his own pockets and had his own posters printed. They were identical, except for a few words at the bottom: "See the other side." The flip side showed the number of colon germs for different meats, and a similar count for manure, which had

The Vegetarian Magazine.

much less. Kellogg realized that controversy would help get his message across.

The meat industry took the bait, and filed a complaint with the Federal Trade Commission to prohibit Kellogg from circulating the posters. The agency sent an attorney to Battle Creek Sanitarium to look into the matter. Kellogg showed him the evidence, and the agency nixed any further action.

The meat industry was concerned and for good reason: Per capita annual consumption of flesh foods has fallen from 225 pounds in 1902 to 170 pounds in 1921, a decline of 24 percent.

To make matters worse for the meat moguls, the United States Department of Agriculture circulated a pamphlet after the war informing people that "It is of course possible to eat meat dishes less frequently (than once a day) or to omit meat from the diet altogether, for it has been determined that all the necessary protein and energy may be obtained from other materials..."

The decline in consumption alarmed meat packers, who fought back in the early 1920s by organizing a nationwide "Eat more Meat" ad campaign that appeared in newspapers and magazines. According to Kellogg, Thomas Wilson from the Institute of American Meat Packers gave some suggestions to "counteract the declining consumption of meat." Among them: request the Department of Agriculture to distribute a booklet to physicians, hospitals, dietitians, live stock leaders, agricultural editors, and scientists; distribute booklets on the value of meat and how to cook it wisely to schools and convince the Federal Reserve and banks that an increase in meat consumption will increase the purchasing power of farmers.

Kellogg was angry and accused the meat industry of "trying to camouflage their alms-asking under the guise of a diet-reform campaign." He wrote: "What right have packers and breeders to undertake to exploit the consumers of food simply to create a market for their products?" Kellogg, in a not particularly prophetic statement, doubted that the efforts of the meat industry would convince consumers to eat more flesh foods.

The story "America Going Vegetarian" in a 1928 issue of *Literary Digest* seemed to back his words. Shoe manufacturers, according to the piece, complained that the decline in meat consumption posed a menace to their supply of leather.

The Vegetarian and Fruitarian magazine addressed the leather issue with humor by stating: "The dying wail of the packers; hurry and eat a lot of corpse else you'll go barefooted." The magazine, which was published by Jean Roberts Albert, who lived in a vegetarian commune in Juliaetta, Idaho, also featured stories and news articles on animal rights, antivaccinations, antivivisection, and medical reform. *Vegetarian and Fruitarian* established a Meatless Week to urge Americans to not eat meat for an entire week. Magazine contributors included William Howard Hay, M.D., of the East Aurora Sun-Diet Sanitorium in New York, who advocated a vegetarian diet, and physician Charles A. L. Reed, former president of the American Medical Association, who wrote favorably on veganism.[52]

The 1928 *Digest* story had stated "Since the war ended, America has gone vegetablewise with a vengeance."[53] But the vegetarian heyday that was decades in the making wouldn't last. Storm clouds were on the horizon.

Chapter 8

The Depression to the Sixties: The Lean Years

Farms in Oklahoma and other parts of the Midwest farm belt were swirling in dust storms during the Great Depression. The region was often called the dust bowl, where drought and storms wreaked havoc with this once-fertile area. Meanwhile, people in the cities were standing in lines at soup kitchens, bowl in hands, hungry. Many people were struggling to eat whatever they could get their hands on, whether it was a carrot or a piece of chicken.

The golden era of vegetarianism was about to end. The progress of the movement would dry up like the parched earth of the dust bowl. Perhaps the hard times endured by the Battle Creek Sanitarium in the Depression foreshadowed the plight of vegetarianism over the next few decades. In 1933, the institution fell into receivership and steadily declined until Kellogg lost control at the end of the decade.

EAT MORE MEAT

The increasing clout of the meat industry and the medical establishment chopped away at vegetarianism like a butcher slicing a turkey. *Hygeia*, a magazine founded by the American Medical Association, featured numerous stories that disparaged meat-free diets. One of them, "The Folly of Vegetarianism," called vegetarians food faddists, remarked that some of them were excluding all animal products, and stated that the extremists among them abhorred cooked foods.[1] The story classified adherents of anti-meat campaigns, alluding to the efforts of Kellogg and others, as "lacrimose sentimentalists who cannot bear the thought of a poor pig's anguish in the slaughter house; religious fanatics who base their vegetarian practices on some chance reference in Scripture...and most of all, the uncritical readers of pseudoscientific medical literature." And once again, the issue of polar explorers and their all-meat diets was mentioned.

Another *Hygeia* article that appeared in 1940 quoted a dietetic expert as saying "vegetarianism is harmless enough although it is apt to fill a man with wind and self-righteousness," and used the words food cranks and freak diet.[2] In *Much Taboo About Nothing,* a writer describes her experience of switching back to meat eating and "new mental freedom" after years of social hardships, such as "starving at banquets."[3]

The "Eat More Meat" campaign crafted by the meat packers became increasingly visible in newspapers, magazines, and radio. But sometimes the meat companies brought their message directly to consumers.

Visitors to the Armour Building at the 1934 World's Fair were handed a 63-page booklet on how to select, prepare, and serve meat. The booklet, *Meat Selection Preparation And Many Ways To Serve,* touted the protein benefits of meat, and quoted a sage who said that "No meat—no man!" It also warned that proteins found in plants are not as complete as those found in animal food—"a strong argument against the adoption of a strictly vegetarian diet."[4]

"Just sit a big husky, he-man down to a meatless dinner, and watch him glance around expectantly, wondering when the 'food' will begin to appear," was another one of the booklet's slaps to vegetarianism.

But demand for meat was still sluggish in the early 1930s. *Business Week,* in "We Eat Less Meat, Prices Drop; Industry Unites to Increase Use," outlines how the meat industry united at the time to convince Americans to eat more of their product. "Never before have so many powerful interests joined to step up meat consumption," the story stated.[5] The Institute of American Meat Packers and the National Live Stock and Meat Board united with the National Association of Retail Meat Dealers and other retail associations and launched their campaign in February of 1931, according to the story.

Several years would pass, but the meat industry was successful and consumption of meat would begin a steady climb upwards for the next few decades. That wouldn't have surprised Otto Carqué, a raw food advocate and author of *Natural Foods: The Safe Way to Health.* Carqué predicted in the 1926 book that meat would be a staple food for many years to come "partly because the majority of people are slow in changing their habits of eating and partly because the meat industry with all of its ramifications is so closely interwoven with the present social and economic system that any sudden and radical change in the methods of living of the great masses is hardly probable."[6]

Despite the odds, vegetarian advocates kept vying for the public's attention. And some of them were heralding the wonder bean called soy, sometimes called the meat without a bone.

The soybean, according to experts, arrived in America from the Orient in 1804. But the soybean remained an agricultural novelty in the United States for most of that century, and its role was limited mainly to animal feed. But that changed in the 1920s.

Seventh-Day Adventist T.A. Van Gundy developed a line of soy-based foods that he sold in health food stores. His company, La Sierra Industries, sold an array of products, including soy cereal, soy nuts, soy milk, soy spread, and soy cheese, which was tofu sold in cans. Another Adventist, Jethro Kloss, manufactured five varieties of crackers, breakfast foods, whole-wheat flour, meat, and dairy substitutes based on gluten, nuts, and soy products at his health food factory near Nashville, Tennessee. He became known as a soy food pioneer after figuring out how to remove the beany flavor, which was characteristic of soy products consumed in China.

Kloss held Demonstration Dinners, which were heavy on milk, cheese, ice cream, and bread all made from soybeans. Around 1930, Kloss made and sold three flavors of soy ice cream—strawberry, chocolate, and vanilla—and soy coffee. He sold his products to pedestrians on Pennsylvania Avenue in Washington, D.C., along with other vegetarian lunches.[7]

Through his Tennessee-based company, Kloss supplied health food stores with these products, and was perhaps the first in the United States to sell soy ice cream. He believed that meat was an unnatural food that was poisonous and unfit for consumption.

Joyce Gardiner, Kloss's granddaughter, recalled giving out samples of his food after his lectures. During one lecture in Miami, Kloss brought her out on stage and remarked to the audience that she has never tasted cow's milk and is "100 percent perfect." Joyce's mother, Naomi, was raised on nut milks.[8]

The soy pioneer died in 1946 at the age of 84. But his book, *Back to Eden*, which was first published in 1935, has sold over 3 million copies, making it one of the most influential health books of all time. Kloss's book had inspired many people in the back-to-nature movement in the 1960s and 1970s.

Soy foods received a boost from industrialist Henry Ford, founder of the auto company that bears his name. Ford, not a vegetarian, was obsessed with soybeans: he extracted soybean oil for auto paint and plastics, even creating the body of one of his cars from plastic derived from soy. He served soybean-based dinners and soybean milk at his home. At the 1934 Century of Progress Fair in Chicago, his company served soybean puree, soybean croquettes, soybean milk, soybean coffee, and soybean cookies. Ford lectured frequently on soy foods and products, and once wore a suit made of soybean-derived fabric. John Harvey Kellogg predicted in 1929 that the soybean would one day be one of the most important foods in America.

WORLD WAR II

Food innovations aside, vegetarianism was swimming upstream. A Harris poll taken in 1943 reported that there were 3.5 million vegetarians living in the United States. But that number was likely overblown since the science of polling was inexact in that era. After all, the polls predicted that Dewey would beat Harry Truman in 1946.

Press coverage of vegetarianism waned in the late 1930s and early 1940s. It looked downhill for vegetarians as America's appetite for meat increased. Worse, Americans were not exactly craving soy burgers. The *National Restaurant Association* in the late 1940s released a survey of America's top ten favorite dishes. It was a meat lover's dream: ham and eggs finished first, followed by prime ribs, chicken, lobster, New England boiled dinner, fried oysters, baked Virginia ham, breast of capon, filet of sole, and deviled crab.

But again, vegetarian advocates did not stop trying to convince people to replace sirloin with soy. Opportunistic vegetarians observed people waiting in long lines snaking around buildings to get their food rations. It was 1943 and World War II had ushered in meat shortages and food rationing. Each family was allowed a mere four ounces of butter, four pounds of cheese, and 28 ounces of meat a week. Tuesdays and Fridays were declared meatless days.

Vegetarians were quick to respond and spoke out. Secretary of Agriculture Claude Wickard assured vegetarians that a special rationing plan would be worked out for them.[9] The statement was in response to the efforts of Symon Gould, secretary of the Vegetarian Society of New York, who urged the government to take vegetarians into account under any rationing plan. Gould and the society sent Wickford a resolution "so that all registered vegetarians and other non-meat eating citizens, for religious, hygienic, or medical reasons, will be assured of the proper nutritional quantities of protein substances in view of their surrender of their rights to any meat rations which may be enforced by regulations."

A year later, in December, meat retailers were threatening to shutdown over burdensome government regulations. The Universal Vegetarian Society announced on the 18th that they would mobilize 10,000 vegetarians to "instruct their fellow citizens how to live on a vegetarian diet" if the strike materialized. Dr. Jacob Rose, director of the society, told the *Times* that a series of lectures on the benefits of a vegetarian diet would be held over the next couple of weeks.[10]

Vegetarians were doubling their efforts to win converts in the wake of meat shortages, said the writer of "Heyday for the Vegetarians," a story that appeared in a 1945 issue of *New York Times Magazine*.[11] The writer sat with a gathering of vegetarians, including Symon Gould, an editor of *American Vegetarian* magazine and future candidate for U.S. president who in the 1920s produced sell-out lectures at Carnegie Hall featuring lawyer Clarence Darrow. Gould outlined the caste system within vegetarianism. The writer described it this way:

First, and noblest, is the ethical vegetarian, who refuses to eat meat on moral or philosophical grounds. These, said Mr. Gould, "are the elite."

Second is the religious vegetarian. He does not eat meat because of the dictates of his religion. They're O.K., too, said Mr. Gould.

Third is the esthetic vegetarian, who would rather avoid what Mr. Gould called the grey, parboiled flesh of a dead animal. With him, said Mr. Gould, it's a matter of art.

Fourth is the scientific vegetarian, who has compared the anatomies of the animal world and decided that man is by nature a herbivorous animal and not meant to eat meat at all. Take the elephant, suggested Mr. Gould. Does the elephant eat meat?

And fifth—the untouchables—are the dietetic vegetarians, who eat no meat only because its healthier not to. Ulcer vegetarians, snorted Mr. Gould. Like Hitler. He sneaks in a pig's knuckle every time he feels better.[12]

The story also stated that vegetarians liked to marry other vegetarians. In the case of mixed marriages, the nonvegetarian "secretly consumes his meat outside the home for fear of revolting his spouse," wrote the reporter. Children of vegetarians are raised on meatless diets, she wrote, "and their portraits are proudly displayed in the vegetarian publications, which comment on their vigor, intelligence and spirituality."

Gould moderated a debate sponsored by The League for Public Discussion on meat eating versus vegetarianism on October 1946, in New York City. The debate, "Is Meat Essential to Health?" featured John Maxwell and Dr. Christopher Gian-Cursio on the vegetarian side, and Thomas Gaines and Professor Frank Sauchelli on the meat-eating side. Physical culture king Bernarr MacFadden gave the foreword.[13]

Vegetarians in all eras like to point out famous people in history who were vegetarians, and 1946 was no different. The first speaker, Maxwell, an 84-year-old Chicago naturopathic physician who established a number of vegetarian restaurants in Chicago, told the audience that Ferdinand de Lesseps, the engineer of the Suez Canal, became a vegetarian after noting how the workers who ate little or no meat outperformed the "beef-fed Englishmen." Maxwell also mentioned the horrors of slaughter, and steel leg hold traps, and called meat eating barbaric.

Thomas Gaines, a health journalist, followed Maxwell and talked about the nutritional value of meat, how vegetarians and vegetarian animals weren't as peaceful as people believed, how meat-eating civilizations dominated vegetarian ones, and also mentioned that Hitler was a vegetarian.

Dr. Christopher Gian-Cursio, a New York natural hygienist and raw food vegetarian, took the podium and declared that cancer became prevalent in societies that abandoned vegetarianism, and that his sick patients did better under a meatless diet than a meat diet. Frank Sauchelli, a New York City chiropractor and a former vegetarian, stated that the proteins in meat were superior to those found in vegetables and legumes. And Sauchelli, like meat-eating proponents of past decades, brought up Stefansson, the arctic explorer, who was seemingly healthy after eating mostly meat for nine years.

The second half of the debate featured rebuttals. Gaines recounted his experience in a health food store where ladies were lauding products such as choplets, stakelets, and other meat analogs. Gaines then said that meat eaters were honest and when they want a piece of meat, "we ask for it." The Californian then said that the lion, a carnivore, was the king of beasts, not the elephant, an herbivorous animal often lauded by vegetarians. Gian-Cursio's rebuttal was that man and beast have become perverted by meat eating, and that meat eaters get vitamins secondhand rather than directly from fruits and vegetables.

Meanwhile, some familiar faces were still around trying to convince people not to eat meat. One of them was Herbert Shelton, the twentieth century's premier natural hygienist. He advocated veganism, one of the pillars of natural hygiene, the Grahamite-like way of life that also includes fasting, proper food combining, positive thinking, rest, exercise, and the avoidance of allopathic medicine, coffee, chocolate, tea, and other stimulants.

As a teenager, Shelton, born on a farm in Texas in 1895, picked up a copy of *Physical Culture* magazine from a newsstand. His interest was peaked by stories on the benefits of fasting and the combination of a raw food diet and weight training. Shelton then read the works of Russell Trall, including *The True Healing Art*, and then the teachings of Trall's mentor, Sylvester Graham. He was also influenced by a highly publicized fast by Sinclair, who said the fast and healthy living cured his chronic indigestion.

After serving in World War I, Shelton went for training in hydrotherapy (water cure) and interned at health and fasting sanitariums. He received a degree in naturopathy from Benedict Lust's American School of Naturopathy, and later, earned a doctorate from the American School of Chiropractic. But Shelton, apparently dissatisfied with naturopathy and other nature cure healing systems, began advocating pure natural hygiene. In the 1920s he went to work for Macfadden as a columnist for the *Evening Graphic*, was a staff member of *Physical Culture*, and wrote the fasting section of Macfadden's eight-volume *Encyclopedia of Health*.

Shelton began lecturing on hygiene and opened Dr. Shelton's Health School in San Antonio, Texas. In 1939, Shelton founded *Dr. Shelton's Hygienic Review*, a monthly magazine devoted to hygiene that ran until 1980. The natural hygiene champion was gaining recognition. He also wrote many books, including a three-volume set titled *The Hygienic System*. That was the book, according to Jean Oswald, Shelton's biographer, that was read by Mahatma Gandhi. The Indian leader invited Shelton to lecture in India before the onset of World War II, but the hygienist declined when war broke out.[14]

Shelton was arrested several times in his career, mainly for practicing medicine without a license. But Shelton did not practice medicine. Like those drugless doctors who came before him, he instructed his patients on how to help the body heal itself, and how to prevent illness from developing in the first place. He didn't have many friends in the medical establishment, or in government. In the Shelton biography, *Yours for Health*, his wife Ida recalled that President Franklin D. Roosevelt once said, "Shelton can stay in jail for the rest of his life."

A decade after he launched the *Review*, Shelton founded the American Natural Hygiene Society and served as the first president. The Society's first convention was held at the Diplomat Hotel in New York City in 1949. Symon Gould was one of the promoters, and the event attracted about 800 people. There were four days of lectures, two of them titled "The Failure of a Vegetarian Diet If Not Based on Hygienic Principles" and "Living Hygienically in an Unhygienic Environment." A banquet and a dance wrapped up the event.

Other conventions featuring vegetarianism occurred in the late 1940s. The Naturopathic Association held the Golden Jubilee Congress in New York City's Commodore Hotel in 1947. The event ran seven days, and featured lectures called "Some Frequently Overlooked Aspects of the Vegetarian Movement, Vivisection—Its Uselessness and Harm to Humanity" and "The Effect of Nicotine on the Human Body." The east ballroom of the hotel had a booth called "Tribute to Bernarr Macfadden, Father of Physical Culture," stacks of pamphlets on the dangers of cigarettes and coffee, and boxes of wheat germ and non-animal gelatin.[15]

Dr. Jesse Mercer Gehman, president of the association, told a reporter that naturopaths don't believe in "vaccination, inoculation, contagion, infection or drugs of any kind." Gehman also replied to a reporter, who remarked that many of the participants looked old.

"That's just one more thing we have to fight," he said. "Outsiders taunt us by saying we ought to be able to live forever if we really believe in and follow our principles, but when we do live a long time, they complain about how old we look."

Gehman was also the chairman of the First American Vegetarian Convention, which was held at Lake Geneva, Wisconsin, in August of 1949. Speakers included John Maxwell, who was appointed president; Scott Nearing, who would become known for his homesteading efforts in Vermont; and Henry Bailey Stevens, author of *Recovery of Culture*. The Millennium Guild selected *Recovery* for its M.R.L. Freshel Award, mainly because its assertion that humans first engaged in war only after abandoning veganism.

That same month in 1949, the Millennium Guild held a dinner at the Ambrosia House in Wisconsin, which was a vegetarian restaurant owned by Guild member Henry L. Nunn, who cofounded the Nunn-Bush Shoe Company. Nunn, a prominent businessman, drew national publicity in 1953 when he implemented a plan in which he guaranteed his workers wages for 48 weeks a year, even during shutdowns. The guest list at the dinner included Kaj Dessau of Copenhagen, who was secretary of the International Vegetarian Union; Roy Walker, author of several books relevant to vegetarianism; and Curtis Freshel, whose wife, M.R.L. Freshel, had died a year earlier.

The gathering honored Stevens and his book *The Recovery of Culture,* which received the Guild's M.R.L. Freshel award. The Guild liked the author's assertion that humans first engaged in war only after abandoning veganism, and they liked Stevens's putting the spotlight on the slaughter of animals.

The book received accolades. For example, eminent London critic Hugh l'Anson Fausset wrote, "Unlike Spengler, who could trace only the rise and fall of civilizations always doomed by what he supposed to be an innate self-destructiveness, Mr. Stevens, by looking more deeply into history, reveals that man is not inherently pugnacious or predatory, but has only acquired the so-called 'tiger qualities' through violating his true nature for a comparatively short period in his history."[16] Another admirer of Stevens's work was George Bernard Shaw, who wrote, "Mr. Stevens has a new and convincing argument for the constructive and non-predatory."[17]

Stevens, who was director of the University of New Hampshire's General Extension Service, argued in *Recovery of Culture* that it was not humanity's discovery of metals that instigated war, it was "the mind set connected with the weapons." He held that once all human beings lived in harmony with each other and animals. Stevens further explained in his book: The ancient people were organized, enough to build megalithic structures still existing today. These peaceful people feasted on fruits, nuts, and other delectable foods of the plant kingdom. Eventually, some kept animals for milk, eggs—and meat. "Man had gone into business as a butcher," wrote Stevens.[18]

He also explained that, like in the Biblical tale of Cain and Abel, the meat-eating keepers of the herds waged war upon the gardeners or orchard-keepers for more land for animals to graze upon. Thus, war came about only after human beings had slaughtered animals for their flesh.

To solve the perennial problem of war, then, people must return to the diet of the peaceful people, and solve conflicts using nonviolence, as Gandhi did in India, wrote Stevens. "All that may be necessary to rid ourselves of trouble is to take up again our membership in the primate family," he wrote.

Stevens, like his spouse, Agnes Ryan, was a strong advocate of nonviolence and human rights. For example, he was at one point an editor of *The Woman's Journal*, a Boston weekly founded by Lucy Stone, Thomas Wentworth Higginson, William Lloyd Garrison, and Julia Ward Howe. Ryan, a well-known pacifist, organized the New Hampshire Peace Union, and she was a radio broadcaster.

Members of the Millennium Guild were not alone in their struggle against meat eating or vivisection. They had allies among naturopaths, natural hygienists, and poets. Although Millennium Guild friend Ella Wheeler Wilcox was not a vegetarian, another poet was an abstainer. Poet–philosopher Sarah Norcliff Cleghorn was a potent foe of animal experimentation and she ate no meat. In her 1945 book *The Seamless Robe*, first published in 1934, Cleghorn wrote: "Our children, potentially gentle and inclusive, begin early to notice our inhumanity to animals. Often they first sharply realize the slaughter of animals for food when they accompany us to the butchershop. Or if living in the country, when they see pigs or poultry killed."[19] Cleghorn, an advocate of peace among people and between people and animals, in her book also condemns hunting, fishing, and vivisection. Youngsters, she wrote, "see pain." "How glaring a thing pain is to those who endure it! How placidly overlooked by those who cause it! When a child first realizes that it is the butcher's truck into which his father's old cow is being pushed and prodded, he will sometimes ask 'Do we *have* to eat meat?' "[20]

THE AMERICAN VEGETARIAN PARTY

The American Vegetarian Party was founded in 1948 by Symon Gould. Its first presidential candidate was John Maxwell, who promised to push for legislation that would sharply curtail the ability of farmers to raise poultry or cattle for slaughter.[21]

Gould designed the party to be more of a public relations ploy than a bona fide third political party. After all, Maxwell couldn't serve as president since he was born in England. But Gould's idea worked: Publications such as the *New York Times* and *Newsweek* published stories on the party. The latter published an oversized photo of Maxwell, with a long and gray beard, sitting at a table with a salad plate and a glass of carrot juice, holding celery—not exactly a positive image of vegetarians. The expanded caption informed readers that Maxwell's restaurant on Chicago's South Wabash Avenue serves vegetarian food to about 500 patrons a day, and that his views are mildly socialistic.[22]

The reference to socialism was only partially correct. The platform of the American Vegetarian Party, as outlined by Gould in an official statement, was built around the pacifist philosophy of antikilling or reverence for life. Vegetarians, he wrote, are "opposed to the killing of animals for sustenance, sport or style." The platform also stated that vegetarianism and other humanitarian ideals, if widely adapted, would put an end to war and help end human suffering. Under a humanitarian system, social ills such as segregation in the United States would end, predicted Gould.[23]

In 1952, the party's platform remained the same, but it had a new presidential candidate. Ironically, the choice was Retired General Herbert C. Holdridge, a 1917 graduate of West Point. But Holdridge was a pacifist, and he promised that he would urge foreign governments to create ministries of peace that would be "guided by the ideal of non-slaughter." The general also said that he would hire the best vegetarian chef in the United States to cook meals at the White House that would make guests "wonder why they ever thought meat edible."

That year, there was a controversy among vegetarian leaders surrounding the party. Jesse Mercer Gehman, president of the American Vegetarian Union, denounced both Gould and the American Vegetarian Party as too political and lacking the support of organized vegetarians. In a *Times* interview that took place in Gould's office on New York City's West Forty-eighth Street, the location of the AVP headquarters, Gould said that he wanted to give vegetarianism social dynamics. Gehman, on the other hand, didn't want vegetarianism embroiled in politics.[24]

The American Vegetarian Party disbanded after the 1960 election, when Symon Gould took the top spot on the ticket. John Maxwell, the party's first candidate whom the *Times* described as a "peppery, pink-cheeked and bright-eyed" man, fell on hard times during the 1950s.[25] By some accounts, he worked as a door-to-door salesman to try to earn enough money to qualify for social security.

Meanwhile, vegetarians coped with ridicule from the nutritional establishment and especially the media. Television was not exactly kind to vegetarianism in the 1950s. An August 1951 episode of the *George Burns and Gracie Allen Show* featured a vegetarian meal as appetizing as a plate of cardboard. The episode, "Gracie's Vegetarian Plot," revolved around Gracie and her neighbor Blanche taking the advice of a book by Professor Heywood Bradford, who urged people to eat just raw fruit and vegetables. They tried the diet on themselves and their husbands. But Blanche's husband, looking over a plate of raw vegetables, told her that he couldn't live on "this stuff." George Burns, talking to the audience, said that there wasn't anything wrong with being a vegetarian. But, he added, it's difficult to stick with it. The episode ends when Gracie and Blanche dump their new diet and instead dine on steak.

By the 1950s, meat consumption was on the rise. The shortages of World War II were fading from memory (or long gone). On the social front, the United States was changing rapidly. Americans were moving to the suburbs in great numbers, spurred on by the G.I. Bill. Rock and Roll and stars like Elvis Presley transformed popular music. On the food front, the first McDon-

ald's restaurants opened, TV dinners were introduced, and backyard barbe-
cues were becoming as American as apple pie. The science of animal agriculture was becoming more sophisticated, and the cost of putting chicken
and steak on the supermarket shelves would decline in the years ahead.

The meat industry and the scientific community were attacking vegetarianism with vigor in magazine articles, newspapers, lectures, and sym-
posiums. W. H. Sebrell, of the National Institutes of Health, called
vegetarianism a food fad during a lengthy address before the American
Institute of Nutrition symposium on April 14, 1954. "Vegetarian diets," he
said, should be categorized as "fads derived from fear of foods" and an
"ancient superstition." He also disparaged natural foods and organically
grown produce.[26]

Sebrell also decried the "shaken confidence" in white bread and the
exaggeration of the value of dark bread, which he attributed to the "zealous advocacy" of Sylvester Graham. He urged the audience to use education to fight food faddism and legal action through the Food and Drug
Administration to combat food quackery.

The decade of the 1950s wasn't exactly a boom time for vegetarianism.
Stories on the topic were far and few between, mainly reporting on meat-
free Thanksgiving dinners and Vegetarian Party Candidates. One story
that did present a lengthy and favorable case was titled "The Case for
Vegetarianism," which ran in the April 1950 issue of *American Mercury*.
Neil Ehmke, president of the Vegetarian Society of New York, along with
a New York physician, argued in favor of a meat-free diet, and Tufts Medical School professor Dr. Joseph Wassersug presented the case against.[27]

The proponents, who stated that there were between three and four million vegetarians in the United States, said vegetarianism would solve the
world's food production problems, and would vastly improve people's
health and well-being. Wassersug, on the other hand, said that it was not
impossible to obtain a complete diet from plants, but that it was difficult
and unnecessary.

"Besides, most human beings would prefer not to vegetate like a potato
or onion... such a vegetative existence signifies the end of living and the
beginning of death," wrote Wassersug.

Vegetarians weren't exactly embraced by the mainstream. Many of
them had to come up with excuses why they were not eating the burger
that was put in front of them.

"In those days, your vegetarianism didn't arrive before you did," said
Muriel Golde, a life-long vegetarian and official of the North American
Vegetarian Society who was born in 1925 to Rosicrucian parents. "When
that burger arrived and you wouldn't eat it, you had to say it was a private
thing.... I always tried to bring my own lunch."[28]

Sometimes, vegetarians had hellish experiences. Joann Scanlon recalls
witnessing one while working in a Missouri hospital in the early 1950s

while she was a high schooler. According to Scanlon, a 10-year-old boy who was anemic was admitted. He and his parents were vegetarians, but the doctors said he had to eat some meat. The parents tried to stop the physicians, but a court order barred them from the hospital. The physicians force-fed meat to the boy. Scanlon said he was absolutely terrified and that his only security—his parents—were taken away from him.[29]

Vegetarians at least had their own publications, most notably The *American Vegetarian*. The newspaper-style publication included the usual fare such as the evils of meat, accomplishments by individual vegetarians, and coverage of events. *American Vegetarian* favored veganism and carried ads for vegan products such as nonleather shoes. Advocates occasionally urged vegetarians not to be silent.

Writing in a 1953 column, Gould alerted readers to necessity of advocacy, but not before they can serve as model vegetarians. "Vegetarians must first transform themselves into true and complete examples of the principles of their faith before they can impress and convince others of the virtues of their belief and the truth of their ideals.... Not a day should go by without some act performed which would spread the message of vegetarianism to your neighbors or in your community." This, Gould argued in his column, can be done by distributing pamphlets, explaining the benefits of a meatless diet, or "taking the time out to reason with your fellow man in a calm and patient manner."[30]

Seventh-Day Adventists were still active in promoting meat-free diets. One of their members, Mervyn G. Hardinge, gave advocates much-needed scientific backing for their efforts. Hardinge was working towards his doctorate in nutrition at Harvard University, and wanted to study vegetarian nutrition. But most of the studies were negative or what he called prejudiced against vegetarians. He found a few gems, including Chittenden's dietary experiments and Jaffa's studies on fruitarians, but little else.[31]

The chairman of the department, a man Hardinge said made fun of vegetarianism, gave Hardinge the go ahead. Teamed with Dr. Frederick Stare, a nonvegetarian, Hardinge assembled 200 adolescents, pregnant women, and men and women between the ages of 45 and 65. The group consisted of 86 lacto-ovo vegetarians, 26 vegans, and 88 nonvegetarians.[32]

After studying his subjects, Hardinge found that cholesterol levels are more correlated to the consumption of animal fat rather than total fat. The vegans had the lowest serum cholesterol levels, and the nonvegetarians the highest. Hardinge also found that the pure vegetarians weighed on the average 20 pounds less than the other two groups, and that adolescents and pregnant women were healthy. Vegetarians were found to consume 50 percent more fiber than meat eaters, and vegans took in 80 percent more than the vegetarians.[33]

Dr. Hardinge's work was summarized in *Time* magazine. The writer reported that pure vegetarians (vegans) have strikingly less cholesterol than meat eaters. "This might mean something if doctors can ever figure out the tie-up between cholesterol and heart and artery disease."[34]

Born in 1914, the doctor was raised as a vegetarian by parents who gave up meat eating at the urging of an Adventist missionary. Hardinge continued to avoid eating meat for several reasons, including health and consistency. "Later my decision was reinforced by the teachings of Scripture and Ellen White. Today it is cemented by scientific findings." Hardinge died in 2002.

The decade of the 1950s closed with nothing spectacular happening on the vegetarian frontlines. But H. Jay Dinshah, one of the board members of the Natural Hygiene Society, was about to blossom into a key figure in vegetarian advocacy of the late twentieth century.

Dinshah in the late 1950s began corresponding with members of vegetarian and vegan societies in England. He was raised as a vegetarian, but became a vegan and rejected the use of animal products such as leather after learning that animals raised for milk and eggs were treated cruelly.

In 1960 Dinshah founded the American Vegan Society at Malaga, New Jersey. He named the fledgling organization's newsletter *Ahinsa* (later named *Ahimsa*), a term that he defined in the first issue as a Sanskrit word meaning without slaughter, and more broadly, a nonviolent way of life. "The highest religious and ethical view must include a profound love and compassion for fellow creatures—the very antithesis of carnivorism, which is a complete denial of the rights of all living beings other than man, (and is a reversion to the jungle)..." wrote Dinshah.[35]

The AVS newsletter was infused with Dinshah's nonsectarian spiritual and philosophical views. "Go ahead—till the soil; mulch the plot; and compost 'til the moon turns blue. But do not forget the soul; do not ignore the improvement of the lot of others; do not neglect the fertilizing of the conscience. Let a man change his diet and live 100 years: yet is his life wasted if he has not learned to treat his fellow beings as he would desire them to act toward him," Dinshah wrote in the June issue.

That year Dinshah married Freya Smith, another vegetarian from birth. Ms Smith, who was from Epsom, England, was a veteran activist who cofounded the Epsom Youth Campaign for Nuclear Disarmament and the Epsom Animal's Friends group. Like her husband, Freya Dinshah saw vegetarianism as just one aspect of the overall moral imperative of *Ahimsa*. The duo spent their days lecturing across America and Europe, writing articles and overseeing AVS activities such as the organization's annual convention. The Dinshah's were assisted in their crusade with essays and commentaries from distinguished writers, including Dr. Catherine Nimmo, who formed the first vegan society in the United States in 1948.

The Dinshahs participated in the 1961 American Natural Hygiene Society Convention in Chicago, which featured a display of vegan clothing and a lecture by Shelton. Dr. Shelton denounced the idea that every food, particularly meat and dairy, is fine in moderation. The Dinshahs later recalled "no Old Testament prophet ever spoke with more fire."[36]

In 1962 Freya, Jay, and his brother loaded up their automobile Faithful Fwances and moved AVS across the country from New Jersey to southern California. They lived with other vegans in shared housing in hope of forming a community. John Maxwell spent the hundredth and final year of his life with these vegans. In 1964 the Dinshahs and AVS moved back to New Jersey where they would remain for the rest of the century.

Despite their efforts, vegetarianism was almost invisible to the mainstream. There was one gem, however. In 1961 the *JAMA* (*Journal of the American Medical Association*) reported, "a vegetarian diet can prevent 90 percent of our thrombo-embolic disease and 97 percent of our coronary inclusions."[37] Not surprisingly, this statement has appeared in countless vegetarian publications over many years.

After a long and prolonged drought, vegetarianism was about to enter a third golden era. A new breed of advocacy was just over the horizon and getting ready to blow in with gale force.

Chapter 9

Peace, Love, and Vegetarianism: The Counterculture of the 1960s and 1970s

The tide had been against vegetarianism during the meat-laden, macho 1940s and 1950s. Then the 1960s came rushing in, turning upside down common meanings in the culture, such as what it meant to be an American, and what it meant to eat meat.

The earliest years of the decade were a near-continuation of the previous decade. But then sharp differences, such as the Vietnam War, the assassination of U.S. president John F. Kennedy, and growing discontent among a sizable segment of the younger generation with materialistic values would erupt in the mid-sixties into social upheaval and usher in radical new ideas and ways of life.

Some who had sought solutions were seeking to share them with the masses. In those days, when television had already conquered the country, vegetarians who sought to share ideas had to be media savvy, a skill that would be even more important to advocates as the decades advanced.

At least in New York City, vegetarian advocacy was a force on talk radio. Socialites Pageen and Ed Fitzgerald were famous talk radio hosts who started out in the 1940s. They broadcasted from their 22-room triplex home, and the husband-and-wife team were the most popular and highly paid talk show hosts in the New York City area for many decades, and they are said to be originators of the conversational format.[1] Pageen was an animal rights and vegetarian advocate, and a socialite who refused to wear furs and would not accept advertisements from furriers. She dined exclusively on vegetarian meals at the finest New York City restaurants while her dining companions ate meat.

In 1968 she became the head of the Millennium Guild, after Curtis Freshel died. Several years later Pageen, who was born in 1913 and was a close friend of Curtis and M.R.L. Freshel, led the Guild's campaign to stop Revlon from using animals in product safety tests. She was author of *Meatless Cooking Pageen's Vegetarian Recipes* (Gramercy, 1968), which she wrote at the request of her radio audience.

THE CALIFORNIA SCENE

Millions of viewers of the *Steve Allen Show*, a popular nationally televised comedy-variety show in the early 1960s, had a few laughs when Gypsy Boots came dancing onto the stage. Well, dancing probably is not the precise word. On the first of many appearances on the show, Boots burst onto the stage singing "I'ma the Gypsy Boots, I eat lots of fruits. I live in a hut. I feel like a nut. I'ma the Gypsy Boots..."

Allen, the show's host, writing in the foreword to Boots's 1965 book, *Bare Feet and Good Things to Eat*, said that he would never forget how Boots came "bounding on the stage with the energy of a dozen men, carrying loads of organic fruits and vegetables or what-have-you, spouting poems with random rhymes...throwing our theater into an immediate uproar."[2]

Boots, who had a scraggly beard and long hair before it was fashionable, prepared vegetarian foods on the show, such as alfalfa sprout sandwiches and carrot juice—cuisine that might have seemed bizarre to viewers, but Allen seemed to enjoy the food. In 1958, Boots had opened a restaurant, Back to Nature Health Hut. The signs were hand painted and customers had to sit on apple crates—spartan accommodations that didn't deter Hollywood's finest from patronizing the restaurant and choosing from a menu that included baked wild rice, baked soybean casserole, fruit juice blends and a variety of sandwiches. Red Buttons, John Agar, Gloria Swanson, Susan Oliver, Tina Louise, Angie Dickenson, Burl Ives, Jim Backus, and many other stars of the era ate at the restaurant. The CBS television show "On the Go" did an interview with Boots at the restaurant.

The showman clowned for the public, at times subjecting himself to ridicule, but anything that would bring people's minds to the topics he was addressing was okay with him. On his clown-like antics, Boots explained that "underneath it all was a serious effort to promote health." Rather than dwell upon negatives such as animal suffering for the sake of meat, Boots's approach was to entertain people while introducing them to vegetarianism and organically grown food.[3]

Some viewers of the *Steve Allen Show* were listening to Boots's message: young people in 25 cities formed Gypsy Boots fan clubs. The Beverly Hills club picketed the *Steve Allen Show* when they thought that Boots wasn't featured enough, even though he appeared on the show 22 times.

Boots, a lifelong vegetarian, was born Robert Bootzin in 1911 to Russian immigrants. He was one of the Nature Boys, a band of half-naked and bearded fruitarians of the 1940s who foraged through the farms and lush woods of California for nuts, berries, and other edibles. Songwriter Eden Abhez, one of the members of the band of bare-chested men, penned the hit song "Nature Boy" sung by Nat King Cole.

When Boots wasn't appearing on television shows such as the *Steve Allen Show* or the *Groucho Marx Show,* he kept active by performing stunts such as putting on pass and punt demonstrations during halftime at San Francisco 49'ers football games—activities he continued well into the 1990s—to demonstrate his plant-based vitality.

California of the 1960s had no shortage of colorful vegetarian advocates. While Boots was busy showing that vegetarians were no weaklings, a chiropractor and naturopathic physician named Pietro Rotundi was at work in Los Angeles.

The popular drugless doctor, who started practicing in 1919, was a founder of the Los Angeles Vegetarian Society with Bianca Leonardo. The doctor was a well-known lecturer on health issues, but health and other event organizers let him lecture under the condition that he not advocate vegetarianism. But with a twinkle in his eye and smile upon his face, he told the crowds that meat is another word for "blood, pus, poison, nerves, and red rot." Italian-born Rotundi had many celebrities as patients, including ex-Beatle John Lennon.

Vegetarianism turned up in some of the landmark events of the hippie era. Lisa Laws, filmmaker, photographer-archiver of the 1960s counterculture, recalls vegetarianism at Woodstock, the legendary August 1969 three days of peace and music festival held in upstate New York.

Members of the Hog Farm commune of New Mexico were flown in to the festival to help feed the over-capacity crowd. Then a member of the Hog Farm, established by Wavy Gravy, Laws, and Peter White Rabbit, purchased 1,500 pounds of bulgar wheat and an equally enormous quantity of rolled oats, almonds, dried apricots, and other ingredients they prepared and served as granola to the hungry audience of young people.

While The Hog Farm served vegetarian food at the festival primarily because it was low cost, natural not artificial, and easy to prepare, at least one vegetarian at Woodstock promulgated the practice of vegetarianism for another reason.

Legend has it that Lewis B. Marvin attended Woodstock with a lamb. He took the baby sheep among the massive crowd to spread the message he succinctly stated in the slogan: "Love Animals Don't Eat Them." Likely hundreds of thousands heard or saw his vegetarian message, many for the first time.

Months later, Marvin jumped on stage at another famous event held in 1969. At the Doors concert in Miami, Marvin, with a lamb in his arms, asked lead singer Jim Morrison to consider the lamb and animal liberation. That moment was depicted in director Oliver Stone's popular film *The Doors* and viewed by millions.

Animal liberation was in the 1960s and early 1970s a loosely knit movement. The Millennium Guild lost cofounder Curtis Freshel, and the vegetarian movement, long established and always concerned about animal liberation, had lost the momentum it had enjoyed at an earlier time. Marvin, who resided in California, was the unofficial leader of animal liberation movement of that era, especially on the West Coast, recall advocates.

Marvin, whose family was well-to-do, explained in a newspaper interview that he became an advocate of animal liberation after a hunting trip. Shocked by the extreme distress of a young monkey, after he shot the monkey's mother, Marvin was transformed. He said in an interview that one of his inspirations was Saint Theresa, who was a vegetarian.[4]

In the late 1960s, Marvin held Moonfire Happenings to protest the Vietnam War, and to show the film footage that had been clandestinely shot inside slaughterhouses. About that time, someone, perhaps Marvin, established a vegetarian restaurant in Laguna Beach named Love Animals Don't Eat Them. Live animals were permitted to roam the restaurant to remind people of the origins of meat. People who could not afford a meal were allowed to eat for free.

Lewis B. Marvin brought live cows into a fast food restaurant, which did not go over well with the police. He topped that feat during the 1973 meat shortage when he brought a Sherman tank to the restaurant, borrowed from a movie studio, for the purpose of protecting cows.

Marvin also coordinated a protest at a Kentucky Fried Chicken outlet on Thanksgiving Day, with activists dressed as chickens and one as Colonel Sanders. The California crusader brought a vegetarian lion to the Los Angeles Press Club as part of the signing of a Declaration of Independence of animals from exploitation. Animal liberation, and more often, spiritual practice, was a motivation for hippies to remove meat from their diets.

"By the time a child is 17, he has seen over 180,000 one-minute ads telling him to eat meat. We've created a system where the average child, by the time he is 11 years old, has seen 134,000 murders. If we stop killing animals, there would be less of a tendency to kill one another (in war)," Marvin told the *Los Angeles Times* in 1992. "There's a lack of compassion. It's chased away when (we) were little children," he said.[5]

Laws, creator of the award-winning documentary and photography book titled *Flashing on the Sixties*, became a vegetarian in 1960 with her husband Tom through their association with Yogi Bhajan, who taught Kundalini yoga in Los Angeles. The Yogi advised his students to permanently abstain from smoking marijuana and eating the flesh of animals. A substantial number of hippies were attracted to yoga.[6]

The Yogi's group of Sikhs established the Golden Temple restaurant in Los Angeles, recalled Laws. The restaurant served such foods as veggie burgers, granola, fruit smoothies, and other so-called hippie food typically associated with vegetarianism of the 1960s and early 1970s. Restaurants like The Golden Temple gave nonvegetarian patrons the opportunity to experience foods other than meat for dinner, and, therefore, such eateries were one of the factors in the rise of vegetarianism.

Los Angeles was not the only city with vegetarian activity. Further north, San Francisco's Haight Ashbury became a Countercultural magnet for the alternative community that had flowered from the Beat generation of the 1950s into the hippie culture of peace and love. Hippies rejected materialism, war, and conformity. They believed in ecology, simplicity, and individuality—doing one's own thing. Hippies called the Diggers founded a store in Haight Asbury named the Diggers' Free Store, where all the merchandise was free of charge.

One writer who had observed the hippies stated: "No matter how naive and inconsistent they may have been, the hippies lived by a code of gentleness and brotherhood. They showed a deep concern for fellow hippies, a reverence for nature, a compassion for all living things (which led many hippies to become vegetarians)."[7]

In 1970, *Time* magazine reported on the food of the youth of Woodstock nation. "With almost religious zeal, they are becoming vegetarians. They are also in the vanguard of the flourishing organic-food movement, insisting on produce grown without chemical fertilizers or pesticides." Some characterized by the press or themselves as "hippies" subscribed to the idea of "hip capitalism," which was based on ideals like handcrafting products.[8]

One business that qualified was *Rags*, a counterculture magazine published in San Francisco. In 1971 *Rags* reported, "To many Americans, vegetarianism represents another weirdo protest of the head generation against mom-and-apple pie-ism." In other words, not eating meat symbolized rejection of "the establishment and institutions," that is, the traditional values of the mainstream culture by younger generation rebels who used drugs.[9]

San Francisco had several restaurants that catered to vegetarians. One of them, the *Messiahs's New World Crusade's* The Here and Now Natural Foods Restaurant, featured signs with the words "All Pure Vegetarian Food" and "Our purpose is to serve all on one high standard." The menu featured roasted wheat germ with fresh fruit for 50 cents, sprouts and avocado for 65 cents, whole grain brown rice and vegetables for 60 cents, and a Macroburger for 70 cents, all available with a choice of freshly baked unleavened sesame, carrot, buckwheat, or nut bread.[10]

Haight-Ashbury was also the home base of a man who would go on to form the most successful vegetarian commune in the nation's history.

Stephen Gaskin, a Marine veteran, was at the time an English professor at San Francisco State College who drew thousands to his "Monday Night Class," which was a free series of lectures on topics such as psychology, psychedelic drugs, and spirituality.

As Gaskin and his followers explored ways to improve society and humanity, they realized that no lasting improvement would occur if they didn't include animals in the equation. "Monday Night Class" devotees became vegetarians. Some believed that the use of psychedelics, that is, hallucinogenic drugs, enabled them to perceive existence beyond every-day reality and to see beyond the illusions of the American culture. There-fore, "Many discovered that a chunk of juicy steak didn't look so appetizing any more," recalled Gaskin.[11]

In late 1970, Gaskin and more than 200 of his devotees left Haight-Ashbury and joined their leader on his speaking tour of colleges and churches across the nation. Along the way, the contingent, some of them riding in psychedelically-decorated vans and converted buses, attracted more followers.[12]

After months on the road they returned to San Francisco, but a short time later, ventured East again. In 1971, the hippie caravan rolled into Tennessee's Lewis County and settled on a piece of borrowed land south of Nashville, in the rural town of Summertown.

Some of the residents of Summertown were suspicious of the newcom-ers. As Gaskin, who then had more than shoulder-length hair, later recalled, this was just about the time when the media was full of stories about Charles Manson—the so-called hippie—who was accused, along with some of his followers, of the murders of actress Sharon Tate and sev-eral other people.

But the newcomers soon earned the respect of the Tennessee townsfolk by gaining a reputation as hardworking and trustworthy. Gaskin and his followers purchased 1,000 acres of woods and founded The Farm. He told the *New York Times* that his community had "made a spiritual agreement to live in harmony with animals" and, therefore, would not kill or eat them.[13]

Or drink their milk. Community members realized that it would be dif-ficult to keep animals for milk without the animals multiplying beyond the capacity of the people to care for them. "We should be able to make it on our own life force," Gaskin maintained. He and the community rea-soned if everyone on the planet consumed fruits, vegetables, legumes, and grains of their labors, and did not tie up valuable food resources raising animals for their meat, there could be an end to world hunger.

Much misinformation and superstition about food, and particularly about the vegetarian diet, was circulating in society, wrote Farm residents in the community's first book *Hey Beatnik! This is The Farm*. Instead of fol-lowing the diet fads of the day, such as macrobiotics and fruitarianism,

The Farm developed a diet free of animal products that would be nutritious enough for pregnant women and growing children, inexpensive enough to be afforded by anyone in the world, and delicious enough to win over devotees of Big Macs.

In 1976 Farm residents planted about 250 acres of soybeans, producing soy products such as soy burgers, soy loaf, and soy sausage. The community built a soy dairy that churned out soy milk, soy yogurt, and soy ice cream. They used soybeans to make cooking oil and margarine, mayonnaise, salad dressing, whipped cream, and dessert frosting.

The Farm spread the word about vegetarianism, particularly through their publishing company, known as The Book Publishing Company. Their books were instrumental in the 1970s in introducing thousands of Americans to tofu, tempeh, textured vegetable protein, and other foods, especially through the book *The Farm Vegetarian Cookbook.* Later, the commune's food company, Farm Foods, made a soy-based ice cream named Ice Bean, which was sold through numerous natural food stores, and even some supermarkets, throughout the nation.

In the mid-1970s other books had revealed the culinary possibilities of the versatile soybean, creating a surge in demand for tofu cuisine. One of them was *The Book of Tofu* by Bill Shurtleff, who learned the art of tofu-making while living in Japan in the early 1970s. The others included The Farm's Book Publishing Company's *The Tempeh Cookbook, The TVP Cookbook, Tofu Cookery,* and *Tofu Quick & Easy.*

The Tennessee community played a major role in introducing Americans to tempeh, a soy-based food rich in vitamin B12. The Farm's tempeh laboratory provides tempeh cultures to producers worldwide, who make this fermented soybean substance into burgers and bacon substitutes. The Farm also became known for its midwifery skills, and as the founders of PLENTY, a nonprofit charitable organization that gives aid to victims of disasters in the United States and abroad.

Hippies making The Farm their home were not the only ones interested in self sufficiency and living simply. The back-to-the-land movement gained strength in the 1970s and participants looked to Helen and Scott Nearing for inspiration.

Like hippies and some others of the late 1960s and early 1970s who chose to not eat meat, and to instead eat organically grown, unprocessed natural foods, the Nearings did so for a combination of reasons. One of these was to boycott the takeover of food production by unscrupulous big business that altered food through technologies to maximize profits. Critical of the "pre-cooked, mixed, prepared" foods sold at grocery stores, the Nearings reflected that "an entire generation of humans is being raised, from infancy to maturity, chiefly on processed, prepared, canned and packaged factory foods." Specifically, the Nearings, and eventually significant numbers of Americans, objected to the denaturing of flour or "refining" that removed the bran and added bleach and synthetic vitamins. Just as Sylvester Graham had, the Nearings and like-minded people of the twentieth century rejected white bread for the whole grain, naturally healthful variety. Bread was no longer chewy and rich in nutrients, and the modern-day natural people were opposed to the use of artificial flavors, colors, and preservatives rountinely used in food production.[14]

The Nearings spent most of their lives living off the land as homesteaders. They were popular lecturers at vegetarian conferences, and they influenced countless people in the 1960s and 1970s who were seeking a simpler life. The couple moved from New York City to a farm in the Green Mountains of Vermont in 1932, during the height of the Great Depression. "The Society from which we moved had rejected in practice and in principle our pacifism, our vegetarianism and our collectivism," they wrote in *Living the Good Life*.

They practiced what they called the good life: natural hygiene (they were never sick), organically growing their own food, fasting on Sundays, hard work, and writing. The Nearings raised cash by selling maple syrup, and at times bartered some of this syrup for products such as citrus fruits, walnuts, or olive oil.

Helen Nearing was born in 1904 in Ridgewood, New Jersey. She was raised as a vegetarian by Theosophist parents. Scott Nearing was born in 1883 and before World War I was a respected Pennsylvania College professor who was fired for speaking out against child labor in the coal industry, and against the war, and for his socialist views. He became a vegetarian in 1917 at the age of 35. He told *Vegetarian World* that he figured if it was wrong to kill people "it wasn't right to kill animals." Scott also read about vegetarianism in *Physical Culture* magazine when he was a young man.

The Nearings wrote and lectured on vegetarianism and cofounded the *North American Vegetarian Society*. "We believe that all life is to be respected—nonhuman as well as human. Therefore for sport we neither hunt nor fish, nor do we feed on animals. Furthermore, we prefer, in our respect for life, not to enslave or exploit our fellow creatures," they wrote in *Living The Good Life*, which sold over 200,000 copies.[15]

They also wrote "Carnivorism involves (1) holding animals in bondage; (2) turning them into machines for breeding and milking; (3) slaughtering them for food; (4) preserving and processing their dead bodies for human consumption. We were looking for a kindly, decent and simple way of life. Long ago we decided to live in the vegetarian way, without killing or eating animals, and lately we have largely ceased to use dairy products and have allied ourselves with the vegans who use and eat no animal products, butter, cheese, eggs or milk. This is all in line with our philosophy of the least harm to the least number and the greatest good to the greatest number of life forms."[16]

In the early 1950s, the Nearings left Vermont when developers started buying land near their farm for ski resorts. They moved and established a homestead on the Maine Coast, where they received thousands of visitors. At age 100, Scott was finally slowing down, so he stopped eating until he died. Helen died from injuries sustained in a car accident in 1995 at the age of 91.

The Nearings' homestead and the Farm's commune attracted thousands of visitors. The vegetarians among them, however, had few books to guide them. Classic works such as Kellogg's *Natural Diet of Man* were long out of print, and bookstore shelves had little or nothing to offer. But this changed in 1971.[17]

Numerous vegetarians, including advocates, credited Francis Moore Lappé's best-selling *Diet for a Small Planet* as a major influence in their lives. The book, which has sold over 3 million copies, detailed the practice of feeding millions of tons of the world's grain to livestock instead of to the hordes of hungry people. Moore, who was 27, reported that at the time, a cow had to be fed 21 pounds of protein to produce one pound of protein for human consumption. She called the raising of cows "protein factories in reverse."[18]

The timing of the book could not have been better. America's concern over world hunger was peaking. Images of starving masses in places such as Bangladesh were beamed into living rooms on news programs. Growing alarm over environmental issues and the rising interest in plant-based cuisine paralleled this concern over hunger. Ethical concern for the treatment of farmed animals was also awakening.

Diet for a Small Planet, although not specifically a vegetarian book, presented compelling environmental and economic arguments for not eating meat. Environmentalists had *Silent Spring* by Rachel Carson, and now vegetarians had *Diet for a Small Planet.*

"Some of the 20th Century's most vibrant activist-thinkers have been American women—Margaret Mead, Jeannette Rankin, Barbara Ward, Dorothy Day—who took it upon themselves to pump life into basic truths. Frances Moore Lappé is among them," wrote *Washington Post* columnist Colman McCarthy in 1989.[19] Lappé, although she was not a consistent vegetarian since she eats fish, became famous and a celebrity especially to vegetarians and advocates. Now some succinct arguments for the plant-based diet were in one paperback book. "We carried it around like it was our Bible," recalled one advocate, Connie Salamone.

Diet also caught on with the media, which ran stories on the ecological and economic ramifications of animal agriculture. Undoubtedly the book did much to forward the economics argument for plant-based agriculture, an argument that had been known by previous generations of vegetarian advocates, but one that had evidently remained dormant for decades.

"All of a sudden, people whose closest contact with a cow was a carton of milk, knew how many pounds of soybeans were needed to feed a cow and how many hungry people around the world those same pounds of soybeans could have fed," said Victoria Moran, writer and popular lecturer, especially at North American Vegetarian Society Summerfests.[20] No one wanted cows to be deprived of food; the problem was that the number of cows, created to fill the demand for their flesh, was unnatural, and feeding them required enormous quantities of food.

Meat was pricey; some people called for boycotts, if not specifically vegetarianism. In 1974, Bread for the World (BFW), a Christian organization, urged Christians in the United States to abstain from meat on Mondays, Wednesdays, and Fridays. Catholic Auxiliary Bishop Thomas Gumbleton of Detroit stated that a reduction in meat consumption would increase the amount of grain in the world available to the hungry.

In 1975, *Vegetarian Voice* reported that United Nations Secretary General Kurt Waldheim called affluent consumption, or meat eating, one of the causes of world hunger. The magazine reported that if the United States became a vegetarian nation, "hunger would be something that children anywhere in the world would know about only if they read history books."[21]

Food for Life, a project for bringing food and life to the needy of the world through the liberal distribution of karma-free vegetarian meals, did much to distribute food to the hungry. Established in 1974, Food for Life is a project of the International Society for Krishna Consciousness (ISKCON), a branch of Vaisnava Hinduism, also known as the Hare Krishna movement, and called a cult by some critics. The Food for Life project, active in 60 countries, serves 30,000 vegetarian meals per day, and more than half of them are vegan. About one out of three volunteers who serve meals are people from outside of the Hare Krishna movement.

SHRIVER AND SALAMONE

In the early 1970s the vegetarian movement began splitting into two separate but related causes: animal liberation and vegetarianism. Nellie Shriver and Connie Salamone, even though their names aren't known to most vegetarians, helped create the split. Not content sitting around discussing the beta carotene content of carrots or sipping tea at socials, the two women were instrumental in bringing vegetarianism to the masses by distributing leaflets and using guerrilla tactics to gain the media's attention.

The movement to liberate animals from the meat industry, experimentation, hunting, zoos, circuses, and every other form of exploitation and killing was slowly beginning to reach the mainstream. Salamone and Shriver were activists in a movement that was yet to be named. Even though the Millennium Guild was still active, it was founded in another era.

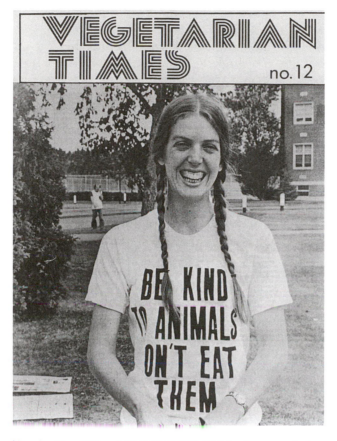

Constantina "Connie" Salamone: Pioneering vegetarian (vegan), animal liberation advocate, ecofeminist, and feminist advocate.

A DIME AND A PHONE BOOTH

Like advocates of the past, Shriver and Salamone had to rely on creativity and cleverness, instead of cash, to promote their cause.

Nellie Shriver, founder of American Vegetarians, showed advocates how they could get their message to millions of people with just a pocketful of dimes. In 1974 Shriver and her small organization American Vegetarians targeted the Oscar Mayer television commercial theme song "I'd love to be an Oscar Mayer Weiner" with a four-line press release stating that her organization had asked the Federal Trade Commission to halt the company's ad because it "makes a mockery of the involuntary suffering" of pigs slaughtered for food.[22]

With assistance from others, and at a cost of 40 cents, Shriver called the *Washington Post*, the *Washington Star News*, the *United Press International*, and the *Associated Press*. The strategy worked because the wire services picked up Shriver's press release. Shriver estimated that at least 10 percent of the papers in the country carried her message, and that 25 million readers heard that there was a connection between meat and the suffering of animals. *Vegetarian World* magazine reported that hundreds of subscription requests to the newspaper were made shortly after Shriver's media blitz. Shriver speculated that the media attention could have been behind the disappearance of the Oscar Mayer ads.

Vegetarian Times credits Shriver and American vegetarians with placing public service announcements (PSA) on 500 radio and television stations. "We also operate on the assumption that one person with no money can do an incredible amount of organizing and free seed planting," wrote Shriver in *Times*. "Even if you are a committee of one in your community you can get public service time. PSAs can be used as an organizing tool and as an educational medium. They can be used to advertise your need for fellow workers, to tell of the world grain shortage statistics, to speak of the slaughterhouse cruelty, heart disease and meat, insecticide ratios in animal flesh, the four kinds of animals killed for Chanel No. 5 perfume fixatives, etc."[23]

One of Shriver's radio PSAs reached Maynard Clark, a Harvard student who credits the announcement with starting him on the road to vegetarianism. In the 1980s, Clark established a vegetarian hotline and an organization that was the precursor to the *Boston Vegetarian Society.*

Shriver appeared on national television as early as 1970, when she and fellow activist Dudley Giehl were guests on the *Today Show*.[24] Host Edwin Newman gave the pair eight minutes to talk about the benefits of vegetarianism. One of the ways Shriver managed to gain air time on popular television programs was to write to the host and offer a rebuttal to issues concerning diet or animals. The strategy worked: she appeared on television's *Phil Donahue Show* during a segment on the Stillman Diet, a widely-publicized, meat-based diet. After the show aired, she received thousands of letters from people curious about vegetarianism. Shriver also appeared on *The Tomorrow Show*.[25]

Interest was burgeoning, yet being a vegetarian could be a challenge in the early 1970s. "It wasn't only that we couldn't buy our dinners at the same restaurants as our friends—we ourselves were considered different. Although non-vegetarians weren't exactly rejecting us, they weren't accepting us either," wrote Victoria Moran and Lucy Moll in 1990 in *Vegetarian Times*.[26]

Although the medical community knew the scientifically proven health benefits of the plant-based diet, it was "reluctant to acknowledge these benefits," the women wrote, noting vegetarians were always having to explain themselves. The inconvenience of the diet at that time was "wearying," wrote Moran and Moll. Moran, a writer and organizer, was spreading the word, as was Shriver and her friend Connie.

WOMEN, WHY DO YOU BUY MEAT?

While Shriver was attracting the media, Constantina "Connie" Salamone was trying to persuade women not to eat meat. Salamone, an editor of the *Majority Report*, a feminist newspaper in New York City, wrote in a 1972 issue that women need to take back their role as protector of the animals and planet. "A feminist kitchen should be a place where the dead bodies of others do not abound."[27]

During the Great Meat Boycott of spring 1973, when Americans were dissatisfied with the high price of meat, Salamone's ecofeminist essay entitled "Why Do You Buy Meat?" drew a favorable story by the *Associated Press* and appeared in several hundred newspapers. Salamone connected the oppression of women with the use of animals for food.

Salamone, born 1940 in Boston, Massachusetts, founded two New York City-based organizations, Vegetarian Feminists and Vegetarian Activist Collective. These two organizations were unique and radical, and consisted of people from 16 to 80 years old, most of whom were "full-time workers without class or upper educational privileges," explained Salamone, who credited her "English and Scottish heritage and working class labor sensibilities" as a factor in her organizing ability.[28]

Powered by Salamone, the two organizations connected "vegetarianism, socialism, feminism, animal liberation, Earth spiritualism, and Native indigenousism." This message of ecological wholism they brought to the masses through street theater, slide shows, and by calling radio talk shows. Salamone said that this approach to activism was "decidedly and consciously non-academic—a university philosophy was not the siren call—we were true street activists by night and by week end."

"Feminists," wrote Salamone, "are still very much 'Human Chauvinists' in their outlook and concept of a completely humane way of life when they still continue to mimic male superiority in their social structures by excluding non-human beings as part of their political societal structure of co-living on the Earth."

Salamone, who was impressed with the "organic health movement seen on communes, and by the wholesome (vegetarian) food served to a half million of us at the Woodstock festival by the 'Hog Farmer' commune residents of New Mexico," became a vegan while working as a feminist activist. She attended a meeting where women were discussing the issue of rape when she realized that the chicken pieces served as a snack were the "remains of a violated being."

Not all feminists agreed with her, she recalled. Members of her Vegetarian Activist Collective and Vegetarian Feminists distributed literature on animal liberation issues at "New Left" gatherings, only to be ignored. "They thought it was a joke."

Salamone's two organizations, though they were disbanded in the next decade, left a mark on vegetarian and animal rights advocacy. For example, VAC published papers on feminism and animal liberation, factory farming, circuses, and vivisection. "VF and VAC had cutting edge movement activists and left a legacy swallowed up later by others, often with no credit to the original work," she said. Some do credit the two pioneering activists. People for the Ethical Treatment of Animals' (PETA) cofounder Alex Pacheco wrote that two brilliant activists—Salamone and Nellie Shriver—were his teachers in the Animal Rights Movement.

Salamone and other leaders readily give accolades to their numerous unsung colleagues in the movement at that time; for example, they applaud the New Jersey-based Vegetarian Association of America. *Dr. Shelton's Hygienic Review,* which was natural hygienist Herbert Shelton's magazine, was another source of information for people abstaining from animal flesh, when information was not readily available, as it is today.

The work of advocates, whether as official spokesperson on television programs, or unofficially, as in talking to friends about food, gradually had an impact on the nation. The *New York Times* alluded to this in 1975. "Not long ago, vegetarians were viewed by many people as weird, wiry crusaders for carrot juice who ran around in tennis shoes rather than wear the leather off some animals back," the paper reported.[29]

Attempts over the centuries to silence or ignore vegetarians had failed. They were slowly beginning to become more vocal and visible. More than 100 years after Russell T. Trall, M.D., established the New York Vegetarian Society, the city's "veggie" groups were still going strong. The Vegetarian Society of New York in 1975 had 400 members, reported the *New York Times.* It was a year when some people, especially among the younger generation, were concerned about world hunger and cut back on or eliminated meat in their diets in solidarity with the hungry, and as protest against the injustice of one nation enjoying abundant grains and legumes, while others overseas were suffering from starvation.

The year 1975 was a volatile one for vegetarianism. One of the ground-shaking events of that year was the publication of a book bearing the same name as Dudley Giehl's organization: *Animal Liberation.* The book, by Australian philosopher Peter Singer, would galvanize people to become a part of the modern animal rights movement, a movement he had observed in the work of Salamone, Shriver, Giehl, and others, and then helped to enlarge.

While no exact numbers can be determined as to how many people were inspired by Singer's book, the number was either significant, or those who were affected by it particularly effective in promoting the cause, since shortly after the book was published the Animal Rights movement in America caught fire.

Singer's book alone did not cause the blaze; the sparks had been fanned for years by activists across the nation. In the original edition of the book, Singer gave some credit to activists such as Salamone.[30] The movement for animal liberation is as old as that for vegetarianism, dating at least to 1817, when Reverend Metcalfe in Philadelphia was preaching abstinence from the flesh of animals, and kindness to them, as a Christian duty.

Animal Liberation provided a powerful argument for the liberation of animals. It presented scenes of factory farming and slaughter, as well as vivisection, in graphic detail—surely motivating a percentage of its readers to become vegetarians, and vegans, or at least to consider the possibility, since the book called for people to eschew not just meat but all food derived from animals.

The graphic details in the book, taken from Singer's own observations, and from food industry publications, were shocking to people who believed animals raised for food led the idyllic farm life. Details like those Singer wrote about were publicized beyond the book; they had been disseminated in society through literature produced by animal rights and welfare groups and vegetarian organizations.

Ironically, the book that helped bring the animal liberation movement to vibrant life was not advocating the liberation of animals for the sake of the animals, but from a utilitarian point of view that emphasized the benefits of their liberation to the greatest number of human beings.

During this same time period, regional leaders such as Dixie Mahy, Bianca Leonardo, Marcia Pearson, and many others were working hard on the West Coast for vegetarianism. Pearson founded the Seattle Vegetarian Society in 1976.[31] When not organizing events, writing, or lecturing before groups about vegetarianism, she was an in-demand fashion model. Pearson chose to restrict her modeling career by turning down jobs modeling for companies that sold furs, cigarettes, liquor, and meat. She organized vegetarian dinners and made numerous appearances on television and area radio talk shows. Some vegetarians have called Pearson "the Godmother of Vegetarianism" in the Seattle area, which now has one of the highest concentrations of vegetarians in the United States.

Vegetarian societies from California to Cape Cod were going strong. They presented public potluck dinners and lectures, organized other events, distributed literature, and used other creative means to get the word out.

The word was getting out in a variety of ways. Jews, like those of other faiths, were working for vegetarianism on the local and national level.[32] In 1975 Jonathan Wolf founded the Jewish Vegetarian Society of America, which was affiliated with the Jewish Vegetarian Society of England. "In a real sense, vegetarianism is the highest form of Judaism.... Intrinsic values in the Jewish religion—compassion for animals, concern about world hunger and ecology—are exemplified by vegetarianism," Wolf said in 1980.

Perhaps the most prominent Jewish person to advocate vegetarianism was Isaac Bashevis Singer, the 1978 recipient of the Nobel Prize for literature who was also a force for animal liberation. For example, he wrote the foreword to Dudley Giehl's 1979 book *Vegetarianism: A Way of Life.*[33] When asked why he ate no meat he would quip that he was a vegetarian for health—the chicken's health. Singer mentioned his beliefs in press interviews and included vegetarian and animal liberation themes in some of his short stories and novels. In one interview he stated that slaughtering animals for food was one small step away from killing people, as in the mass murdering by Hitler and Stalin. Singer had left Poland because of the Nazis.

NORTH AMERICAN VEGETARIAN SOCIETY

The growth of vegetarian advocacy gave rise to the need for organization, and leaders met the challenge by forming the North American Vegetarian Society in 1974. A year earlier, Jay Dinshah and representatives from four other vegetarian groups from North America attended the 22nd World Vegetarian Congress held in Sweden and invited the International Vegetarian Union to hold the next Congress in the United States. The invitation was accepted and the North American Vegetarian Society was formed by Dinshah and a committee to serve as a host for the Congress.

NAVS established a program designed to support and assist all vegetarian groups in North American and to encourage the starting of new groups. Brian and Sharon Graff were named directors of the society, and soon established annual gatherings called Summerfests.

The year 1975 was an important year for vegetarian advocacy. With the formation of the NAVS, the stage was set for the 23rd World Vegetarian Congress held in the late summer at Orono, Maine. The event marked the first time that the International Vegetarian Union held its congress on American soil. Arguably, it was the most important gathering of vegetarians in the United States of the twentieth century.[34]

All three major television networks of the era, ABC, NBC, and CBS, along with dozens of newspaper and magazines, covered the event, which was held at the University of Maine and lasted about two weeks. About 1,500 people attended the Congress, a count said to eclipse any attendance mark of any conference held that century. Lecturers included a who's who list of world vegetarianism: environmentalist Richard St. Barbe Baker; Helen and Scott Nearing; writer and philosopher Henry Bailey Stevens; IVU president Dr. Gordon Latto; Ann Wigmore, founder of the Hippocrates Health Institute; International tennis star Peter Burwash; Nellie

Shriver; Connie Salamone; Paul Obis, founder of Vegetarian Times; Vegetarian organizers Dixie Mahy and Brian Graff; Seventh-Day Adventist leader Stoy Proctor; and writer Victoria Moran. The Dinshahs were the chief organizers of the conference.

The vegetarian heavyweights, with the press at hand, were not about to let an opportunity to sound a message on world hunger get away. The event featured a Funeral For Famine, complete with casket, hearse, and pallbearers. Jay Dinshah, in a eulogy delivered at the event, said "Shall we, through reverence for life, and through vegetarianism, banish famine once and for all time from the face of this planet?"

Media coverage of the 1975 World Congress was generally favorable, but some of the coverage was critical. *The Christian Century* reported that the event was disappointing because there were more workshops on feeding meatless diets to pets and using vegetable-based cosmetics than on strategies for ending famine."[35] The *Century* also reported that there was a cadre of young, freewheeling activists, particularly from the Vegetarian Activist Collective, who wanted to focus more on politics.

Congress officials did not exactly warm up to the idea of political action. Dinshah, according to the *Century*, objected to a pamphlet that he found politically offensive. He believed that it was best to keep politics out of vegetarian advocacy. However, Salamone told a *Harper's Weekly* reporter that "you're making a political statement by being a vegan." She and other VAC members were part of a small but vocal group of advocates at the Congress calling for the inclusion of animal rights on the agenda.

A writer for a British vegetarian society stated: "The impact of the 23rd Vegetarian Congress reaches far beyond the dining hall, the lecture rooms, and the auditoriums.... CBS television cameras bring it all into the homes of millions across the nation, with local radio programs and newspapers also spreading the world. The whole of America is talking vegetarianism—watch out for repercussions on the rest of the world!"

THE PRESS

Like branches in the wind, the progress of vegetarianism swayed back and forth over the decades. In the 1970s, these winds were blowing in the favorable direction, but media coverage was still blowing in all directions.

The *New York Times*, arguably the most influential newspaper of the era, published an article about the rising numbers of vegetarians, especially among the young.[36] The paper reported in 1975 that the young were embracing vegetarianism for one or more reasons: they abhorred the idea of killing animals for their flesh, they disapproved of the use of chemicals found in meat, they could not afford meat, and they belonged to religious groups that were vegetarian. However, reported the *Times*, young people were mainly concerned about the ethics of wasting grain that could be used to feed the world's malnourished masses, but was fed to animals slated for the dinner table.

The *Times* piece also alerted readers to the increasing availability of vegetarian foods: the number of natural food stores, vegetarian restaurants, and nonvegetarian restaurants offering meatless options on the menu was rising. The articles also noted celebrities who did not eat meat, such as Pegeen Fitzgerald, musician and ex-Beatle George Harrison, and actors Cloris Leachman and Dennis Weaver, as well as famous figures from history such as da Vinci, George Bernard Shaw, Gandhi, and Hitler, who historians have discovered was no vegetarian, even though he on occasion refrained from eating animal flesh out of concern for his health. The article also noted the dietary studies conducted by Doctors Mervyn G. Hardinge and Frederick Stare.

A year later the *New York Times* and the *Associated Press* reported on the upsurge in demand for meat-free meals on a college campus.[37] Mount Holyoke College, a trend-setting college in South Hadley, Massachusetts, had established a vegetarian lunch center, and a student newsletter containing recipes and articles to accommodate interest in meals without meat.

Change was definitely occurring in the country, but not without a struggle against formidable odds. The wind more often blew against vegetarianism than in its favor. Quite a few articles about vegetarianism, in mainstream publications, that at superficial glance might have appeared favorable to removing meat from the menu, and that were read by millions of people, were actually not positive, but they did keep the idea of vegetarianism in the media.

These type of articles, published during the 1970s, placed laborious conditions on the vegetarian diet that made it seem that eating no meat and avoiding nutritional deficiency were mutual goals. Although the articles often began on a favorable note, they tended to deteriorate into "yes, but" paragraphs or statements that might have caused some curious or skeptical readers to shy away from the plant-based diet.

Most of the stories questioned whether a diet free of meat provided adequate protein, even though science decades earlier proved that vegetarians get more than enough protein. The deficiency myth lingered.

Life and Health magazine, an Adventist magazine, noted this obstacle, and called the protein question the most frequently asked question among skeptics. For decades to come that question would frustrate vegetarians, who among themselves turned it into a joke since just about every vegetarian heard the question from relatives, friends, coworkers, classmates, and anyone else who knew they did not eat meat: "Where do you get protein?"[38]

One example of the "yes, but" brand of reporting on vegetarianism appeared in *McCall's* in January of 1972. The article began: "As more and more people become vegetarians, either because they think it is healthier not to eat meat or because they oppose killing of any kind, a legitimate nutritional question arises. Simply, can you have an adequate diet without animal protein?"[39]

The writer explained that a vegetarian diet containing milk, eggs, and cheese, but no meat was adequate, except that it was "likely to be low in...iron...and zinc." More problematic, was the strict vegetarian diet because "plant proteins are not as high in quality as animal proteins, but they can be combined so as to produce a balanced protein mixture,"[40] wrote the nutrition expert.

However, the writer further warned, lack of vitamin B_{12} in the vegan diet could lead to degeneration of the spinal cord and "loss of brain function." Some vegans supplement their diets with a non-animal source of B_{12}, such as fortified cereal, while others do not. The vitamin B_{12} issue became a much-debated one in the late twentieth century among vegans and nutritional experts, vegan or not. But the warning that one's brain might cease to function as a result of not eating meat and all foods derived from animals harkens back to Sylvester Graham's days as a crusader for vegetarianism in the 1830s, when his opposition within the medical community claimed vegetarianism caused insanity. It is a warning still issued today.

Some articles in the popular press directly disapproved of vegetarianism. In "When a Vegetarian Diet Can Be Dangerous," published in the May 1976 issue of *Good Housekeeping* magazine, the reporter noted "Lately more and more people have become vegetarians, partly for health reasons, partly, perhaps, because of the rise in the cost of meat." Vegetarian diets containing cow's milk or eggs were qualified as "completely nutritious diet," but only if the vegetarians "carefully select foods in the four food groups..."[41]

"Pure (strict) vegetarians," the article stated, "can have serious nutritional problems, and they have to eat a highly varied diet that includes grains...vegetables...and nuts." They also must eat these foods in varied combinations and in large amounts because plant foods aren't concentrated sources of nutrients." Lack of particular nutrients "could lead to anemia and neurological disorders."[42]

Such warnings, complicated combining of foods, and instruction to eat large amounts of food might not have deterred people determined to abstain from animal flesh, but whether it scared away those less dedicated seems likely. If, after all, people were seeking to eliminate meat from their diets as a measure to improve their health, then why would they risk their health by doing the same?

Vic Sussman, a journalist and author of *Vegetarian Alternative* (1978), later recalled in a *Washington Post* column how families reacted upon learning parents would be raising their children as vegetarians.

Portly uncles and wattled aunts educated largely by talk shows and hearsay suddenly become nutrition experts, popping up with dire warnings that dwarfism and loathsome diseases will be visited on your meatless, deprived children. And your in-laws will start acting like outlaws, though they were sure you were crazy to begin with. Your poor child, they assure you, will be an outcast when the other kids are pigging out at a Burger King. The kid also won't get enough protein or vitamins or minerals, and will end up a hollow-eyed poster for CARE.[43]

Vegetarians of the 1970s, as they did in the past and would do again, publicized lists of celebrities and famous figures from history who did not eat meat. The more extraordinary a figure, the better. Men at the time liked to point out that professional wrestler Killer Kowalski was a vegetarian. Advocates believed that such publicity was a necessity since the stigma attached to vegetarianism—that it somehow made one suspect, or weak—had not been vanquished from society, even in the 1970s. Also on the list of celebrities who were noted for their vegetarianism, and who at least sometimes advocated it: television star actors Dennis Weaver, Cloris Leachman, Susan Saint James and comedian and peace and civil rights activist, Dick Gregory. Popular comedian-turned-social activist Gregory was a 1968 write-in candidate for the U.S. presidency who fasted and ran across the nation to publicize the problem of hunger in the United States. His book *Dick Gregory's Natural Diet for Folks Who Eat: Cookin' With Mother Nature* (Harper & Row, 1973) advocated veganism. Gregory stated that he became a vegetarian for health and abhorred the violence inherent in a diet containing animal flesh. In the 1970s Gregory predicted the eventual takeover of vegetarianism by big business and the establishment of 24-hour natural food supermarkets.

Throughout history a person's diet meant more than mere food intake. The personal is political, A. Bronson Alcott had taught and practiced in the past. Dick Gregory alluded to this principle in his book. He explained that preventable diseases associated with meat eating are destructive to African Americans as a group. Gregory wrote: "The quickest way to wipe out a group of people is to put them on a soul food diet. One of the tragedies is that the very folks in the black community who are most sophisticated in terms of political realities in the country are nonetheless advocates of 'soul food.' They will lay down a heavy rap on genocide in America with regard to black folks, then walk into a soul food restaurant and help the genocide along."

A booklet, *Facts of Vegetarianism*, published in the early 1970s featured inspiring quotations from the world's celebrated leaders in ethical living of the past, as well as a list of contemporary celebrities who were not meat eaters. Written by movement leaders Nellie Shriver, Dudley Giehl, Nathaniel Altman, and Jay Dinshah, it was published as a joint effort of their respective organizations, American Vegetarians, Animal Liberation, Inc., and American Vegan Society.

The organization Vegetarian Society, Inc., which was founded in 1948 by Bianca Leonardo, put a light touch in its brochure on vegetarianism. "To become a vegetarian, it is not necessary to make an oath of allegiance to the Great Turnip over a sack of soybeans," the brochure stated, followed by practical suggestions for changing one's diet.[44]

VEGETARIAN WORLD

Vegetarians of the 1970s were similar to their counterparts of yesteryear when it came to motivations for abstaining from meat. William Blanchard, founder and publisher of *Vegetarian World*, listed the modern-day motivations in a 1975 issue:

- Environmental—"humanists who are aware that civilization's billions of food animals are wasting up to 100 times the protein plants alone can supply in the human diet."
- Health—"the best known variety, have long been numerous and range from movie stars and sports champions...to armies of senior citizens concerned about heart trouble and other threats to longer happier living."
- Ethical—these vegetarians "feel a kinship with all forms of sentient life."
- Aesthetic—"instinctive aversion to fleshfoods but most of them are at last overcome by the pressures of social custom and adapt to the omnivorous diet."
- Religion—"Meat abstention has deep spiritual significance for many devout Americans. In addition to hundreds of thousands of Seventh-Day Adventists, there are vegetarian Buddhists, Hindus, Mormans increasingly, Rosicrucians, Theosophists, and Unity followers. Numerous 'occult' or 'metaphysical' groups are actively vegetarians."
- Natural vegetarians—"subscribe to the belief that the human species is physiologically non-carnivorous."[45]

Blanchard also noted that a "new main vegetarian element is being made up by today's many food-conscious young subculture adults who enthusiastically support avant-garde food stores, restaurants..." He also mentions that some people became vegetarians in protest over the high cost of meat.

The Millennium Guild handed Blanchard their M.R.L. Freshel Award for the first issue. The Guild's president, Pageen Fitzgerald stated: "For more than 50 years the millennium Guild has pressed the point that man's civilization cannot be built upon a slaughterhouse diet. We now bestow the Guild's Freshel award upon you and trust that you will play well the part of David to overcome the clumsy Goliath."

Vegetarian World, which had a circulation of 35,000 at its peak, featured most of the top advocates of the day, including Dr. Paavo Airola, a naturopath and nutrition researcher; Ann Wigmore, a pioneer in the use of wheat grass juice; and Robin Hur, a frequent contributor credited with uncovering facts about health, nutrition, and ecology that were used by vegetarian advocates. The publication also featured celebrity interviews and profiles, including Dennis Weaver, Mary Tyler Moore, Carol Burnett, Cloris Leachman, Dick Gregory, and film legend Gloria Swanson, who said it was easy to be a vegetarian.

Like vegetarian publications of the past, *V-World*, as it was often called, covered extraordinary feats by people who did not eat meat. One of them was Marine Captain Alan Jones, who broke records in activities such as sit-ups, swimming, and strength. Jones, who was featured in several issues, once swam for 150 consecutive hours, and performed 51,001 consecutive sit-ups. Scott Smith, *V-World's* editor, called him "superman."[46]

The publication merged with *Vegetarian Times* in 1978. The latter was established as a four-page black and white newsletter in 1974 by Paul Obis, and distributed free. Obis, who knew no other vegetarians, was inspired by Lappé's book and George Harrison's Concert for Bangladesh. The publication he started grew rapidly as the interest in vegetarianism proliferated, and by 1976, it had 10,000 readers. In this era, *Vegetarian Times* frequently featured stories on world hunger, and contributing writers included Nellie Shriver. *Vegetarian Times* was an educator and a clearinghouse, providing facts and connecting people to products, services, and organizations.

Over the next two decades, the *Times* featured many contributors who would still be promoting vegetarianism at the start of the twenty-first century. One of them, Victoria Moran, began writing for the magazine after meeting Obis at the World Vegetarian Congress at Orono. Moran wrote several books on vegetarianism and related themes and became a popular motivational speaker who has appeared on *The Oprah Winfrey Show*. Susan Smith Jones was a frequent contributor to *V-World* and the *Times* who has become a leader in the health and human potential movement.

VEGETARIANISM GOES TO WASHINGTON

In 1976 America was celebrating its 200th birthday, and Nellie Shriver, along with the America Vegetarians and Alex Hershaft, joined the party by organizing The Bicentennial Luncheon. The event was designed to introduce Congress to vegetarianism, and drew close to 200 senators and representatives. Speakers included Congressman Andrew Jacobs, an Indiana representative who was the only openly vegetarian member of Congress (and who abhorred the violence of the Vietnam War, as well as violence against animals), Robert Pinkus of the Metropolitan Vegetarian Society of New Jersey, and Ann Wigmore, advocate of vegan living foods and wheatgrass as a panacea. Volunteers handed out copies of *Vegetarian World* and literature calling for a ban on the promotion of meat and refined foods. That same year, Paul Obis testified before the U.S. Senate Committee on Agriculture and Forestry, urging the panel to educate food stamp recipients that vegetarian food choices were the most economical.

Meanwhile Hershaft, Blanchard, and Nathaniel Altman, author of *Eating for Life*, formed the Vegetarian Information Service to disseminate information and the latest vegetarian news to the press. They distributed *Vegetarianism Like It Is*, a brochure listing the reasons for not eating meat. VIS sponsored a three-day Eating for Life conference where advocates, journalists, scientists, consumer groups such as the Center for Science in the Public Interest, government representatives, and personnel from the American Meat Institute gathered to discuss vegetarianism, world hunger, and other similar issues.

A year later vegetarian advocates were enthusiastic about the U.S. Senate Select Committee on Nutrition that was exploring the links between diet and illness. The committee was poised to recommend that Americans "decrease their consumption of meat and increase consumption of fish and poultry," but watered it down to cutting back on fatty meat in favor of lean meat, poultry, and fish.

Advocates believed that any government recommendation to cut back on meat of any kind was akin to a de facto stamp of approval of a vegetarian diet. So they were disappointed by the watered-down version of the McGovern Report, which was named after Senator George McGovern, the committee's chairman. Vegetarian leaders cried foul, and stated that the panel buckled under pressure from the meat industry. T. Colin Campbell, a Cornell nutrition scientist, later recalled that there was an enormous political furor over the report.

However, the committee arranged a subsequent hearing during March of that year for the meat industry and vegetarians to air their views. Meat industry representatives, after given an eight-week extension to submit additional evidence, presented the panel with about 300 pages of articles and statements that cast doubt on the link between animal fat consumption and disease.

Vegetarian advocates were allowed input. Altman, on behalf of American Vegetarians, explained that a diet without meat provides adequate nutrition. Hershaft testified on the scientific evidence that a meat-based diet plays a significant role in the development of heart disease, cancer, and other diseases. Robert Rodale, publisher of Organic Gardening, testified that it was more efficient to convert soybeans directly into food rather than using them as feed for food animals.

In the 1970s, even more than today, vegetarianism was a cause promoted on many levels, from potluck dinners to politically oriented events. Dinshah and the others at NAVS organized week-long Summerfests, and in 1977 Connie Salamone did too, sponsored by the Vegetarian Recreation Committee, VIS, Metropolitan Vegetarian Association, and Salamone's

Vegetarian Activist Collective. The Vegetarian '77 Festival and Conference was held at Star Lake Center in Galilee, Pennsylvania.

Besides workshops on practical topics such as movement building, media relations, cooking, nutrition, and health, Vegetarian '77 offered workshops on "Animal Liberation: The Invisible Oppression (Speciesism)"; "Political Nutrition: The Four Food Categories in American Nutritional Charts, and How They Got That Magic 'Four' "; "Ecology & Energy: A Society Loving Mother Earth Will Be a Vegetarian One"; "History/Lifestyles: Women as Vegetarian Advocate"; "Economics: Planning a Vegetarian Meal Budget"; and "Organic Food Co-op and You."

At the time, these subjects were perceived by people outside the movement as odd, even radical. For example, this was long before America had natural food store supermarket chains or provided any organically grown foods at supermarkets.

While ecology was a topic in the news, the idea of animal liberation was considered absurd, even by most environmentalists and even some animal welfarists, when it was considered at all.

Vegetarian '77 employed the egalitarianism espoused by other movements. Therefore, provided for all at the gathering was a five-minute open mike speak-out on several topics: vegetarian generations and family traditions; ethical vegetarianism; animal rights and human obligations; and ecology and energy.

Another feature of Vegetarian '77 was Vegetarian Encounter Theatre with participants depicting situations such as "My first time in the health food store"; "I am a monkey in a laboratory"; "Deprogramming a meat-eating stranger"; "In the A&P, Main Street, USA"; "The frustration of buying vegan clothes in a store"; "Getting a fur coat and leather hat for presents"; and "I dreamt I was Ronald McDonald."

Salamone had plenty of help executing the 10-day event. Among those on hand to lecture or assist in other ways were Nat Altman, Neil Ehmke, Joy Gross, Robin Hur, Bob LeRoy, Allen Schoenfield, Ellen Spivack, Dudley Giehl, Nellie Shriver, and Jay Dinshah.

In 1978 vegetarian advocates once again lobbied lawmakers on the benefits of a plant-based diet. That year the American Association for the Advancement of Science held the "Question of Meat," which was a debate between vegetarian advocates and the meat industry. Hershaft believes that it was the first time that the issue was debated "in a balanced setting with qualified representatives for both sides of the issue."[47]

On the vegetarian side, Dr. John Scharffenberg, a professor of applied nutrition at Loma Linda University, argued that "next to tobacco and alcohol, meat is the greatest single cause of death." Jim Mason, who represented Friends of Animals, pointed out that animal agriculture was inhumane, and that a wide adaptation of a plant-based diet would help feed the hungry.

On the meat industry's side, Dr. George Mann, an associate professor of biochemistry and medicine at Vanderbilt University, said there was no direct link between meat eating and the development of cancer or other diseases. Robert Angliotti of the department of Agriculture questioned the benefits of any move away from a meat-centered diet when much of the economic system was based upon the public's demand for meat. American Meat Institute's Richard Lyng, who would later become U.S. Secretary of Agriculture, argued that the meat industry provided jobs and food that the public wanted, and that ethics were an individual choice.

Vegetarian advocates were not the only ones promoting a plant-based diet in the nation's capital. CSPI organized a Food Day event at the White House. Several high-ranking elected officials, including U.S. Senator Mark Hatfield, attended the vegetarian dinner, which featured black bean soup, broccoli nut casserole, vegetables and dip, fruit salad, and whole grain muffins.[48]

Whether Food Day succeeded in raising lawmakers' consciousness is debatable, but it sure raised the ire of cattlemen. The National Cattlemen's Association sent a telegram to then-president Jimmy Carter, calling the event bizarre and stating that the menu should be modified. The telegram stated : "The last thing we need is the president of the United States advocating a vegetarian diet for all Americans," according to the *New York Times*. Hatfield, an Oregon Republican, replied: "If one food day buffet would threaten the tradition, then we ought to question that tradition." A CSPI spokesman told the *Times* that he believed that "meat has a place in the American diet, but a much smaller piece than it currently occupies."

The decade closed with another top advocate making a case for not eating meat. Jim Mason and Peter Singer's *Animal Factories* (Crown, 1980) grabbed a share of media attention—bringing disturbing images of animals in crates and cages into the living rooms of millions of Americans, thus providing more power to animals rights activists' and vegetarian advocates' arguments that the vast majority of cows, pigs, and chickens raised for the American dinner table no longer lived the Norman Rockwell-like farm existence depicted in ads for animal products.

The issue of animal rights was becoming increasingly prevalent in vegetarian advocacy, giving it new strength and momentum. Vegetarianism was about to reap a harvest like it had never seen before.

Chapter 10

Vegetarianism Has Arrived

The new decade began, and vegetarianism was on the verge of blossoming. Ground planted and cultivated during the 1960s and 1970s was sprouting new forces for cultural change.

At the start of the 1980s, mainstream America was still largely unfamiliar with vegetarianism. However, change was under way, and the work of the advocates of the previous decades would result in people realizing that entrées other than sirloin, shrimp, fish fillets, and chicken cutlets existed, even if they were not about to eat them themselves.

A large percentage of the population became aware of vegetarianism, even if just in a peripheral way. They learned of it from a number of sources, some reported accurately, while others perpetuated stereotypes and misconceptions. For example, some had read or had heard of *Diet for a Small Planet* and its argument about the inefficiency of using land to raise animals for slaughter, along with its emphasis on the supposed inferiority of protein from plants in comparison with animal-derived sources. Other people, more interested in cuisine than economics or ecology, purchased popular vegetarian cookbooks like *Moosewood* or *Laurel's Kitchen*. Still others learned about vegetarianism from leaflets on health, hunger, or animal liberation found at health food stores. Then there were those people who read *Animal Liberation* or other books describing factory farming, which presented a strong case for passing on the meat entree.

Many more people became aware of vegetarianism from reading one or more magazine or newspaper articles on the topic. It can be assumed that a great many people read of it in one of several columns popular *Washing-*

ton Post columnist Colman McCarthy wrote on vegetarianism, farmed animals, and other related topics.

Word was getting out. But a 1980 Thanksgiving column by McCarthy revealed just how many miles the movement had yet to travel to change public perception of cuisine without meat. Stereotypes of vegetarians—what they ate, who they were as people—remained stiffly in place, prompting McCarthy to quip, only half in jest, "Meat-eaters, equate vegetarianism with starvation. They think it's all sunflower seeds, garbanzo beans, and tofu, and if we lose control of ourselves, we mulch it with brewer's yeast."

This was not such a problem in places like New York City and San Francisco, where vegetarian food was beginning to be trendy. But in the small cities, suburbs, and rural towns of America, it was still the Dark Ages for vegetarianism. It was as if the golden age of the early twentieth century had never occurred, so bereft of knowledge of vegetarianism was most of the United States. Countercultural ideas about eating, however, were still seeping into the mainstream. Yet, the prospect of Americans changing their eating habits must have seemed like an impossible quest to many advocates of vegetarianism at that time.

This new decade of the 1980s seemed on the surface the antithesis of the 1960s and 1970s counterculture. It featured Ronald Reagan conservatism, corporate raiders, cordless phones, personal computers, and hit television shows such as *Dallas* and *Dynasty*, which celebrated wealth and other materialistic values. The often-heard slogan "Greed is good," a line from the hit movie *Wall Street,* seemed to characterize the era. The decade ushered in such trends as designer brands for the middle class and gourmet cooking by celebrity chefs who were more inclined to whip up liver pâté than lentil loaf.

The 1980s introduced the nation to *MTV,* Madonna, Morton Downey, Jr., and the mainstreaming of pornography. It was also a decade when public relations and advertising industries were using shock value and celebrities to sell goods and services, including more meat.

At first glance, the situation might have looked grim for vegetarianism. Nellie Shriver's televised public service announcement (PSA) linking vegetarianism with Gandhi, da Vinci, and other great minds, an ad that generated thousands of inquiries to her *American Vegetarians* during the seventies, was in the past. Talk of collectives, communes, and the counterculture, except as food for stand-up comics' monologs on late-night television, was also gone.

Although sales of beef slumped, sales of chicken soared. Other entrees, especially ethnic cuisine, traditionally prepared with vegetables or grains, and a much smaller portion of meat than Americans typically were accustomed to, or none at all, started to increase in demand, even though people were still consuming plenty of meat. Interest in vegetarianism was

Ingrid Newkirk: PETA's cofounder and leader.
Used with permission from PETA.

increasing, but the number of animals slaughtered annually was also rising, as was the number of people who developed dietary-related disease
such as cardiovascular disease and certain forms of cancer.

However, a growing undercurrent of concern about cholesterol, environmental destruction, and animal liberation ran concurrent in the nation
with interest in comedy clubs, video games, and nouvelle cuisine. As a
result of the crass, even vulgar, tactics used by advertisers and others in
the media during the 1980s, vegetarian advocacy changed. Although
grassroots groups and individuals still organized public potluck dinners,
lectures, and other events to promote the cause, a national animal rights
organization became the leading promoter. It promoted vegetarianism
using a combination of sixties' counterculture street theatre and slick, sexy
media techniques—a sort of Abby Hoffman-style irreverent activism combined with girlie magazine and horror movie shock value.

Vegetarianism would get attention, even if it meant offending some
people. The methods used by 1970s and 1980s advocates of vegetarianism
were worlds apart, but the underlying message was the same: what you
eat affects animals, the Earth, and humanity, as well as your own health.

The time was right for the emergence of People for the Ethical Treatment of Animals (PETA, pronounced pē-ta), an organization that used sometimes outrageous, sometimes silly methods to convince the public of their serious message that "Animals are not ours to eat, wear, experiment on, or use for entertainment."

PETA was founded in 1980 by Ingrid Newkirk and Alex Pacheco and made headlines after exposing filthy and cruel conditions in a primate laboratory in Silver Spring, Maryland, a case that eventually went all the way to the consideration of the Supreme Court of the United States.

Before cofounding PETA, Alex Pacheco was a member of the Sea Shepards, an organization renowned for protecting sea animals. Pacheco had become a vegetarian, and then a vegan, after touring a very large slaughterhouse. He recalled the cries and screams of the animals and the river of blood that covered the slaughterhouse floor. A man who says he was a fan of action and war movies "the bloodier the better," Pacheco said that he had "walked through this living nightmare."[1]

One of PETA's first major protests on behalf of farmed animals occurred outside of a Washington, D.C., chicken slaughterhouse.[2] The local media ridiculed the effort, but it became the talk of the town. "They couldn't believe that anyone cared about chickens. But we couldn't go anywhere in the Capital without hearing people talk about the protest," recalled Newkirk, who was on her way to becoming one of the most important figures in vegetarian—and animal rights—history.[3]

The slaughterhouse protest "ignited a spark," said Newkirk. Animal rights gave vegetarian advocacy "the jolt it needed."[4]

PETA brought the graphic details of factory farming and slaughter out of the shadows and into the light of public scrutiny. Objecting to the slaughter of animals was not new for vegetarians, but PETA did it on a scale never before seen. Part of the organization's method was to grab the attention of the public, and their leaflet *Factory Farming: Mechanized Madness*, which was widely distributed by activists in every state, did just that.[5]

The leaflet revealed facts such as that five to six chickens, kept in cages the size of a folded newspaper, "are severely crowded, they are kept in semi-darkness and their beaks are cut off with hot irons (without anesthetics) to keep them from pecking each other to death. The wire mesh of the cages rubs their feathers off, chafes their skin, and cripples their feet."

Pigs were no better off, according to the leaflet, since nearly all of them in the nation are kept closely confined at some point, or for their entire lives. The females, called sows, "are kept pregnant or nursing constantly and are squeezed into narrow metal 'iron maiden' stalls, unable to turn around. Although pigs are naturally peaceful and social animals, they resort to cannibalism and tail biting when packed into crowded pens and develop neurotic behaviors when kept isolated and confined."

Cattle and their calves, too, lived anything but bucolic lives for people to have meat and milk, PETA told whoever cared to know, and those who did not want to know. "They are castrated, de-horned, and branded without anesthetics. During transportation, cattle are crowded into metal trucks where they suffer from fear, injury, temperature extremes, and lack of food, water, and veterinary care." The young females became biological milk machines, kept pregnant and hooked to machines, while the males were sent to the veal factory where "Taken from their mothers only a few days after birth, they are chained in stalls only 22 inches wide with slatted floors that cause severe leg and joint pain. Since their mothers' milk is usurped for human consumption, they are fed a milk substitute laced with hormones but deprived of iron: anemia keeps their flesh pale and tender but makes the calves very weak. When they are slaughtered at the age of about 16 weeks, they are often too sick or crippled to walk."

Activists passed out leaflets containing this disturbing information, and they also distributed PETA's publications promoting the benefits of veganism, including healthful, appealing recipes and practical information on becoming a vegan.

People for the Ethical Treatment of Animals decided that the facts about factory farming needed to be disseminated much more widely, and through the use of creative campaigns—that is, campaigns in tune with the times that would attract attention, even if that meant offending some people's sensibilities to get out the message of animal liberation. From the start Newkirk and PETA created controversy with campaigns featuring slogans like "Did your Food Have a Face?" The bold slogan was accompanied by even bolder graphics: a living calf, and a baby pig, sandwiched between two slices of bread.

PETA leader Newkirk, now the sole leader since Pacheco retired from the organization after 20-plus years, believes that the popularity of animal rights revived vegetarianism in America, propelling it into the mainstream. "Vegetarianism was just little meetings of health vegetarians who were by and large not activists. The infusion of animal rights activism did an awful lot of good."

Soon after its founding, PETA began placing its slogans and graphics on eye-catching posters, placards, T-shirts, and other displays designed in a young, trendy style. Some of the most controversial PETA campaigns have featured scantily clad young women, including a few celebrities. "People want blue jeans, rock 'n' roll, and beer. Maybe we can sell vegetarianism the same way," says Newkirk, explaining the organization's activist style.

British-born Ingrid Newkirk was called the Mother Teresa of Rabbits by *Fortune* magazine, who also named her as one of "the year's most 25 fascinating business people" in 1990 for her business acumen in building her organization from a tiny grassroots concern into a powerful, international organization.[6]

Newkirk means business. Case in point: At a 1988 animal rights conference she stated that she was unhappy about talk of animal rights activists keeping a low profile and not doing things like placing the latest PETA campaign bumper stickers on their vehicles. Animal rights, stated Newkirk, "is not a tea party. It's a revolution." Her fellow activists knew what she meant: Human beings make war upon animals, and the Animal Rights movement calls for a cultural revolution in the way human beings regard other animals, and that it can only happen if people are not timid, but are assertive, about pointing out cruelty and exploitation, and in their belief in animal liberation.

In 2003 Newkirk was characterized in a magazine article as being like Malcolm X was to Dr. Martin Luther King, Jr. Newkirk is akin to King in that she strives for peace among people and animals, as he strived to bring peace among people. A more apt analogy is that Ingrid Newkirk is to the animal liberation what William Lloyd Garrison was to liberation of slaves—both crusaders have used the term *abolitionist*. Both, in describing their crusades, have used this phrase, "I do not wish to think, or speak, or write, with moderation...I am in earnest—I will not equivocate—I will not excuse—I will not retreat a single inch—AND I WILL BE HEARD."[7]

Vegetarianism, and especially veganism, is fundamental to animal liberation. Newkirk and PETA advocate veganism and for an end to the use of animals. "Human beings are unthinkingly brutal towards animals. Some are doing things to make us ashamed to use the word 'civilized.' We are giving the animals a voice they do not have. By being rude and in your face, the activists are turning up the volume on abuse. You need to shake people up a little bit to get people to pay attention," she told the press.

Shaking up the public and being "in your face" attracts critics and animosity, something PETA has often used to their advantage. For example, PETA took on the Dairy Industry's "Got Milk?" popular advertising campaign, which depicted celebrities sporting milk moustaches. PETA crafted a parody campaign featuring Rudolph Giuliani, who was not a willing participant in the campaign, and who was then the mayor of New York City mayor, and who had been diagnosed with prostate cancer.

The parody ad, which featured a photo of the mayor with a milk moustache, and was accompanied by the slogan "Got prostate cancer?" caused an uproar. Giuliani fought back by holding a press conference where he drank two glasses of milk. Before PETA pulled the ads, their mission was accomplished. The controversy resulted in an avalanche of press stories and more than 75,000 hits to one of PETA's many Web sites: www.dumpdairy.com. Newkirk called the campaign hugely successful.

PETA again challenged the cultural tide when it took on the McDonald's fast food restaurant chain with its Unhappy Meal campaign. It was a take off on the burger giant's famous children's Happy Meals, which featured a cardboard lunchbox, brightly decorated with an image of clown

Ronald McDonald and typically filled with a hamburger, French fries, and dessert. According to Newkirk, the fast food giant fails to give an accurate account to children of how animals it turns into meat are treated. The Unhappy Meal box was designed to look like the Happy Meal box—with a difference: it contained a Ronald McDonald figure dressed as a blood-drenched butcher who had slaughtered some tiny toy animals in the lunchbox, whose throats had been slit.

Crusaders of PETA were not the only ones using attention-grabbing promotional tactics in the 1980s. The Farm Animal Reform Movement (FARM) in 1985 established the Great American Meatout, an event held annually on the first day of Spring (March 20) to urge Americans to "kick the meat habit, at least for a day, and explore a more wholesome, less violent diet." FARM, founded by Alex Hershaft in 1981, enlisted television game show host Bob Barker to serve as chairman of the event the first year. Barker's name gave credibility to the fledgling campaign.

Fashioned after the Great American Smokeout, an annual day when people are encouraged to quit smoking, each Meatout features advocates across the nation handing out recipes and leaflets, giving food demonstrations at supermarkets, festivals, and other public events, and urging mayors to sign Meatout proclamations. In 1987 McCarthy devoted his column to the day and stated that meat eating was more lethal than smoking tobacco.[8]

Clearly, the American public was learning about vegetarianism, whether they wanted to or not. But public perception was slow to change. Peter Burwash, a professional tennis star in the 1960s and 1970s, knew this fact all too well. "There is an illusion surrounding vegetarianism, a wall of ignorance, that is centuries thick. I like to call it the 'myth of vegetarianism.' " Meat eaters think vegetarians "are a bunch of scrawny weirdos who carry around bags of nuts and eats lots of seaweed—in a word "health nuts," said Burwash. In fact, Burwash, who was frequently featured in *Vegetarian Times* and *Vegetarian World,* admitted that he had once believed vegetarians were "scrawny know-it-alls."[9]

Burwash's description of the depiction of vegetarians was not far removed from a description by John Harvey Kellogg, in 1900. "Vegetarians are sometimes pointed out, less frequently now than formerly, as being just a little 'short' intellectually, and many people who are not personally acquainted with those who abstain from the use of flesh expect to find the typical vegetarian a pale-faced, weazened-looking individual, wearing his hair long, and parting his name, as well as his hair, in the middle, signing himself 'J. Jonathan Jones, V.E.' (vegetable eater)."

Kellogg thought it would not be inappropriate for meat eaters to be labeled "pigarians." He also wrote:

Those who ridicule vegetarianism and vegetarians evidently do so without an intelligent view of the thing which they make the butt of their scoffing. Vegetari-

anism is not a fad or a fancy: it is no sense a dietetic novelty.... From the stand-
point of common sense, whose bill of fare is most worthy of approval—that of a
man who prefers to eat his corn, wheat, and other comestibles just as they come
from the hand of the Creator, bread from heaven direct; or that man who first feeds
these sweet, pure, heaven-born foods to a scavenger, a wallowing-hog, and after
he has rolled them around in the mud for six months or more, then brutally kills
the hog; and in gnawing his bones only gets back a small fragment of the original
food, perhaps one twentieth, and that in a deteriorated and polluted form?[10]

One of the ways that advocates of vegetarianism were in the 1980s trying to dispel stereotypes was by showing films that would appeal to a
mainstream audience. Two documentaries produced in the era became a
popular tool for promoting vegetarianism: *Healthy, Wealthy, and Wise*, produced by the International Society of Krishna Consciousness, and *The Vegetarian World*.

The latter film presented archival film footage of three outstanding representatives of the millions who did not eat meat: Count Leo Tolstoy, the
novelist-turned philosopher and Christian; George Bernard Shaw, the
witty playwright who was also renowned as an antivivisectionist, anti-
vaccinationist, and vegetarian; and Mohandas Gandhi, the Indian leader
who used nonviolence (ahimsa) to free his people. The film showed Shaw
quipping that "Animals are my friends...and I don't eat my friends," and
Gandhi saying, "The greatness of a nation in its moral progress can be
judged by the way its animals are treated."

The *Vegetarian World* was hosted by actor William Shatner, who was best
known for his role as Captain Kirk in television's *Star Trek*, a science fiction
series set hundreds of years into the future. At least one episode of the
original series had portrayed meat eating as a barbaric relic of the past. In
one episode of *The Next Generation*, the Trek series that aired 20 years after
the original, First Officer William Riker revealed that human beings no
longer slaughtered animals for food. Meanwhile, in real life, PETA,
FARM, and other organizations were providing Americans with facts
about animal slaughter and human health and diet.

The health system of natural hygiene that was championed by Herbert
Shelton received phenomenal publicity in 1985 with the publication of *Fit
for Life*.

Shelton died that year, but he had, along with grassroots natural
hygiene groups and the national organization American Natural Hygiene
Society, tried to keep the flames of the movement lit over the decades, yet
most people had never heard of natural hygiene. That is, until *Fit for Life*
was published. The book presented a vegetarian, natural hygiene regimen, though it did contain some meat recipes. Sales of the book topped
two million and it remained on the *New York Times* bestseller list for about
a year.

Harvey and Marilyn Diamond, the authors, became celebrities but were widely attacked by doctors and dietitians in the press. A story in the *Times* called them "graduates of unaccredited correspondence schools" and their advice "filled with inaccuracies." The couple appeared on nationally televised programs such as ABC-TV's *Nightline,* and were guests on television shows such as *Merv Griffin, Phil Donahue,* and *Hour Magazine.* Merv Griffin, in particular, helped boost sales of the book since he had worked successfully with the program.

The *Fit for Life* regimen follows vegan dietary principles pioneered by Graham, Jackson, and Trall. The Diamonds had been students of natural hygienist T.C. Fry, Dean of the American College of Health Science in Austin, Texas. Their regimen consisted of eating only fruits in the morning and other unprocessed foods from the plant kingdom for lunch and dinner, with no dairy products. Meat was not mentioned in the plan.[11]

The Diamonds, who credited past natural hygiene advocates, explained in a *Vegetarian Times* interview that by including a few meat recipes that they hoped to reach many more readers than if the book had been labeled as a vegetarian book.[12]

CRUSADE FOR THE ENVIRONMENT

The purity of the diet was a concern for vegetarians, and so was the purity of the environment.

While the Diamonds were pitching their book and ringing up sales, John Robbins was walking away from a multimillion-dollar fortune and the prestige that comes with running an international company. Robbins, who was the heir to the Baskin-Robbins ice cream empire, decided to teach people that eating products derived from animals was not a good idea.

Robbins not only gave up his claim to Baskin-Robbins, but in 1987 he took on the very industry that had provided fortune and fame for his family. That was the year his book, *Diet for a New America,* made it to the bookshelves. *Diet* gave compelling economic, environmental, and animal rights arguments for vegetarianism and veganism.

In *Diet,* Robbins decried what he calls the Great American Food Machine for keeping Americans in the dark about the health and the environmental consequences of meat eating, and he provided a first-hand account of how animals are raised and slaughtered for food. The book featured statistics to fortify Robbin's arguments. For example: one acre of land could yield up to 20,000 pounds of potatoes but only 165 pounds of beef; 75 percent of the nation's topsoil has been lost, the vast majority of it due to livestock raising; and the nation's water supply was threatened by the meat industry that drank up more than its share, were some of the statistics and facts, which were later summarized into a widely distributed booklet titled *Realities.*

Raised in a mansion that had an ice-cream cone shaped swimming pool, John Robbins became a vegetarian while he was enrolled at the University of California at Berkeley in the mid-1960s, where he participated in student peace demonstrations. The most immediate connection to the violence that he abhorred was the violence done to animals condemned and killed for the dinner table. "The Vietnam War made me very aware of the violence and destruction in our world. I wanted my life to be a testimony of different values. How can I live in a different way? The clearest was to stop eating animals," he said.

Robbins, who has made several appearances on television talk shows such as *Donahue,* and who has said he will not tell people what to eat, used a more subdued approach to educating the public than many of his contemporaries. Robbins summed up his approach: "There is no need to attack the people who produce beef or to depreciate the labor of anyone who works to feed others. I have very strong feelings you don't fight violence with violence."[13]

A documentary based on his book was broadcast by a California public television station in 1991. *Diet for a New America: Your Health, Your Planet* featured T. Colin Campbell, John McDougall, M.D., and Michael Klaper, M.D., medical authorities who discussed the health and environmental ramifications of a meat-based diet. The documentary video also aired in several other cities, such as Seattle and San Francisco.

Klaper, who helped with the documentary, teaches vegetarian nutrition to doctors across America through his Institute of Nutrition Education and Research, based in Manhattan Beach, California. Dr. Klaper, a popular and influential figure in the vegetarian movement, and an expert on vegan nutrition, also lectures on the environmental implications of animal-based agriculture, which he says also have an effect on human health. Outspoken in his scientifically, environmentally, and ethically based belief in veganism, ironically, Klaper grew up on a dairy farm. Known for his wit and expertise, he has quipped in his lectures that "the human body has absolutely no requirement for animal flesh. Nobody has ever been found face-down 20 yards from the Burger King because they couldn't get their Whopper in time."

The meat and dairy industries at the time were facing changing consumer habits—annual beef consumption declined about 12 pounds per person from 1986 to 1990. Robbins was not the only one sounding the environmental alarm on meat eating. Another wake-up call rang in 1992 with the publication of *Beyond Beef.* The book, written by Jeremy Rifken, warned of the tremendous environmental consequences of the world's ever increasing appetite for beef. *Beyond Beef* took a more global approach than *Diet for a New America,* and alerted readers to what many believe is the livestock industry's role in the increasing desertification of not only the Western United States, but also of Africa and Australia, and the destruction of South American rainforest. Rifkin's book also traces the history of cattle-raising, including the cowboy image, and how it became an icon in the Western world.[14]

The book was at the forefront of an international campaign by Rifken and his Washington, D.C.-based organization, Beyond Beef, to cut world-wide beef consumption by one-half by the year 2000. Rifken formed a coalition of environmental, animal rights, and vegetarian groups to help with the campaign, which took place in 17 countries.

The campaign generated a frenzy of coverage by hundreds of major magazines and newspapers, including *Time, Newsweek, USA Today, The New York Times, Esquire, Publisher's Weekly* and the *Chicago Sun-Times.* Popular television shows such as *The Today Show* and the *Cable News Network* (CNN) gave the campaign air time.

Television stations aired a public service announcement that featured a photo series of cattle herds alternating between images of overweight people eating beef, starving people, open heart surgery, and rainforest trees being cut down. The *Beyond Beef* campaign also placed full-page ads in major newspapers.

The beef industry swiftly responded to the campaign by forming the Food Facts Coalition of industry groups, including the American Meat Institute and The National Live Stock and Meat Board. The coalition dubbed their opposition "Beyond Belief" and placed their own full-page ads in the *New York Times,* depicting cattle as "Mother Nature's recycling machines" and U.S. cattlemen as "America's original conservationists."

The goal of the *Beyond Beef* campaign was to reduce worldwide beef consumption by one half, but it failed. However, Rifken succeeded in raising the vegetarian-environmental consciousness another notch, even if the notch was small.

DOES AN ENVIRONMENTALIST EAT MEAT?

Some environmental groups have agreed with the premise that animal agriculture threatens the environment. Generally, they don't dispute the evidence that was popularized by Lappé, Robbins, and others. But they have been reluctant to recommend vegetarianism or "eating low on the food chain" to members.

Environmental groups treated it as a side issue, choosing instead to concentrate on educating their members on ecosystem destruction, source pollution, endangered species, and advocating solutions such as stricter government regulations.

The fear: advocate vegetarianism, and you'll turn off most of your members. Convincing people to recycle bottles and newspapers is one thing, but convincing them to drop meat from their diet is another. Environmentalists quoted in a 1991 *Vegetarian Times* story believed that their members can only handle so much.

From the vegetarian point of view, mainstream environmentalists had either sold out, or failed to get the message that meat poses a menace to the planet. Organized events like Earth Day, which had grown enormously in acceptance and participation since the first was held in 1970, were now in some cases sponsored by corporations, some of which even sold meat.

Vegetarians cringe when some environmentalists state that raising animals for food doesn't do much to harm the environment. However, there was dissent among the membership of the Sierra Club when some initiated a referendum in 1997 to place vegetarianism into the organization's creed, but the effort failed.

It had been long clear to vegetarian advocates that there was a need for an environmentally aware organization to offer an alternative to the typical American diet dependent on large-scale animal-based agriculture. The void was filled when John Robbins founded EarthSave in 1989. After receiving tens of thousands of letters following the publication of *Diet*, Robbins founded EarthSave in 1989 to give people information on how they could improve their health and help halt environmental destruction by choosing a plant-based diet. The California-based organization over the years added almost three dozen chapters and branches across the United States and in Canada, Australia, and Germany.

One of EarthSave's achievements was placing a full-page ad in the *New York Times* on June 18, 1989. It was titled "How to Win an Argument With a Meat Eater" and featured an illustration of a Tyrannosaurus Rex with a knife in one hand and a fork in the other. The text of the ad presented several arguments for vegetarianism—hunger, environment, cancer, cholesterol, natural resources, antibiotic, pesticide, ethical, and the survival argument—that were taken from *Diet for a New America*. "How to win an Argument With a Meat Eater" was also reprinted as a flyer.[15]

Modern vegetarians, like those of the nineteenth century, connected animal-based agriculture with environmental consequences. Some share other similarities to Victorian-era advocates of abstinence; among both eras of vegetarians were ties to the peace movement and to women's liberation.

A prominent promoter of peace and women's rights among renowned vegetarians is award-winning writer Colman McCarthy, who, in 1985 with his wife, Mavoureen, founded the Center for Teaching Peace. The curriculum, taught to high school and college students, includes lessons on the world's peacemakers, facts on why vegetarianism (veganism) is a form of peacemaking, and a rejection of violence.

Vegetarians today are a diverse population with diverse beliefs, including on non-violence. McCarthy, like nineteenth century vegetarians had, connects all forms of non-violence: "Too many people in the antiwar movement focus only on decreasing wars among nations, while ignoring the daily and murderous violence inflicted on animals. Little good is accomplished by going to an antiwar march and then coming home to a meal of slaughtered animal," McCarthy said.[16]

During his several decades with the *Washington Post* and writing for other publications, McCarthy has addressed a wide variety of topics of concern to vegetarians. He wrote about *The Sexual Politics of Meat*, a 1990 book by Carol J. Adams that introduced the term *absent referent*, meaning meat eaters don't think about the fact that the meat they eat is the remains of a butchered animal. The *Sexual Politics of Meat* integrated literary theory into feminism and vegetarianism. *Ms* magazine hailed it as a "powerful" book that might influence readers to become vegetarians. Adams was not the first to recognize patriarchal society tends toward exploitation and violence against animals and women, treating both as "pieces of meat"; however, her book was a pioneering and influential work that McCarthy believed broke "new ground...whole acres of it."[17]

Another vegetarian who has brought vital information on eschewing meat to readers is journalist Corydon Ireland, whose "Against the Grain" column is featured in Gannett newspapers. Word was getting out.

BATTLE IN THE HEARTLAND

When the calendar changed from 1989 to 1990 more than just a new decade began—a new age of invigorated vegetarian advocacy was born.

People for the Ethical Treatment of Animals emerged as an increasingly strong force for vegetarianism and veganism. Under the leadership of Newkirk and Pacheco, the organization had grown by 1990 to 325,000 members and a budget of $8 million. "Ten years ago I used to say our efforts for animal rights were like bubbles in a pot...(now) the pot is really starting to boil," stated Newkirk in *People Weekly* magazine.[18] Synonymous with bold activism, the organization and its often sensational tactics were largely responsible for bringing the ethical aspect of vegetarianism into public discussion.[19]

Such discussion was not pleasing to every one. "Vegetarians, once a fairly passive population, have grown fangs. They've become outspoken, some would say strident, railing against the clogged arteries of a gluttonous nation, the massive exploitation of animals, and the looming destruction of the environment," stated *USA Today*. Robin Walker, PETA vegetarian Campaign Coordinator, told the paper that her organization "hoped for a meat-free America."[20]

In 1990 PETA hired singing star k.d. lang as a spokesperson for their ongoing "Meat Stinks" campaign. lang appeared in a television commercial in which she had her arms wrapped around a cow named Lulu and said: "We all love animals. But why do we call some of them pets and some of them dinner? If you knew how meat was made, you would prob-

Did your food have a face?: Popular vegetarian slogan of the late twentieth century. Used with permission from PETA.

ably lose your lunch. I'm from cattle country—that's why I'm a vegetarian. Meat stinks, and not just for animals, but for human health and the environment."[21]

A preview of the commercial aired on the popular television show *Entertainment Tonight* after PETA invited them for a taping. The commercial, which Ingrid Newkirk called too "hard hitting," never aired. But the preview reaped a bonanza for PETA: millions of viewers saw the preview at a millionth of the cost it would have been if they had to pay a network to run the ad, she said.

The commercial, however, did not go over well in America's heartland. Dozens of radio stations in Oklahoma, Kansas, Missouri, and Nebraska, bowing to pressure from cattlemen, refused to play lang's songs. A station program director told the media that they didn't care if k.d. lang is a vegetarian, but that her "meat stinks" campaign hurts everyone who lives in the area.

A spokesperson for the National Cattleman's Association said that cattlemen do not oppose vegetarians, but "when people like k.d. lang use their public position to put out unjustified false claims, then we must respond." The beef industry at the time could have been concerned about declining beef consumption and trying to recover from bad publicity generated by celebrities who appeared in the Beef Council's 1987–1988 ad campaign. One of them, actor James Garner, had quadruple bypass surgery, and another, actress Cybill Shepard, said in a media interview that one of her beauty secrets was that she didn't eat meat.

The battle heated up when PETA enlisted rock star Chrissie Hynde of the Pretenders and ex-Beatle Paul McCartney and his wife, Linda. The McCartneys, veteran animal rights, vegetarian, and environmental activists, recorded phone messages for PETA campaigns and allowed the organization to set up exhibits at their concerts.

Meat producers were not happy, and they greeted McCartney in the summer of 1990 when he arrived in Ames, Iowa, for a concert.[22] They handed out leaflets comparing the rock 'n' roll legend to Adolf Hitler, erroneously said to be a vegetarian. McCartney told the press "I'm very pro-corn," while Hynde said "they'd have to put a gun to my head and pull the trigger" to stop her from promoting vegetarianism.

Whatever the methods, outrageous or pragmatic, promotion of vegetarianism was having an earth-shaking effect. The National Restaurant Association reported to the press results of a survey: one in five restaurant patrons now preferred a vegetarian entrée.

THE SCIENTIFIC EVIDENCE

The decade of the 1990s also began with a flood of scientific evidence supporting vegan diets. That year, the press reported that scientists had succeeded in reversing severe heart disease, the leading killer of Americans, without the aid of drugs or surgery. "People with blocked coronary arteries who adhere to a strict vegetarian diet, engage in mild exercise and practice stress reduction can reverse the blockage," reported the *Times*.[23]

This prescription might seem to have originated in the nineteenth century from Dr. Caleb Jackson's *Our Home on the Hillside*, but it was the work of Dr. Dean Ornish, M.D., a California internist. Ornish in the late 1980s enlisted volunteers suffering from severe heart disease for a study and brought them to his Preventive Medicine Research Institute in California. The study, Lifestyle Heart Trial, also had help from researchers at the University of California at San Francisco, and the University of Texas Medical School.

Patients in the experimental group were put on a vegetarian diet that reduced fat intake to 10 percent of total calories—a significant decrease from the 30 percent recommended by the American Heart Association and a level that's nearly impossible to reach with meat in the diet. They also meditated, practiced some yoga techniques, and exercised daily. Patients in the control group were put on the AHA's 30 percent diet.

The year-long study ended with 18 of the 22 patients in the experimental group showing unclogged arteries and no chest pains, while the patients in the control group experienced increased blockage and more pain. The results were published in *The Lancet*, and similar studies done by Ornish a few years later, with similar results, were reported in the *Journal of the American Medical Association.* Ornish told the press that a 30 percent fat diet might help prevent heart disease in some people, but it might fall short in reversing the condition.

In 1993 Mutual of Omaha, a large insurance company, began funding additional studies and established the program as a health plan benefit to members. Ornish's program, which was available at his Preventive Medicine Research Institute and at some hospitals at a cost of $3,500 a year, was about one-tenth of the tab for conventional coronary care such as angioplasty. Ornish's book *Dr. Dean Ornish's Program for Reversing Heart Disease* (Random House, 1990) became a best seller.[24]

The year 1990 turned out to be a good one for positive news about vegetarianism. While word was spreading about Ornish's work, T. Colin Campbell released the results of the China-Cornell study, a landmark epidemiological study that verified the health benefits of a plant-based diet. It was widely-credited with being the most comprehensive study ever done on the link between diet and disease. *New York Times* writer Jane Brody called it the Grand Prix of epidemiological studies.[25]

The study, which was established in 1983 by University of Cornell biochemist T. Colin Campbell and a team of scientists from Oxford University and China, examined the diets of 6,500 people from 65 largely rural counties in China. The study reported that diseases such as diabetes, osteoporosis, heart disease, and some cancers such as breast and colon cancer were rare or virtually nonexistent among Chinese who ate little or no meat or milk. China-Cornell gave vegetarianism additional scientific credibility, and Campbell told the press that human beings are a vegetarian species.[26]

Other high-profile studies were favorable to vegetarianism, particularly the Framingham Heart Study, which was established in Massachusetts in 1949. William Castelli, M.D., former director of the study, told the media: "We've never had a heart attack in Framingham in 35 years in anyone who had a cholesterol level under 150." The average cholesterol level in Americans at the end of the twentieth century was 205, and 244 in heart attack victims. Castelli also said: "Diets are like the Sears catalog—there's good, better and best, and vegetarianism is best."[27]

Science confirming the health benefits of vegetarianism and veganism continued making headlines the following year as a group of physicians

Neal Barnard, M.D.: Founder and head of PCRM.

attacked the Four Food Groups, the federal government-issued set of eating guidelines that were widely followed for decades. Neal Barnard, M.D., and his organization, the Washington, D.C.-based Physicians Committee for Responsible Medicine, unveiled their New Four Food Groups on April 8, 1991.

Barnard, at a press conference, called for the U.S. Department of Agriculture to revise its long-time four food groupings and relegate meat and dairy to optional status, leaving whole grains, vegetables, legumes, and fruits. He had based this announcement on decades of dietary studies, published in medical journals, which had verified the power of a plant-based diet to prevent, and in some cases reverse, leading killer diseases such as cancer. PCRM's dietary recommendations were a drastic departure from the milk and dairy-laden four food groups that had dominated nutritional advice for the previous four decades and were political.

But Barnard did not go out on this dietary limb alone. He was joined by T. Colin Campbell, Ph.D.; oncologist Dr. Oliver Alabaster, cancer specialist at George Washington University; and Denis Burkitt, M.D., the world-renowned British physician widely credited with discovering the link between a deficiency of fiber in the diet and colon cancer. Burkitt, who Barnard credits as an influence, helped prove what Sylvester Graham had proclaimed about fiber more than 100 years earlier—that it is essential in the human diet.

The doctors' message to the public was that the typical Western diet, high in fat and animal protein, and low in fiber, leads to increased risks of cancer, heart disease, obesity, diabetes, and osteoporosis. Cut meat and dairy from the diet, and these risks are drastically reduced, they said. The recommendation was based on decades of studies from medical journals of the human diet proving the health benefits of vegan foods and demonstrating the detrimental effects associated with meat eating.

The announcement of the New Four Food Groups came just days after the U.S. Department of Agriculture's introduction of the Food Pyramid. But the pyramid eating guide was withdrawn after complaints from the meat and dairy industry. The USDA's Food Pyramid was released in 1992 after revisions. In the final version, the pictorial representations of the meat and dairy groups were slightly altered. The graphics for these groups were slightly enlarged, and the serving recommendations were placed outside of the pyramid. Vegetarians and some nonvegetarian nutrition experts believe that these industries tainted the USDA recommendations.

Neal Barnard was raised in North Dakota. Some members of his family were doctors and others cattle ranchers. Barnard recalled an experience while working as an assistant in a morgue—an experience that propelled him on a path to vegetarianism. "One day I had to prepare a cadaver for examination. This was a heart attack victim. I cut in and removed a section of ribs. Then the mortician opened the heart, and the arteries were clogged with fatty deposits. Later, I went upstairs for lunch and in the hospital cafeteria they were serving ribs. The sight of those ribs was so similar to the section of human ribs I had just handled that I just couldn't eat them."[28]

Barnard and PCRM continued to advocate their New Food Groups, even after a member of The American Medical Association responded in the press by calling the groups irresponsible and absurd. Ironically, Barnard drew upon dietary studies that were published in prestigious medical journals. In 2004, the AMA would take back its accusations.

Past advocates of vegetarianism such as William Alcott and John Harvey Kellogg did not mince words. Neither does Neal Barnard. "The meat industry has long tried to dictate what America should eat. When the U.S. Department of Agriculture (USDA) unveiled the first 'food pyramid' in 1991, cattlemen objected to its seemingly small section allotted to meat and actually managed to have the graphic withdrawn. After being held hostage in back rooms at the USDA, the Food Guide Pyramid as we know it today slinked cautiously back into view a year later," stated Barnard.[29]

Suzanne Havala: Top dietitian and author. Courtesy
of Suzanne Havala Hobbs.

Some other experts on nutrition, that is, those not associated with vegetarianism, have expressed similar concerns. One is Marion Nestle, a
highly regarded expert who managed the editorial production of the Surgeon General's Report on Nutrition and Health and wrote about the meat
industry's connection to federal dietary guidelines in *Food Politics*. She
stated that she was instructed not to recommend eating less meat to
reduce consumption of saturated fat, nor to recommend restrictions for
other food categories.[30]

"This scenario was no paranoid fantasy...federal health officials had
endured a decade of almost constant congressional interference with their
dietary recommendations." Nestle stated the agency had to put a "positive spin to any restrictive advice about food." For example, a suggestion
to eat less beef would raise the ire of the industry, but eating less saturated
fat would not.

A year after the food pyramid controversy, Physicians Committee for
Responsible Medicine once again made headlines. This time around, Dr.
Barnard took on the dairy industry. If meat eating is perceived as an

American tradition, then milk drinking is more a patriotic duty, at least it seemed so the way the media reacted with swift and opinionated response to Barnard's message. At a press conference in late September of 1992, Barnard was joined by Benjamin Spock, M.D, the beloved and influential pediatrician, author of *Baby and Child Care*, and political activist; Dr. Frank Oski, director of pediatrics at Johns Hopkins University in Baltimore, and author of *Don't Drink Your Milk*; and Suzanne Havala, R.D., the coauthor of the *American Dietetic Association's Position Paper on Vegetarianism*. The doctors and the dietician urged parents to stop giving their children cow's milk, and the media erupted like a volcano.

Barnard said that the fat, protein, and sugar in milk is unnecessary and can cause health problems. Cow's milk should not be given to children, nor should it be included in nutrition programs for poor children, or in school lunches, he said.

The doctor and his colleagues held the press conference to alert the public about a study published earlier that year in the *New England Journal of Medicine,* one that revealed a link between a protein in cow's milk and the onset of juvenile diabetes, a disease that afflicts youngsters genetically predisposed to it.

"The dairy commercials tell us milk has something for everyone," said Barnard. "But what we don't know is if that something could be iron-deficiency or allergies, even something as serious as insulin-dependent diabetes." Several milk cartons, each featuring labels such as "51 percent of calories from fat," "diabetes," and "heart disease," were placed on a table at the press conference. The photo of the conference participants and their altered milk cartons made the news around the world.[31]

The conference was held in Boston, where a century and a half earlier, in 1837, bakers and butchers reportedly mobbed health reformer Sylvester Graham at a temperance hotel for his advocacy of whole wheat over refined flour, and for recommending a vegan diet. The bakers and butchers were thwarted by Grahamites who, up on the roof of the hotel where Graham was scheduled to lecture, spilled sacks of lime and sawdust, ingredients then in store-bought bread, onto the mob below.

Barnard, as outspoken as Graham was in his day, told reporters that he intended to tell the truth about milk even if it raises the blood pressure of dairy advocates.

The doctor's statements that day apparently did more than raise their blood pressure. The AMA and dairy industry officials didn't mob him or drench him with milk, but they counterattacked with harsh criticism.

The war of words was like a tsunami that swept through the media. Most reporters and editors seemed to have taken sides against Barnard, or perhaps, rather, for cow's milk. Headlines screamed "Some doctors frown on milk; colleagues say they're all wet," and "Milk Shake-up."

The issue was the hot topic of the week. Many newspapers, including heavyweights such as the *New York Times* and the *Washington Post*, pub-

lished commentaries on the topic. PCRM's assertion that milk is unwholesome was widespread.

The message was ubiquitous, although not necessarily framed in the
most flattering words. One editorial in a major newspaper stated that "the
important thing, though, is what once was parental dogma is now open to
challenge, and what used to be called whining will now be elevated to the
status of reasoned debate." The editorial did not list PCRM's fact-based
reasoning against cow's milk for children. Instead it ended thus: "Parents
facing a resourceful and often desperate adversary may wish to counter
by serving up some items from Dr. Oski's list of calcium-rich alternatives
to milk. They include anchovies, prunes, broccoli, collard greens, kale,
mustard greens and kelp. Go heavy on the kelp and prunes—big, steam-
ing mounds—and see how the debate goes."

Largely due to public demand and by publicity generated by PCRM,
other groups and grassroots advocates, and by individual advocates,
nutritionists were recognizing that diets without meat and milk could be
healthful. In 1993 the American Dietetic Association released their *Position
Paper on Vegetarianism*, a report that listed the benefits of a plant-based
diet. It was the first time that the 70,000-member ADA officially approved
of a vegetarian diet.

Registered Dietitian Suzanne Havala, the primary writer of the paper,
had convinced the association to form a vegetarian practice group in 1988.
Havala, a vegetarian and author of several books on vegetarianism, was
certified as a charter Fellow of the American Dietetic Association, a status
granted to fewer than one percent of the ADA's membership.

For most of the twentieth century, the medical establishment had
warned Americans that a vegetarian diet, and especially a vegan diet,
could lead to nutritional deficiencies. However, such warnings waxed and
waned as time passed and scientists uncovered more evidence of the
healthfulness of vegetarian diets.

In 1995 the United States Departments of Agriculture and Health and
Human Services for the first time mentioned vegetarianism in its *The
Dietary Guidelines for Americans* (4th Ed.). The guidelines stated: "Vegetarian diets are consistent with the dietary guidelines for Americans and can
meet Recommended Dietary Allowances for nutrients."

The American Dietetic Association in its series of *Position Paper on Vegetarian Diets*, and in subsequent papers, stated that vegetarian diets are
healthful and nutritionally adequate. The 1997 paper stated: "Studies
indicate that vegetarians often have lower morbidity and mortality rates
from several chronic degenerative diseases than do non vegetarians.
Although non dietary factors, including physical activity and abstinence
from smoking and alcohol, may play a role, diet is clearly a contributing
factor."

A good number of Americans were apparently at least curious about
eating meals without meat, largely because of extensive media coverage

and the work of the grassroots as well as individual people. Vegetarian organizations were more than happy to provide information. One of them, The North American Vegetarian Society, was helping people form grassroots groups, providing literature, and offering inspiration to advocates and the public through its annual week-long Summerfests of lectures, workshops, and cooking demonstrations. The NAVS also published a magazine, *Vegetarian Voice*.

Havala has been a popular featured lecturer at Summerfests, as has Dr. Klaper, Peter Burwash, and the cofounders of the Vegetarian Resource Group. Havala, Reed Mangels, Ph.D., and Mary Clifford, R.D., have lent their expertise on nutrition to the organization, especially by writing for its periodical *Vegetarian Journal*.

The Vegetarian Resource Group (VRG) was reaching out to the public and to people in particular professions, through their magazine *Vegetarian Journal*, available on newsstands. VRG became instrumental in disseminating information about the vegetarian diet—nutrition and cuisine—to teachers, doctors, dietitians, food manufacturers, book publishers, cafeterias, and professional organizations.

Debra Wasserman, cofounder of the group, stated. "Our goal has always been to work in the mainstream with all types of professional organizations...we have been able to promote vegetarianism in a positive way and have made it easier for anyone to follow a vegetarian lifestyle whether it be when they visit a doctor's office, attend college or camp, go to a bookstore, or simply go out to eat."

The Vegetarian Resource Group was formed by Wasserman and Charles Stahler in 1982 as the Baltimore Vegetarians. Both were former members of the Vegetarian Society of the District of Columbia, an organization founded in 1927. Baltimore Vegetarians organized veggie potluck dinners and meals for the homeless, and convinced a major supermarket chain in Upstate New York to distribute some 60,000 booklets on vegetarianism to its customers.

About the time when the organization became the VRG, demand for information about vegetarianism was reaching new heights. When VRG participated in conferences for dietitians, physicians, or educators, they were so swamped with requests for information that they would run out of materials before the conferences were over, even though they had brought with them thousands of leaflets and other fact sheets.

Vegetarianism was fast streaming into society, but it still had rapids to ride.

PUTTING A FACE ON THE FOOD

Demand might have reached new heights, but Americans were digging their forks into meat at a record rate. America's per capita meat consumption was still rising. Beef consumption was declining, but poultry consumption was soaring, unlike the birds.

Like their nineteenth-century counterparts, vegetarian advocates realized that meat eating remains a habit rooted in tradition, convenience, and familiarity. If people who ate meat were motivated to contemplate what—or rather whom—they put on their plates, they might have second thoughts, reasoned advocates.

Like PETA and FARM, another animal rights organization would make a major contribution to the forwarding of vegetarianism, and veganism. Tangible evidence, that is, presenting to the public living animals, would help move people away from meat, sparing the animals, hoped Gene and Lorri Bauston, founders of Farm Sanctuary. The Baustons and the "animal ambassadors" of Farm Sanctuary, as they are known, most having been debeaked, crippled, and deformed by genetic tampering to make them have more flesh, milk, or eggs, and having been rescued from factory farming, helped to put a face on the 10 billion animals then slaughtered annually in America for their flesh.

The Baustons were thrust into the national spotlight shortly after founding Farm Sanctuary in 1986. Earlier that year, the couple had visited Lancaster stockyards in Pennsylvania, and found dead and decaying animals, and other horrors such as goats with their legs twisted and maggots everywhere. The couple, then in their early twenties, documented what they saw by taking photos. They rescued a sheep they named Hilda. Subsequent visits to other slaughterhouses yielded video footage of downed animals and filthy conditions, and some of the film footage was aired on television.

At first, the Baustons ran their organization out of a house in Wilmington, Delaware, and later from a run-down barn and five acres borrowed from a soybean farmer in Pennsylvania. With money that they raised by hosting walk-a-thons and selling vegetarian hot dogs at rock concerts, the Baustons in 1989 purchased a defunct hog farm in Watkins Glen, a sleepy town in the Finger Lakes section of upstate New York.

The farm, which they bought for $100,000, included a decrepit seven-bedroom house and plenty of space for animals. Over the years, Farm Sanctuary took in hundreds of cows, pigs, turkeys, and other animals that were either rescued by the Baustons and Farm Sanctuary volunteers or given to them by other people or organizations. In 1994, the Baustons established a second sanctuary in Orland, California.

Vegetarian advocates like the Baustons rocked tradition in the 1990s, as much as William Metcalfe and the other advocates from the nineteenth century. Farm Sanctuary became one of the organizations to use the media to challenge the tightly-held tradition of eating turkey on Thanksgiving.

Lorri Bauston spent several Thanksgiving mornings being interviewed by a major television network, an opportunity she used to destroy the illusion that farm animals live idyllic lives grazing on grass and sunning themselves in pastures.

On one of her appearances on the television show *CBS This Morning*, Bauston was surrounded by turkeys who were busy pecking away at the pumpkin pies that she was holding in both hands. Bauston, wearing a sweatshirt embossed with the words "Farm Sanctuary, Adopt a Turkey," smiled and continued talking as the crowd of turkeys gobbled while taking their turns at the pumpkin pies.

The "Adopt a Turkey" program, designed to allow people to either take a turkey as a companion, or support one at the farm with a modest financial contribution, came about to show people that turkeys are animals "capable of feeling fear and pain just like a dog or cat," stated Bauston. "Most people would never consider eating Fido for holiday dinner, and we're hoping that once they meet Harry that they wouldn't want to eat him for dinner either."

At the conclusion of the show, the host said: "People are sitting out there this morning and saying this is all just a little too politically correct for me." But Bauston laughed, and replied: "Well, of course, we want to have fun, but also it does have a very serious message. Most people don't realize that turkeys are treated very cruelly, and of course we're hoping that people will realize that it would be a happier way to celebrate the holidays if they have a vegetarian Thanksgiving. Harry has convinced a lot of people to save a turkey rather than serve a turkey this Thanksgiving." The turkey was named Harry because he had been adopted by Harry Smith, then host of *CBS This Morning*.[32]

With a staff of volunteers and some hired hands, the Baustons ran their farm, hosted thousands of tours, and lobbied for farm animal protection laws in several states. Their first legislative victory occurred in 1995 when the organization successfully urged the California legislature to enact the Downed Animal Protection Act, a law mandating that sick animals be euthanized rather than sold to slaughterhouses.[33]

By the late 1990s Farm Sanctuary had 65,000 members and the help of celebrities. Movie star and former supermodel Kim Basinger and movie star James Cromwell, who played farmer Hoggett in the movie *Babe,* made public appearances on behalf of the organization. Cromwell also served vegan meals to the homeless in Los Angeles on Christmas Day 1996.[34]

Consumption of chicken and turkey was steadily rising, but another animal rights group was trying to convince Americans not to eat poultry, and also to go vegan. During the 1990s, United Poultry Concerns (UPC) and its founder and president, Karen Davis, Ph.D., were featured in hundreds of newspapers, including the *Washington Post, Washington Times, CBS Evening News, Knight Ridder* and the *Associated Press,* and countless television spots.

The slogan of UPC is "a nonprofit organization that promotes the compassionate and respectful treatment of domestic fowl."

Dr. Davis, who lives with companion chickens and turkeys, believes that consumers are more likely to stop eating fowl if they know that chickens, turkeys, and other birds have highly evolved intelligence. People are more likely to stop eating poultry if they see the true nature of these animals: that they are sensitive, and possess individuality, said Davis.

Like nineteenth-century vegetarian leaders Sylvester Graham and Bronson and William Alcott, today's leaders call for veganism, and not just abstinence from flesh foods. Says Davis,

The production of milk and eggs includes as much cruelty as does meat production. Mutilation of beaks and other painful bodily manipulations are performed without anesthetic, for example, and baby birds and other animals are taken away from their mothers. Surplus baby animals and "spent" hens and cows are slaughtered, smothered to death, gassed, or ground up alive according to their size and the convenience of the company or farmer.

Some people think that the only way to get others to adopt an animal-free diet is to emphasize health and environmental reasons. While these reasons may be validly included, especially with respect to industrialized farming and human global population demands, it's a mistake to assume that most people don't care enough about animals and their suffering to respond to ethical concerns. Millions of people stifle their feelings of compassion for fear of social reprisal. For this reason alone it is important to emphasize the ethics of diet so that practical compassion for all animals becomes a normal part of society.[35]

UPC's founder was raised in Pennsylvania in a town known for pheasant hunting and stopped eating meat after reading an essay by Leo Tolstoy on the horrors of slaughterhouses. Davis and UPC campaigns have often yielded results. In 1995, with the help of many smaller animal rights groups, UPC and Davis persuaded the American Honda company to scrap an ad campaign they believed was cruel to chickens. The ad ran on national television and in full-page ads in magazines. It featured a Honda Prelude and a chicken crossing a highway, with the following copy: "If a chicken crosses the road at 3 feet per minute, and pauses to consume 2 kernels of corn placed 9 inches to the right of the road's center, and a Prelude VTEC 1,000 feet away accelerates from a stationary position towards the chicken, do you serve it with potatoes or stuffing?"[36]

Two days after UPC blitzed the media with releases condemning the ad, American Honda told the group that it had taken "immediate steps to stop circulation of the ad." UPC has waged numerous other campaigns, and they sponsor annual vigils outside slaughterhouses to remember the nameless animals who suffer and are slaughtered sooner or later for eggs or meat.[37]

SUPER STAR OF VEGETARIANISM

Another leading advocate of vegetarianism is one who would seem least likely to want people to abstain from meat, milk, and eggs. But by the middle of the decade, former successful cattle rancher Howard Lyman had become the shining star of the vegetarian movement. Who better than a cattle rancher to advocate vegetarianism, thought advocates. In the early 1990s, he began lecturing at vegetarian conferences, and by the decade's end, served as president of the International Vegetarian Union —a most prestigious position in organized vegetarianism.

The fourth-generation farmer was born September 17, 1938 in Great Falls, Montana. After graduating from Montana State University and two years in the army, he returned to the family farm. Lyman's farm eventually grew to a multi-million dollar agribusiness with thousands of acres of crops such as barley, corn, wheat, 30 employees, a thousand head of dairy cows, thousands of beef cattle, turkeys, and pigs.

However, Lyman's fortunes took a turn for the worse. In 1979 he had an operation to remove a tumor from his spine, and it was getting harder to run his farm because the chemicals he had used for years depleted the soil until it, in his words, "looks more like asbestos."

Lyman also ran for Congress in 1982, won the primary, but was narrowly defeated in the general election when news of the bank foreclosing on his farm spread. In 1987 he began work as a lobbyist for the National Farmer's Union in Washington D.C. His health was failing—his cholesterol level topped 300, he had high blood pressure, and weighed over 300 pounds. He decided to become a vegetarian and his health problems gradually faded away.

The transition to a plant-based diet was not an easy one for the former rancher. "Being from Montana. I would rather ride a stolen horse, then to admit to somebody I was a vegetarian," said Lyman in an interview.[38]

Lyman, in his book *Mad Cowboy: Plain Truth From The Cattle Rancher Who Won't Eat Meat*, said his switch to a meatless diet was also spurred on by the realization that factory farming animals led to increased water pollution, water use and even soil erosion from overgrazing. "Suddenly the circle came together.... We were as a civilization making one big mistake.... We were eating dead animals and it wasn't working. If those animals had set out to take their revenge on us, they couldn't have done a better job."[39]

In 1992, Lyman joined Jeremy Rifkin's *Beyond Beef* campaign as executive director, and then later joined the Humane Society of the United States as director of the *Eating With Consciousness Campaign*. By the mid-1990s. Lyman was traveling 100,000 miles a year, lecturing, appearing on radio talk shows, and conducting television and newspaper interviews.

In April 1996, Lyman became known to millions of Americans when he appeared on the *Oprah Winfrey Show,* a top-rated television talk show with

Howard Lyman: The cowboy who won't eat meat. Courtesy of Howard Lyman.

up to 20 million viewers. Lyman at the time was warning people that mad cow disease could occur in America because of the livestock industry practice of feeding cows the ground up remains of other cows, a practice that was banned the previous year. The brain-wasting disease was suspected of killing nearly two dozen people in Britain. Lyman repeated his warning on the show, and said that the disease could make AIDS look like the common cold. Winfrey said "It just stopped me cold from eating another burger."

Cattle prices and cattle futures dropped significantly after the show aired, prompting a Texas Cattleman to sue Lyman, Winfrey and her production company for $10 million. The case went to court in 1998 amid a blitz of publicity and lasted about a month. The judge ruled that Winfrey and Lyman did not defame cattle producers, nor did they provide false information.

Howard Lyman, after a two-year run as president of the International Vegetarian Union in the mid-1990s, was named executive director of EarthSave. The former cattleman believes that most people would not eat meat if they knew how animals are treated at slaughterhouses. "When animals reach the slaughter facility the only concern is to kill as many in as short a period as possible. The animals are terrified at the slaughter plant and the cruelty inflected on the animal in their last moments on earth are indescribable. I believe if viewing of slaughter was required to eat meat, most folks would become vegetarians," said Lyman.

VEGETARIANISM EVERYWHERE

While the Mad Cowboy was stomping around the country, other advocates were increasingly using street theater and showmanship. Pam Rice, who founded New York City's VivaVegie in 1991 on Manhattan sidewalks with a bowl of fruit on her head and a sandwich board, stating "Ask me why I am vegetarian." Rice has distributed over 100,000 copies of her pamphlet "101 Reasons Why I Am A Vegetarian."

Rice and other members of her group have donned a pea pod costume and become Penelo Pea Pod and carried a sign with the words "Give Peas a Chance: Go Vegetarian." VivaVegie members have made appearances at annual events such as street fairs famous for meat-heavy ethnic fare: the Fourth of July hot dog eating contest on Coney Island, the Greenwich Village Halloween Parade, and the Easter Parade on Fifth Avenue.[40]

While VivaVegie was taking advocacy to the streets, a vegetarian from California was asserting his rights. In June of 1996, 38-year-old vegetarian bus driver Bruce Anderson refused to hand out coupons entitling passengers to free hamburgers. His employer, the Orange County Transportation Authority, fired Anderson for insubordination. In turn, Anderson sued the authority when they refused to hire him back, and filed a complaint with U.S. Equal Employment Opportunity Commission.

The case made headlines throughout the world. Anderson told the press that he didn't eat dead cows and that no one else needs to either. The coupons, which were handed out by bus drivers as part of a joint promotion between the OCTA and a fast-food chain to encourage bus riding, entitled bearers to a free hamburger with the purchase of a soft drink.

Anderson said that he would have agreed to keep the coupons—or "heart attack coupons," as he put it—in a tray at the front of the bus, but the authority insisted that they be handed out. However, Anderson said that the act of handing out coupons violated his staunch moral beliefs about the slaughtering and eating of animals.[41]

The U.S. Equal Opportunity Commission agreed with Anderson, ruling that the authority violated the Civil Rights Act of 1964. Under the ruling, the commission found that Anderson's views were not religious in the classical sense, but that his beliefs were just as strong as traditional religious views.

The Anderson case was believed to be the first time that vegetarianism was legally equated with religious beliefs. On the day of the ruling, Anderson said that it was a great day for vegetarians, and that vegetarians

VivaVegie's Penelo Pea Pod. Courtesy of Pamela Rice.

were now being taken seriously. In November of 1996, the transportation authority settled the lawsuit by giving Anderson $50,000.[42]

Vegetarians were vocal about their beliefs, but the very word *vegetarian* was being altered. An increasing number of people called themselves vegetarians even if they ate some fish, fowl, or even an occasional plate of pork with their beans.

Some vegetarians believed that it was a positive sign, signaling that vegetarianism was acceptable, even a goal to strive for, and no longer something to joke about or hide. The changing definition was noted as early as 1987 in a *New York Times* story that stated "vegetarians no longer need to defend their diets at parties" but cautioned that vegetarians now had to defend their name.

Almost a decade later, a story that appeared in *Glamour,* a magazine popular with young women, was just one indication of how rapidly the term vegetarian was being diluted in the late twentieth century. Under a checklist for healthy vegetarians, the writer recommended fish, poultry, meat, dairy products, and eggs as possible sources of protein, along with grains, legumes, and nuts. The story ended with a section titled "There's No Right Way to Be a Vegetarian," where the writer states that some vegetarians "eat fish, poultry or even meat occasionally." Finally, the word *semivegetarian* appears.

The word *semivegetarian* started popping up regularly in the media during the 1990s. In a 1995 article in *Cosmopolitan*, another favorite with young women, which was otherwise favorable to vegetarianism, the writer said that the most popular group of vegetarians were the semis who consume some chicken and fish, and enjoy meat once in awhile. "Don't worry if you eat non vegetarian occasionally. If you can't pass up the stroganoff on a special occasion, go ahead and indulge, then revert back to your vegetarian diet the next day."

George Eisman, R.D., author of *The Most Noble Diet*, founder of VEGEDINE, and another leading advocate of vegetarianism who is active among the dietetic community, has likened semivegetarianism to six-day-a-week Christianity. Despite the mountain still to climb that such challenges as the erosion of the word vegetarian presented, information about how to become a vegetarian was widely available in America, probably more than ever in the past. Yet, the country still had an inconsistent attitude towards the subject of vegetarianism. In fact, like in past eras, sometimes people came under suspicion for just bringing up the subject. Pulitzer Prize-winning writer Alice Walker figured this out incidentally.

A short story by Walker, *Am I Blue?*, was part of a reading test for tenth grade students in California. The president of that state's board of education decided Walker's story was inappropriate because it was "anti-meat eating."

The story is about the narrator's thoughts and feelings as she observes a lonely and distraught horse who was separated from his mate by human beings. The narrator perceives the disregard for the suffering of animals is like the disregard for black people during slavery. Later, while eating meat, the narrator realizes animals suffer for people to have meat, and spits out the meat.

News of the banning of *Am I Blue?* made headlines, and inspired impassioned letters, for and against, to the *San Francisco Chronicle*, which published Walker's short story for its readers.

THE MOVIES AND TELEVISION

While Walker's story was met with hostility, another story—a motion picture—titled *Babe*, was receiving accolades. Released in theaters nationwide in August of 1995, the heart-warming movie meant for children, about a talking pig, attracted audiences of all ages. The movie, which evidently inspired some moviegoers, especially the youngsters, to consider pigs and other farmed animals as more than meat, was a summer smash hit, and nominated for an Academy Award for Best Picture. The movie did not win that award, but it had people talking about the animals, and why they should not be eaten. Popular television talk show host Oprah Winfrey told her audience of millions that after seeing the movie, she would no longer eat pork.

Acclaimed actor James Cromwell, who starred as Farmer Hoggett, and who was a long-time vegetarian, became a vegan after making the movie. He spoke about vegetarianism and animal liberation before several thousand people who attended a Washington, D.C., march for animal rights. "If people saw and experienced what is done to animals, if they saw the atrocities...done to fellow creatures of life, they would stop (eating meat)," were some of Cromwell's words quoted in the media.

For several years movie star, musician, and teen heartthrob River Phoenix had lent his stardom to the promotion of vegetarianism, animal liberation, and environmentalism. The hugely popular young man, who gave exposure to his veganism and ideas on animal rights in numerous media interviews, was even allowed to write an article on such topics for *Seventeen*, a mass circulation magazine for teen girls. The *New York Times* noted Phoenix's veganism, and *Vogue*, the popular fashion magazine, featured Phoenix in a multi-page article "Tofu Guy." River Phoenix's accidental death at age 23 in 1993 was a loss for vegetarianism. The young actor, deemed one of the best of his generation, was reaching youth, and surely would have done more.

On the television scene, vegetarianism was increasingly an issue explored by top-rated television programs such as *Roseanne* and *Friends*. Even when the programs used stereotypes, the popularity of the series guaranteed widespread exposure for vegetarianism. On the top-rated situation-comedy *Roseanne*, actor Sarah Gilbert played Darlene, a character described by *Newsweek* as "the acid-tongued daughter" who lashes out at "the meat-industrial complex." A vegetarian in real life, Gilbert realized that vegetarianism "resonates with kids" who have connected meat eating with "ecological destruction...debeaking chickens and clipping the tails off of pigs... (and) destruction of the rainforest in South America," reported *Newsweek* in 1995.[43] Similarly, in an episode of *The Simpsons*, a popular animated sitcom, Simpson daughter Lisa realized that a lamb she had cuddled at the petting zoo was no different than animals she ate for dinner.

At first she was furious when her family either rejected or didn't understand her newfound empathy for the eaten. She was considered subversive by her school principle and weird by her classmates. Fed up, she succumbs and bites into a hot dog only to discover it's made from soy, and not pigs. Finally she meets animal rights activists Paul and Linda McCartney, who help her to accept her vegetarianism yet tolerate her family's love of barbecued pig.

Television and movies were powerful influences on America's youth. Polls taken in the 1990s indicate that teenagers and young adults have a strong interest in vegetarianism, and consider the lifestyle a positive one. In 2001, the Vegetarian Resource Group sponsored a Roper poll to find out the number of teenagers who are vegetarians. The results indicated that about one million (two percent) youths between the ages of 6 and 17 never eat meat, poultry, or fish. About one-half of them are vegans, VRG estimated.[44]

A poll conducted by Teenage Research Unlimited found that 42 percent of teens from the ages of 12 to 19 believed that vegetarianism was in or hip. Sally Clinton, founder of the Vegetarian Education Network, told *Good Housekeeping* magazine why teens were dumping meat from their diet: "The majority of young people become vegetarians because of deep concern for animals and the environment." Clinton founded a vegetarian newsletter for teens called *How on Earth!* in 1992.

For adults, the market research firm Yankelovich, Clancy, Shulman in 1992 found that 7 percent of the American population, or 12.4 million people, considered themselves vegetarian. The numbers were inflated: Calling oneself a vegetarian and adhering to the classical definition of a vegetarian diet—no meat, fish, or fowl—are two different things. Some of the people polled reported that they have occasionally eaten meat or fish.[45]

About the same time, the National Restaurant Association reported that one out of every five Americans likes to order a vegetarian meal when they dine out. This survey and the Yankelovich results were widely reported by vegetarian societies throughout the 1990s and featured in many newspapers and magazines.

In 1994 and 1997, the Vegetarian Resource Group sponsored a Roper poll to determine how many adults in the United States are vegetarians. Both polls showed that one percent of the adult population, or about 2 million, never eat meat, poultry, or fish. Statistics from VRG and other organizations estimates that anywhere from one-third to one-half of all true vegetarians are vegans.[46] One factor moving the mainstream toward vegetarianism was the increasing excellence of the cuisine.

THE FOOD

Lingering stereotypes equating vegetarian food with culinary hell were beginning to crumble in the 1990s. Culinary masters such as Executive Chef Ron Pickarski helped elevate vegetarian cuisine to legitimacy in the culinary world by proving that it was "more than beans and rice."[47]

At the 1996 World Culinary Olympics held in Europe, Pickarski's cooking team scored 39.9 out of 40 possible points and was awarded the only medal in the first ever vegetarian category. Pickarski's leadership and the work of his team changed the Culinary Olympics. By the 2000 Olympics, all national teams were required to present a vegetarian program.

This change had an impact on chefs worldwide. "Vegetarianism (as a cuisine) is now respected and practiced by professional chefs," explained vegan chef Pickarski, who was a Franciscan Brother (monk) of the Order of Friars Minor from 1968 to 1993. The gourmet scene included the Greens, the San Francisco vegetarian restaurant that made headlines for its cuisine, cookbooks, chefs, and long waiting lines.

On the fast-food front, meatless burgers were making inroads. In 1998, the Oregon-based Gardenburger, maker of the burger that bears the company's name, launched a $14 million, five-week blitz of ads on major television networks. In the week following the ad, Gardenburger sold nearly five times the burgers it sold in the same week a year earlier. In fact, sales of all veggie burgers jumped by 2 million in that week. Worthington Foods, which was founded by the Seventh-Day Adventist Church in 1939, announced that sales of their meat-free burgers increased substantially after the ad blitz.

But Veggie burgers reached new fast food heights in 2002, when Burger King's 8,500 restaurants across the United States began offering vegetable-based burgers called BK Veggie. This marked the first time the fast food chain offered a meat-free burger on such a widespread scale. Some vegetarian advocates hailed the move as a major victory, but Priscilla Feral, president of Friends of Animals, a national animal rights organization, called for vegetarians to boycott fast-food restaurants serving animal flesh and to instead dine at vegetarian restaurants.

Kristie Phelps, a member of People for the Ethical Treatment of Animals, remarked to the press: "We think going vegetarian is the best thing people can do and Burger King has made that easier." Phelps and other PETA activists in various cities wore bikinis fashioned from faux lettuce leaves and stood in front of selected Burger King restaurants waving to motorists and passing out BK veggie burgers.

During PETA's campaign to support Burger King, Ingrid Newkirk was interviewed by television reporters of a popular talk show. When she tried to explain that chickens are like animals people keep as companions such as cats, she was rebuffed by one interviewer who claimed to have no interest in getting to know a chicken.

Undaunted, Newkirk continued, "Beaks are seared off with a red hot wire for these birds. They are in cages so small, they can never raise one wing in a lifetime. What sort of bullies and lousy people are we that we can't extend our compassion, not just to the animals who are in our homes, but to ones who, through no fault of their own, never get to know us?"

The PETA leader also pointed out that the younger generation—and the food industry—are in tune with the times. "Corporations are recognizing that young people think this is an important issue. It's not just human rights; it's animal protection, which is why Burger King today has introduced a veggieburger."

PETA continued to enlist the support of celebrities such as actors Pam Anderson, Linda Blair, Rue McClenehan, Bea Arthur, tennis champ Martina Navratolova, and musicians Paul McCartney, Fiona Apple, and Moby to promote its cause. The voice of PETA was heard. In 2003 the organization's membership exceeded 800,000.

Other organizations, too, plugged into star power. For example, PCRM called upon actors Ed Asner and Marilu Henner, singer Kevin Eubanks, and award-winning writer Alice Walker for ads to promote the health aspect of vegetarianism using the slogan "Do it for someone you love."

But ads, talk shows, and the assistance of untold grassroots activists who spread the message beyond the media were not the only vehicles for promotion of the meat-free diet. Advocates now had a powerful new ally: the Information Superhighway also known as the Internet.

THE NEW FRONTIER

Vegetarian advocates of the 1990s tapped into the rapidly growing Internet by establishing Web sites, bulletin boards, and email lists. National and grassroots organizations and individuals created Web pages containing various aspects of vegetarianism.

In 1996, Jeff and Sabrina Nelson founded *VegSource,* a Web site devoted to vegetarianism. By 2001, a media group rated it the Web's most popular food site—vegetarian and non-vegetarian alike—with 1.4 million visits or hits a month.

Ironically, Jeff Nelson is a direct descendent of the Armour family that made a substantial fortune in the nineteenth century and became famous as the largest meat producer in the United States. Nelson stated that he established *VegSource* to contribute a "new chapter to the Armour history." About his great-great-great Grandfather Herman Ossian Armour, Nelson said: "His goal was to turn more and more people into meat addicts; mine is to help them kick that habit."[48]

PETA has no peer when it comes to attracting attention and featuring sexy women in their campaigns. For example, PETA spokesperson and popular actor and sex symbol Pamela Anderson donned a lettuce leaf bikini—her image appeared on an immense billboard above New York's Times Square with the words "Turn Over a New Leaf: Try Vegetarian." PETA also captured attention when two bikini-clad spokespersons gave away vegan hot dogs outside the Rhode Island State House in Providence on July 3, 2003, to encourage onlookers to "go vegetarian" for Independence Day.

"Eating vegetarian foods liberates people from obesity and diseases like cancer, heart disease and diabetes...By becoming a vegetarian you are

Two PETA spokeswomen outside the Rhode Island State House, promoting vegetarian Fourth of July. Courtesy of Vegetarian Museum Archives. Used with permission from PETA.

also freeing the animals from the savagery of slaughter. "Choose Kindness Over Cruelty," said Kayla Rae Worden of PETA at the event. "Karina," the other bikini-clad spokesperson who also drew dozens of men to the free hot dogs, said, "We humans have a choice about how we use our bodies.... The animals have no choice." "Karina" has starred in an adult film and used her earnings to help animals.[49] This does not please all.

Yet public criticism has not daunted PETA, as it did not stop past vegetarians. At the turn of the twentieth century, vegetarianism seemed to be drawing less ridicule and more acceptance, if not a substantial increase in practitioners.

Award-winning athlete Gary Null, Ph.D., a syndicated New York radio talk host and author of *The Vegetarian Handbook*, stated: "It appears that a real paradigm shift towards an acceptance of vegetarianism is at hand in the United States." Null, an author of over 60 books, became well known over the years for his award-winning documentary exposés on the health industry and his vegetarian advocacy, which included television appearances. In the seventies Null had challenged the misconception that vegetable protein is inferior to animal protein.

Another New York City talk host, Shelton Walden, of *Walden's Pond*, has experienced that shift. The radio show host, whose program features vegetarian, animal rights, environmental, and human rights topics, has observed that American culture has changed since he became a vegetarian in 1980: "People are less likely to sneer at vegetarianism." Walden also noted that there are more vegan and vegetarian-friendly restaurants, particularly in New York City.

During this era, top talk radio programs drew millions of listeners. A number of these hosts—some sympathetic, some not—interviewed guests on vegetarian topics. Howard Lyman's views on mad cow disease and veganism were aired on Coast-to-Coast AM with George Noory in January 2004. He was also a guest on other shows such as *The O'Reilly Factor* with host Bill O'Reilly and *Imus in the Morning* with host Don Imus. Karen Davis, Ph.D., was a guest on the Howard Stern Show, and Robert Cohen, who is known as the Not Milk Man for his vegan advocacy, was a guest on both Howard Stern and Coast-to-Coast AM.

Sometimes the vegetarian advocacy community recognizes the efforts of talk show hosts. For example, Don Imus was named a candidate for the "The Sexiest Vegetarian Alive" on People for the Ethical Treatment of Animals' Web site in 2002, but the honors went to actors Tobey Maguire and Natalie Portman. Imus, a vegetarian, frequently mentions his wife Dierdre's vegetarianism on his show. The couple serves a vegetarian diet to participants in their residential program for children suffering from cancer or blood disorders.

Efforts by Imus and other talk show hosts have helped push the meat-free message to the masses. Such exposure has led some trend experts to predict a rosy vegetarian future for the United States.

Faith Popcorn, founder of BrainReserve, a trend forecasting company, stated that "at first, most, and then eventually all Americans, even those not convinced, or concerned, about potential consequences to their health or the planet, will still want to eat only food from plants."

However, vegetarian advocates face a paradox. On one hand, the vegetarian message has never been more visible in society. On the other hand, never before have Americans dined on so much meat. Meat consumption reached an all-time high in 2001: per capita consumption of red meat and poultry averaged 219 pounds, up from 199 pounds in 1990 and 166 pounds in 1960. Poultry consumption made up a vast majority of this growth.

THE ATKINS ATTACK

Like a hurricane descending upon the vegetarian movement, high-protein diets such as the Atkins Diet threatened the progress made by countless advocates. The Atkins Diet, an eating plan that features high-protein foods derived from animal products, is the antithesis of vegan eating. Demonizing carbohydrates, the Atkins Diet moved swiftly into mainstream America and onto the menus and shelves of chain restaurants and supermarkets, sending seismic waves into the wheat and vegetable food industries. Even Burger King in 2003 introduced a low-carb version of its popular Whopper hamburger sandwich, which was no more than the burger without a bun.

Physicians such as John McDougall, M.D., a long-time crusader for veganism, took on high-protein diets in debates and in the media. The media framed the conflict as a battle between diets and held a press conference that included people whose health had been harmed by such diets. Dean Ornish, M.D., was in the center of the storm, defending the low-fat vegetarian diet. McDougall, like Dr. William Alcott in the nineteenth century and other advocates, fought sickness early in life. He suffered a stroke at age 18, then eventually rebuilt his health with a vegetarian diet. McDougall became known in the 1980s with *The McDougall Plan for Super Health and Life-Long Weight Loss* (New Century Publishers, 1983), and then later for his food company, *Dr. McDougall's Right Foods*, and for his syndicated national talk and television shows.

McDougall blasted high-protein, animal-based diets: "You can't stay on these diets forever, because you can't stay sick or hungry forever." He deemed the diets "Make yourself sick diets." He made these remarks during the Great Nutrition Debate at the U.S. Department of Agriculture in February 2000. That diets such as Atkins have gained a tremendous following comes as no surprise to McDougall. "The foods recommended— steaks, lobsters, fishes, pheasants, eggs, and cheeses—are the ones most of us were raised to enjoy. Preach what people want to hear and you have an immediate following, because naturally we all like to hear good news."[50]

Late in 2003, the nation was shaken by media reports of a cow infected with mad cow disease. Worried meat eaters learned how the meat industry uses "everything but the 'moo,' "—a phrase with origins in the twentieth century. Vegetarian Upton Sinclair, author of *The Jungle*, had described "everything but the squeal," meaning all parts of the dead body of the hog were ground down into merchandise of some type. In Sinclair's day, some people were moved out of fear to reject meat. It is not yet known if the threat of mad cow disease so motivated people in 2003. In the interim, at least one national politician was calling for strict regulation and testing of cows to be designated meat.

In 2003, 186 years after Rev. Metcalfe's arrival in America, a vegan was a candidate for the Democratic nomination for president. U.S. Rep. Dennis Kucinich, an Ohio politician inspired by John F. Kennedy, ran on a platform that might have pleased Rev. Henry S. Clubb, a nineteenth century foe of war. Kucinich called for strict regulation and testing of cows designated for meat. He promised to create a Department of Peace and withdraw U.S. troops from war-torn Iraq. His slogan was "The end of fear and the beginning of hope for America." He also promised to cancel trade agreements detrimental to American jobs, remove profit from health care, assist family farms, and offer free college education. The press mentioned Kucinich's veganism, and that if elected, he would still allow meat to be served at the White House, but he was evidently not belittled for eschewing food derived from animals. The label *vegetarian*, and even *vegan*, seemed to be losing some of its stigma.

The late Dr. Mervyn Hardinge believed that vegetarianism comes in waves or periods of rise and fall. But for vegetarianism to continue on an upswing, there has to be a burning will to maintain a meat-free diet, he said. Hardinge said that most people would slack off any vegetarian regime unless it comes from "something higher than the self."

"If you think your body is the temple of the Holy Ghost, then you're going to try to keep it clean and pure," he said. Fear of disease such as mad cow disease won't work in the long run, said Hardinge. "People who become vegetarians out of fear will give it up once the fear evaporates."[51]

Dietitian Suzanne Havala can verify that people need a higher motivation than health to become vegetarians or vegans. She said people who switch to vegetarianism out of concern for their health are less likely to stay with it then those who avoid meat for ethical reasons.

Hardinge's idea that God has to have a place in the widespread adoption of vegetarianism seems to be one that is alive again in the nation, more than 150 years after Reverend William Metcalfe preached vegetarianism from his Philadelphia Bible-Christian pulpit.

Undoubtedly, religion has played an enormous role in vegetarian advocacy. Jews, like Christians, have a history of contributing to vegetarianism in America. In the late twentieth century, Richard Schwartz, Ph.D., a mathematics professor, and Roberta Kalechofsky, an author and publisher, maintain the tradition of Judaism and vegetarianism derived from the Old Testament.

Schwartz, author of *Judaism and Vegetarianism*, 2nd ed. (Micah, 1988), argues that vegetarianism is the diet most consistent with basic Jewish mandates. He established a Web site on the subject and has lectured and written extensively on vegetarianism and Judaism, here and in Israel. Kalechofsky, through her company Micah Publications, has published and distributed 15 titles on the subjects of vegetarianism and animal rights, including *Vegetarian Judaism—A Guide for Everyone* (1998), *Rabbis and Vegetarianism* (1995), which features a collection of essays, and two books designed to help Jews celebrate Passover as vegetarians. Kalechofsky received an award from the Jewish Vegetarian Society of North America in 1989 for her work in "having advanced the cause of Jewish vegetarianism."[52]

Christian vegetarian and animal rights advocates, too, are working to break down perceived barriers to vegetarianism. Recently established, the Christian Vegetarian Association and allcreatures.org are increasingly active and attracting members, as did the Edenite Society, an Essene organization, during the 1970s.

Bruce Friedrich: PETA's Catholic crusader for vegetarianism. Used with permission from PETA.

To young and old, PETA brought the issue of Christianity and vegetarianism to the masses at the turn of the twenty-first century with campaign slogans such as "Jesus was a vegetarian." The campaign drew upon passages from the Bible, the Gospels of the Essenes, and a number of scholarly books that present evidence that Jesus abstained from meat eating. "The heart of this campaign," wrote coordinator Bruce G. Friedrich, a Roman Catholic, "is Jesus' call for mercy and compassion."[53] This generated controversry.

"No one can know for certain if Jesus was or wasn't a vegetarian, but the evidence that he was is strong...," contends Friedrich. Billboards depicting the classic image of God with a beard and in a robe with the words "I Said 'Thou Shalt not kill' Go Vegetarian" were another campaign.

The *Washington Post* reported that Friedrich had written to 450 U.S. Catholic bishops and several leading Evangelists. The response was mixed. One bishop who replied to Friedrich, James Tillon of the Diocese of Scranton, Pennsylvania, stated "I believe in your cause. I am 95 percent vegetarian and working towards 100 percent myself."[54]

Close to Christmas in 2003, PETA made headlines in Providence, Rhode Island, when they unveiled a billboard depicting the Virgin Mary cradling a dead chicken in her arms. Pasted on the ad were the words "Go Vegetarian. It's an Immaculate Conception." Inside the "o" of the word "go" was a cross. The telephone lines of radio talk show hosts rang with calls, mostly from irate Catholics offended by the ad. Others agreed with the ad and said they were Catholic and vegetarian.

The Most Rev. Robert E. Mulvee, bishop of the Catholic Diocese of Providence, said, "This use of one of the most sacred images of the Christian faith trivializes not only the Mother of Jesus, but also the very cause PETA strives to advance." PETA argued, "If cats and dogs were treated the way chickens, pigs and other farm animals are treated, everybody involved would be charged with felony cruelty to animals and prosecuted." PETA's Friedrich also said, "We need to get over our prejudices and treat all of God's creatures with His kindness and tender mercy."

In 2003, some Roman Catholics were not the only people to take offense at a publicity campaign promoting vegetarianism (veganism). PETA erected a billboard near the New England Holocaust Memorial in Boston, Massachusetts. The scenes depicted horrified some Holocaust survivors who denounced the ad campaign. On the billboard: frightening images of Holocaust victims next to images of factory-farmed chickens and turkeys. "Holocaust on your plate" creator Matt Prescott, who is Jewish, said, "We need to use it as a context for teaching lessons of compassion and kindness." PETA activists pointed out in media interviews across America that it was the late Isaac Bashevis Singer who wrote, "In relation to them, all people are Nazis; for the animals, it is an eternal Treblinka." Singer had often spoken of his ethical vegetarianism in interviews. "Vegetarianism is a major step on the road to world peace.... as long as human beings will go on shedding the blood of animals, there will never be any peace. There is only one little step from killing animals to creating gas chambers, à la Hitler and concentration camps, à la Stalin.... there will be no justice as man will stand with a knife or with a gun and destroy those who are weaker than he is." The Jewish and Christian connections to vegetarianism, like the link between the American and British branches of the vegetarian movement, thrived in 2003, promising to yield more results.

The seeds of vegetarianism planted by Reverend William Metcalfe, William Alcott, Sylvester Graham, and the other pioneers back in the nineteenth century bore fruit. While vegetarianism in America flowed up and down like a wave throughout the nineteenth century, and steadied in the early twentieth century, it traveled rough waters after World War II, and might have drowned out of public sight. However, the winds of change during the countercultural era of the 1960s and 1970s helped blow it back onto a steady course that continues to the present day, rising ever higher.

And if present trends continue, teens will take vegetarianism to a tidal wave level. Author Rev. Professor Andrew Linzey, who holds the world's first post in Christian theology and animal welfare at Oxford University, stated, "What currently spurs on the animal-rights movement in the United Kingdom and the United States more than anything else is this: the realization that it isn't necessary to eat meat. Young animal-sensitive people are now taking revenge on their carnivorous parents. The growth of vegetarianism among the fourteen-to-eighteen age group has been startling."[55] Linzey says people should visit slaughterhouses and see if "what goes on with them is compatible with the spirit of Jesus."[56]

Vegetarianism might have reached the mainstream, but America's insatiable appetite for meat continues.

Will the United States one day become a vegetarian America? No one but a prophet knows. Until that day when the lion lies down with the lamb, advocates of vegetarianism will continue to work towards a vegan world.

Afterword

The vegetarian movement in the United States originated with an Englishman and blossomed under American Sylvester Graham. After Graham's death, and that of William Alcott, M.D., vegetarianism was championed by others. Mary Gove Nichols and Thomas Low Nichols, M.D., brought their advocacy to England, where she died in 1884 and he in 1901. James Caleb Jackson, M.D., lived until 1895, and Russell Thatcher Trall, M.D., until 1877. Bronson Alcott was still promoting abstinence from meat eating in the early 1880s and died in 1888. J. Howard Moore died in 1916. Henry Stephen Clubb's crusade continued nearly until his death in 1922. Members of the Bible-Christian passed away, and, in the 1920s, the church ceaseed to exist. John Harvey Kellogg, who said that he didn't do too bad for a "grass eater" died in 1943. Bernarr MacFadden died in 1955.

Curtis Freshel, with wife Emarel Freshel and their Millennium Guild, worked against vivisection and for vegetarianism, and he brought the world Bakon-Yeast, a smoky flavoring that enhanced vegetarian foods. Freshel was named Vice President of the International Vegetarian Union in 1955. He died in 1968.

Jay Dinshah passed away in 2000, leaving the work of his American Vegan Society to its co-founder, his wife Freya Dinshah. Constantina Salamone continues her work for ecofeminism, animal liberation, and vegetarianism; she formed World Women for Animal Rights Empowerment in the 1980s.

The natural hygiene movement, made more systematic by Herbet Shelton, continues through the work of numerous people, including Dr. V. Vetrano and Victoria Bidwell, and an organization, The National Medical Association, which was Shelton's American Natural Hygiene Society.

Allopaths John McDougall, M.D., Neal Barnard, M.D., Michael Klaper, M.D., continue as leading advocates of vegetarianism (veganism), and others, including Michael Greger, M.D., and Joel Fuhrman, M.D., are also making waves.

The Seventh Day Adventist Church, through its food companies, hospitals and health centers, books, research, restaurants, and local church activities, continues to advance vegetarianism.

Vegetarianism as a movement, one as legitimate and important as other struggles for rights and respect, is slowly moving from the stage of ridicule to that of recognition. Its progress in 2004 America, nearly 200 years past its birth, continues to rise and fall like the tides.

Recently, the high-protein diet trend was rocked when rumbles of discontent began erupting against it. Some reasons include the rumors that it had killed the leading high protein diet guru and the news stories that a few people who had been on the diet had wrecked their health.

Meanwhile, a much smaller trend has emerged: raw food vegan dining is finding favor among some health seekers and fitness enthusiasts, especially Hollywood celebrities.

The word *vegan* is now in the vocabulary of Americans, particularly the young. Punk-rock bands like Earth Crisis and others are educating the rising generation.

Two leading organizations promoting the vegan diet, PCRM for health reasons, and PETA primarily for the sake of protecting animals, became increasingly well-known. Opposition, some from critics with alleged ties to animal industries, grew more vigorous and vitriolic.

Meanwhile, the American Medical Association, once a critic of PCRM's vegan recommendation, stated in 2004 that its criticism was no longer valid since much new scientific data on diet had been accumulated, and the AMA has no policy regarding vegan diet. One of the AMA's earliest leaders, Dr. Mussey, was an advocate of vegetarianism influenced by a Graham lecture.

The American rights and freedoms of vegetarians became an issue of contention early in the twenty-first century when Jerry Friedman, who rejected vaccination grown in chicken embryo on the basis of Ethical Veganism, lost his employment. He sued for violation of his right to religious freedom. The court denied Ethical Veganism as a religious belief.

It is the authors' profound hope that this book will open a portal for vegetarianism scholarship, bringing out of the darkness the people and events of the past, illuminating the Vegetarian America of yesterday, and shining light into vegetarianism's ever-expanding universe for explorers to come: A universe of health, food for all, harmony with the Earth, and peace among people and animals.

Notes

CHAPTER 1

1. The American Indian culture of the past is depicted as dependent upon animal skins and flesh as part of the traditional way of life, yet such may not have always been the case. The lore of Native American tribes includes the belief that originally human beings and animals lived together in peace. Particular traditions of the Native people provide possible evidence to verify this belief, although it is not certain whether any tribe was vegetarian. One example, explains Rita Laws, Ph.D., a Choctaw and Cherokee Indian, is that of the Choctaw Indians of the past; they raised their children as vegetarians until the age of 10. The main food of the Choctaw was a stew consisting of corn, pumpkin, and beans. Corn is a sacred food to the Choctaw and is used in their ceremonies. They did not construct their dwellings out of animals skins; they used plant materials or clay, and their ceremonies tended to be based on crop harvest time.

Several tribes in addition to the Choctaw were farmers before the Europeans came. It seems the tribes might have become nomadic hunters out of necessity. Laws has stated that hunting was a leisure time pursuit rather than a way of life before Spanish explorer Coronado arrived in the United States in the sixteenth century. Rita Laws, "Native Americans and Vegetarianism," *Vegetarian Journal* (September 1994), http://www.vrg.org/journal/94sep.htm.

2. "Vegetarian Indians," *The American Vegetarian and Health Journal* 1 (May 1851): 94.

3. *The Stirling Observer*, 26 September 1850, article republished in *The American Vegetarian Journal of Health and Longevity* 2 (October 1852): 160.

4. Charles C. B. Seymour, *Self-Made Man* (n.p., 1858), 1.

5. *The Autobiography of Benjamin Franklin; The Journal of John Woolman, and Fruits of Solitude*, The Harvard Classics, vol. 1 (New York: P.F. Collier & Son, 1909), 39.

6. Ibid.

7. Johann Conrad Beissel, *Turtle Taube* (Ephrata, Pa.: Ephrata Cloister, 1747).

8. Michael Showalter, "Food at the Ephrata Cloister," unpublished essay (August 2003).

9. Harry Emerson Wildes, "Shattering an Ideal," in *The Delaware* (New York: Farrar & Rinehart, 1940), 85.

10. Ronald Gordon, *Conrad Beisell and the Ephrata Cloister* (Ephrata, Pa.: Church of the Brethren Network, 1996), http://www.cob-net.org/cloister.htm.

11. Francis M. Thompson, "The Dorrellites," in *History and Proceedings of the Pocumtuck Valley Memorial Association* (Deerfield, Mass.: Pocumtuck Valley Memorial Association, 1898), 82–89.

12. Ibid.

13. *The Autobiography of Benjamin Franklin; The Journal of John Woolman, and Fruits of Solitude,* The Harvard Classics, vol. 1 (New York: P.F. Collier & Son, 1909), 181–182.

14. Herman Daggett, *The Rights of Animals: An Oration, Delivered at the Commencement of Providence-College* (Sagg Harbour: Printed by David Frothingham, 1791).

15. L. Du Pre, *The Principles of a New Covenant, or Social Compact; for the Animal Creation* (Poughkeepsie, N.Y.: Dutchess County Agricultural Society Transactions). Potter, Baltimore, May 15, 1809, J. Robinson No 1 No Calvert Street.

16. W.D. Haleg, "Johnny Appleseed. A Pioneer Hero," *Harper's New Monthly Magazine,* November 1871, 830–836.

17. Vasu Murti, "They Shall Not Hurt or Destroy" in *The Writings of Vasu Murti: Animal Rights and Vegetarianism in The Western Religious Traditions* (n.p.), 91.

CHAPTER 2

1. William Alcott, "Society of Bible Christians," *The Library of Health* (1849), 260–264.

2. Ibid., 260–264.

3. The Maintenance Committee, comp. *History of the Philadelphia Bible-Christian Church* (Philadelphia: J.B. Lippincott Company, 1922), 20–24.

4. William Metcalfe, *Bible Testimony, On Abstinence from the Flesh of Animals as Food; Being an Address Delivered to the Bible Christian Church* (Philadelphia, Pa.: J. Metcalfe & Co. Printers, 1840), 16.

5. The Maintenance Committee, *History,* 33–35.

6. W.M. Metcalfe, M.D. *Out of the Clouds: Into the Light* (Philadelphia: J.B. Lippincott & Co., 1872), 13.

CHAPTER 3

1. *The Providence Daily Journal,* 10 July 1832, 2.

2. Ibid., 2.

3. Sylvester Graham, *A Lecture on Epidemic Diseases Generally, and Particularly the Spasmodic Cholera, Delivered in the City of New York, March, 1832, and Repeated June,*

1832, and in Albany, July 4, 1832, and in New York, June, 1833 (Boston: D. Cambell, 1838).

4. Ronald Deutsch, *The New Nuts among the Berries* (Palo Alto, Calif.: Bull Publishing Co., 1977), 23.

5. "National Fast," *The Providence Daily Journal,* 14 July 1832, 2.

6. Graham, *A Lecture,* 33.

7. Ibid., 77.

8. Ibid., 49–50.

9. "One Who Fools," *Genius of Temperance, Philanthropist and People's Advocate,* 11 May 1831, 1.

10. *Genius of Temperance, Philanthropist and People's Advocate,* 13 April 1831, 2, and a famous abolitionist.

11. Origin of word "vegetarian," *Oxford English Dictionary,* 2d ed., s.v. "vegetarian."

12. Ibid., 21.

13. Sylvester Graham, *Lectures on the Science of Human Life,* vol. 2 (Boston: Marsh, Capen, Lyon and Webb, 1839), 21.

14. Ibid., 86.

15. Sylvester Graham, "Material of Bread," in *Treatise on Bread, and Breadmaking* (Boston: Light & Stearns, 1837).

16. Andrew Combe, M.D., "Theory and Laws of Digestion," chap. 5 in *The Physiology of Digestion,* 4th American ed. (Boston: Marsh, Capen & Lyon, 1837).

17. Graham, *Lectures,* 2:239–240.

18. Ibid., 398–399.

19. Ibid., 427.

20. Edith I. Coombs, *America Visited* (New York: The Book League of America, n.d.), 114–115.

21. Ibid., 114–115.

22. Ibid., 236.

23. Ibid., 255.

24. Graham, "Preface," and "Material of Bread."

25. Ibid., "Preface."

26. Ibid., "Material of Bread."

27. P. Gerard Damsteegt, "Health Reform and the Bible in Early Sabbatarian Adventism," *Adventist Heritage: A Journal of Adventist History* 5 (winter 1978): 1.

28. William Alcott, M.D., *Forty Years in the Wilderness of Pills and Powders; or, The Cogitations and Confessions of an Aged Physician* (Boston: John P. Jewett and Company, 1859), 4.

29. John B. Blake and Mary Gove Nichols, Prophetess of Health, *Proceedings of The American Philosophical Society* 106 (June 1962): 221.

30. Benjamin Rush and G. W. Corner, *Autobiography of Benjamin Rush: His "Travels Through Life"* (Princeton, N.J.: Princeton University Press, 1948).

31. Oliver Wendell Holmes, *Medical Essays 1842–1882* (Boston: Houghton, Mifflin, and Company, 1891), 203.

32. Isaac Jennings, *The Tree of Life; Or Human Degeneracy: Its Nature and Remedy, as Based on the Elevating Principle of Orthopathy* (New York: Miller, Wood, & Company, 1867).

33. John B. Blake and Mary Gove Nichols, Prophetess of Health, *Proceedings of The American Philosophical Society*, 106 (June 1962), 221.

34. *The Providence Daily Journal*, 6 January 1834.

35. Sylvester Graham, *Aesculapian Tablets of the Nineteenth Century* (Providence, R.I.: Weeden and Cory, 1834), 37–40.

36. Ibid., 37–40.

37. Ibid., 37–40.

38. Ibid., 37–40.

39. Ibid., 37–40.

40. Ibid., viii–ix.

41. Ibid., author's note on index page.

42. Asenath Nicholson, *Nature's Own Book*, 2d ed. (New York: Wilbur & Whipple, 1835), 6.

43. Ibid., 6.

44. Harvey Burdell and John Burdell, *Observations on the Structure, Physiology, Anatomy and Diseases of the Teeth; in Two Parts*, part 1 by Harvey Burdell; part 2 by John Burdell (New York: Gould and Newman, 1838).

45. *The Providence Daily Journal*, 8 January 1834.

46. "Confectionary, Pastry," *The Providence Daily Journal*, 2 January 1834.

47. *The Providence Daily Journal*, 7 January 1834.

48. The Editors of American Heritage, *The American Heritage Cookbook and Illustrated History of American Eating and Drinking* (New York: American Heritage Publishing Co., Inc., 1964).

49. "Grahamism," *The Hampshire Gazette*, 22 June 1836, 1.

50. William Alcott, "Introduction," *The Moral Reformer* 1 (1835): inside front cover.

51. Samuel Austin Alliborne, *A Critical Dictionary of English Literature and British American Authors*, 3 vols. (Philadelphia, Pa.: Childs & Peterson, 1859), 45.

52. William Alcott, "Fifty Years Ago," *The Moral Reformer* 1 (1835): 49.

53. Ibid.

54. William Alcott, "Dialogue on Flesh-Eating," *The Moral Reformer and Teacher on the Human Constitution* 2 (1836): 89–93.

55. Richard Harrison Shyrock, *Medicine in America: Historical Essays* (Baltimore: The Johns Hopkins Press, 1966), 124–125.

56. Mary S. G. Nichols, *A Woman's Work in Water Cure and Sanitary Education* (London: H. Nisbit, n.d.), 113.

57. Ibid., 36.

58. "Notice of School Opening," *Graham Journal of Health and Longevity* 2 (March 14, 1838): 128.

59. William A. Alcott, *Vegetable Diet: As Sanctioned by Medical Men, and by Experience in all Ages* (Boston: Marsh, Capon & Lyon, 1838), 224–273.

60. Ibid., 223.

61. Anonymous, *Rational View of the Spasmodic Cholera* (Boston: Clapp & Hull, 1832).

62. Alcott, *Vegetable Diet*, 2.

63. Ibid., 3–5.

64. "Vegetable Diet," *Boston Medical and Surgical Journal* 19 (December 19, 1838): 316–319.

65. Ibid., 316–319.

66. Robert Samuel Fletcher, "Bread and Doctrine at Oberlin," *Ohio History: The Scholarly Journal of Ohio Historical Society* 49 (January 1940): 58–67.

67. R. D. Mussey, *Health: Its Friends and Its Foes* (Boston: Gould and Lincoln, 1862), 175.

68. "Speech of Mr. Graham at the Third Annual Anniversary of the American Physiological Society," *Graham Journal of Health and Longevity* 3 (July 20, 1839): 235.

69. Ibid.

70. "One Who Feels," *The Genius of Temperance,* 11 May 1831, 2.

71. "The Science of Life," *Boston Medical and Surgical Journal* 13 (October 21, 1835): 178.

72. Sylvester Graham, "Dr. Copland on the Vitality of the Blood," *Boston Medical and Surgical Journal* 14 (April 13, 1836): 159–160.

73. "Some Facts and Logic Respecting Dietetics," *Boston Medical and Surgical Journal* 14 (April 20, 1836): 169.

74. "The Use of Fruit," *Boston Medical and Surgical Journal* 19 (July 22, 1835): 386–387.

75. "Grahamism a Cause of Insanity," *Boston Medical and Surgical Journal* 14 (February 24, 1836): 38–45.

76. Sylvester Graham, "Grahamism Not a Cause of Insanity," *Boston Medical and Surgical Journal* 14 (June 1, 1836): 266–322.

77. David Cambell, "To the Public," *The Graham Journal of Health and Longevity* 1 (April 4, 1837): 2.

78. "Ultra Abstinence from Animal Food," *The Graham Journal of Health and Longevity* (March 3, 1838): 107–108.

79. *Graham Journal of Health and Longevity* 2 (July 7, 1838): 209–223.

80. Ibid., 211.

81. Ibid., 212.

82. "Grahamism: A Cause Of Insanity," 38–45.

83. Graham, *Aesculapiun Tublets,* 4

84. Ibid.

85. Horace Greeley, *Recollections of a Busy Life* (New York: J.B. Ford & Co., 1863), 103.

86. Ibid., 103.

87. Ibid., 103.

88. Sylvester Graham, "Appendix," in *Lectures on the Science of Human Life,* vol. 2 (Boston: Marsh, Capen, Lyon and Webb, 1839), 1195.

89. Sylvester Graham, *Lectures on the Science of Human Life,* vol. 2 (Boston: Marsh, Capen, Lyon, and Webb, 1839), 5.

90. To be labeled a proponent of an "ism" in those days was similar to being categorized by today's label of "extremist."

91. Editorial, *Botanico-Medical Recorder* 8 (June 13, 1840), 293.

92. Letter to Editor from J.J. Flournoy, *Botanico-Medical Recorder* 9 (January 9, 1840): 113–115.

93. Editorial Department, *Botanico-Medical Recorder* 9 (January 9, 1840): 124–126.

94. Edith I. Coombs, *America Visited* (New York: The Book League of America, n.d.), 297.

95. Ibid., 328.

96. Ibid., 335–336.

97. Larry A. Carlson, "Bronson Alcott's 'Journal for 1837,' " *Studies in the American Renaissance* (1981): 44, 45.

98. Octavius Brooks Frothingham, *Transcendentalism in New England* (New York: G.P. Putnam's Sons, 1876; reprint, New York: Harper, 1959), 150–153 (page citations are to the reprint edition).

99. Odell Shepard, *The Journals of Bronson Alcott* (Boston: Little, Brown & Co., 1938), 115.

100. Odell Shepard, *Peddlar's Progress: The Life of Bronson Alcott* (Boston: Little, Brown and Co., 1937), 441.

101. Franklin B. Sanborn and William T. Harris, *Memoir of Bronson Alcott*, vol. 1 (Boston: Roberts Brothers, 1893), 341–342.

102. William Lambe, "On the Possibility of Supporting Life on a Vegetable Diet," *The Bulletin of Medical Science* 11 (October 1844): 339.

103. A. Bronson Alcott, "Days from a Diary," *The Dial*, 15 April 1842, 426.

104. Kenneth Walter Cameron, ed., *Response to Transcendentalist Concord: The Last Decades of the Era of Emerson, Thoreau, and the Concord School as Recorded in Newspapers* (Hartford, Conn.: Transcendental Books, 1974), 181.

105. "A Lecture on the First Step in Physical and Moral Reform Delivered before the Kensington Physiological Society; in the Bible-Christian Church, on the Evening of the 14th of April, 1842," by the secretary (Philadelphia, Pa.: William Metcalfe, 1842), 20–21.

106. Orson Murray, "Two Heifers 'Polly' and 'Susan Elizabeth'…(Auction of…)," *The Regenerator* 1 (March 25, 1844): 51; Orson Murray Scrapbook, Valentine Nicholson Collection, W.H. Smith Memorial Library, Indiana Historical Society, Box 3 F1, M641.

107. Horace Greeley and Orson S. Murray, *New York Tribune*, 30 December 1843, appeared in *The Regenerator* 1 (January 8, 1844): 6.

108. Thomas Wickensham, "Adventures of a Grahamite," *The Regenerator* 1 (February 19, 1844): 32.

109. William S. Tyler to Edward Tyler, Amherst College, October 10, 1833, published in Thomas H. Le Duc, "Grahamites and Garrisonites," in *Documents, NewYork History: Quarterly Journal of the New York State Historical Association* (Albany, N.Y.: The Association, 1939), 189–191.

110. "A Lecture on the First Step in Physical and Moral Reform Delivered before the Kensington Physiological Society; in the Bible-Christian Church, on the Evening of the 14th of April, 1842," by the Secretary (Philadelphia, Pa.: William Metcalfe, 1842), 14–15.

111. Richard Harrison Shryrock, *Medicine in America: Historical Essays*, 2d ed. (Baltimore, Md.: The John Hopkins Press, 1972), 124.

112. "Graham's Lecture to Young Men," *The Graham Journal of Health and Longevity* 2 (July 7, 1838): 237–238.

113. Ibid., 237–238.

114. "Dr. Graham in Boston," *Hampshire Gazette*, 8 March 1837, 4, col. 3.

115. Graham brought his series of lectures on anatomy and physiology, which included his dietetic system, to black audiences, thus breaking down another societal barrier at a time when many white people disparaged blacks.

116. Rev. William Metcalfe, *Bible Testimony, on Abstinence from the Flesh of Animals as Food; Being an Address Delivered in the Bible-Christian Church, North Third*

Street, West Kensington, on the Eighth of June 1840, Being the Anniversary of Said Church (Philadelphia: J. Metcalfe & Co., 1840), 5.

117. "Flesh-Meat," *Botanico-Medical Recorder* 9 (October 3, 1840): 14–15.

118. Ibid., 14–15.

119. S. Graham, "A Transcript from the Tablets of the Heart," *Hampshire Gazette*, 17 September 1850, 1.

120. William Alcott, "Society of Bible Christians," *The Library of Health* (1849), 260–262.

121. Ibid., 260–262.

CHAPTER 4

1. "Proceedings of the American Vegetarian Convention," *The American and Vegetarian Health Journal* 1 (November 1850): 1.

2. Letter from David Prince, M.D., *The American Vegetarian and Health Journal* 1 (October 1851): 1–2.

3. Letter from Professor Mussey of The Ohio University, Cincinnati, *The American Vegetarian and Health Journal* 1 (October 1851): 1.

4. Letter from Lewis S. Hough, M.A., *The American Vegetarian and Health Journal* 1 (October 1851): 2–3.

5. "Vegetarian Experience," *The American Vegetarian and Health Journal* 1 (October 1851): 5–6.

6. "Second Session. Declaration of Sentiments and Resolutions," *The American Vegetarian and Health Journal* 1 (October 1851): 6–7.

7. Joel Shew, letter, *The American Vegetarian and Health Journal* 1 (November 1850), 12–13.

8. "Dr. Alcott's Address," *The American Vegetarian and Health Journal* 1 (November 1850): 8–9.

9. Ibid., 1.

10. Other historians have reported that this first annual meeting of the Society was attended by many reformers, including Harriet Beecher Stowe, author of *Uncle Tom's Cabin*, and Amelia Bloomer, advocate of women's rights. The group gathered for the meeting toasted to "temperance, women's rights, and vegetarianism!"

11. Joel Shew, preface to the American edition, *Water and Vegetable Diet in Consumption, Scrofula, Cancer, Asthma, and Other Chronic Diseases* (New York: Fowlers & Wells, 1850). American edition of *Additional Reports on the Effects of a Peculiar Regimen in Cases of Cancer, Scrofula, Consumption, Asthma, and Other Chronic Diseases* (London: 1815).

12. T.L. Nichols, letter from Dr. Nichols, *The American Vegetarian and Health Journal* 1 (August 1851): 136.

13. "Address of Cyrus M. Burleigh," *American Vegetarian and Health Journal* 1 (October 1851): 171–173.

14. John Grimes, "A Christmas Vegetarian Banquet and Soiree," *The American Vegetarian and Health Journal* 2 (February 1852): 17–20.

15. "Dr. Grimes' Speech," *The American Vegetarian and Health Journal* 1 (November 1850): 29–30.

16. "Evening Session—Dr. Alcott's Remarks," *The American Vegetarian and Health Journal* 2 (October 1852): 153–155.

17. Ibid., 153–155.

18. William Metcalfe, "Do You Eat Flesh?" *The American Vegetarian and Health Journal* 2 (November 1852): 161–162.

19. "Evening Session—Dr. Alcott's Remarks," *The American Vegetarian and Health Journal* 2 (October 1852): 153–155.

20. "Work for Vegetarianism," *American Vegetarian and Health Journal* 2 (December 1852): 184.

21. Anne Denton, "The Rights of Women," *The American Vegetarian and Health Journal* 2 (December 1852): 186–187.

22. Ibid., 186–187.

23. Ibid., 186–187.

24. Ibid., 186–187.

25. Charles Lane, "Health, Economy, Humanity," *American Vegetarian and Health Journal* 2 (February 1852): 21–24.

26. Ibid., 21–24.

27. William Metcalfe, "Gleizes," *American Vegetarian and Health Journal* 2 (November 1852): 176.

28. "The Economy of Life," *The American Vegetarian and Health Journal* 2 (November 1852): 170.

29. James Caleb Jackson, letter, *The American Vegetarian and Health Journal* 2 (September 1852): 133–136.

30. Ibid., 133–136.

31. W. A. Alcott, "Sylvester Graham," *The American Vegetarian and Health Journal* 1 (December 1851): 216.

32. Seth Hunt, "Death of Sylvester Graham," *The American Vegetarian* 1 (October 1851): 187.

33. R. T. Trall, "Life of Sylvester Graham," *The American Vegetarian and Health Journal* (March 1852): 41.

34. Ibid., 41.

35. Ibid., 41.

36. Stanley Aronson, "The Man Who Invented the Graham Cracker," commentary, *The Providence Journal*, 28 February 2000, B5.

37. Richard Harrison Shryrock, *Medicine in America: Historical Essays*, 2d ed. (Baltimore: The John Hopkins Press, 1972), 124–125.

38. "Vegetarian Festival," *The New York Daily Times*, 5 September 1853, 1.

39. Ibid.

40. "Vegetarian Society in New York," *American Vegetarian and Health Journal* 2 (November 1852): 169.

41. O. S. Fowler, *Religion, Natural and Revealed: Or The Natural Theology and Moral Bearings of Phrenology and Physiology* (New York: O. S. Fowler, 1844), 136–137.

42. Nelson Newland, "On Food and Diet," *Eating Room Portland Pleasure Boat* 9 (September 14, 1854), 1–2.

43. "Portliness Illustrated by Wm. T. Coggeshall," *The Ladies' Repository: A Monthly Periodical Devoted to Literature, Arts, and Religion*, October 1853, 469–470.

44. Thomas Low Nichols, *Forty Years of American Life* (New York: Stackpole Sons, 1937), 43.

CHAPTER 5

1. Vegetarian Settlement Company, *Kanzas, Containing Full Information for Inquirers* (New York: Fowler & Wells, 1856).

2. Henry S. Clubb, "Vegetarians for Kanzas," *The Water-Cure Journal* 19 (April 1855): 87.

3. Miriam Davis Colt, *Went to Kanzas; Being a Thrilling Account of an Ill-Fated Expedition* (Watertown, N.Y.: L. Ingalls & Co., 1862), 95–102.

4. "The South and the Union," *Debow's Review, Agricultural, Commercial, Industrial Progress and Resources* 19 (July 1855): 742.

5. James C. Jackson, appendix in *Fruit & Bread: A Scientific Diet*, by Gustav Schlickeysen, translated by M.L. Holbrook, M.D. (New York: M.L. Holbrook & Company, 1877), 211.

6. Caleb Jackson, "To Allopathic Physicians," *The Water-Cure Journal and Herald of Reforms* 25 (April 1858): 52.

7. J.C.B., "Grahamism," *The Water-Cure Journal and Herald of Reforms* 27 (July 1859): 11.

8. James C. Jackson, *Flesh as Food for Man in Dyspepsia and Its Treatment* (Dansville, N.Y.: Our Home Publishing, 1862), 1.

9. Ellen G. White, *Counsels on Diet and Foods*, no. 111 (Washington, D.C.: Review and Herald Publishing Association, 1946), 81.

10. R.T. Trall, American preface to *Fruits and Farinacea: The Proper Food of Man*, by John Smith (New York: Fowler & Wells, 1892).

11. R.T. Trall, *The Scientific Basis of Vegetarianism* (Catherines, Ontario: The Provoker Press, 1970), 43.

12. Ibid., 20.

13. Ibid., 21.

14. "Goal of Hygienic Movement," *The Water-Cure Journal and Herald of Health Reforms, Devoted to Physiology, Hydropathy, and the Laws of Life* 26 (December 1858), 87.

15. Ibid., 88.

16. O.W. May, "To Dr. Henry Glasspool," *The Water-Cure Journal* 26 (November 1858), 67–69.

17. Ibid., 67–69.

18. Ibid., 67–69.

19. The idea, but not the rhetorical style, that doctors were grossly ignorant about diet would still be heard from advocates of vegetarianism for generations to come. For example, John McDougall, M.D., an internist/allopath, in his bestselling book *The McDougall Plan*, pointed out that physicians received only a few hours of training in nutrition out of hundreds of hours of medical school.

20. Trall, *The Scientific Basis*, 34–35.

21. Russell T. Trall, "Rambling Reminiscences, Hunting and Fishing," *The Herald of Health* 4 (October 1864): 1.

22. R.T. Trall, "Volume Thirty-Eighth," *The Herald of Health* 4 (July 1864): 241.

23. College Department, *The Herald of Health* 3 (May 1864): 188–189.

CHAPTER 6

1. John B. Hamilton, "Life and Times of Doctor Reuben D. Mussey," *Journal of the American Medical Association* 26 (April 1896): 1.

2. E.P.M., "A Vegetarian Clergyman," *The Herald of Health* 3(April 1865): 152.

3. Henry Ward Beecher, "A Discourse to Medical Students," *The Herald of Health and Journal of Physical Culture* 9 (April 1867): 177.

4. "Irritability and Meat," *The Herald of Health and Journal of Physical Culture* 9 (April 1867): 190.

5. "Dr. Drake, the Quack, and His Victim," *The Herald of Health and Journal of Physical Culture* 9 (March 1867): 120–121.

6. "Popular Fallacies Concerning Hygiene," part 1: Dietetical Fallacies, *Appletons' Journal: A Magazine of General Literature* 1 (June 26, 1869): 398–400.

7. Ibid., 398–400.

8. Ibid., 398–400.

9. E. T. Youmans, "John Stuart Mill on the Women Question," *Appletons' Journal: A Magazine of General Literature* 1 (June 24, 1869): 536–537.

10. M. G. Kellogg, "Meat-Eating," *The Health Reformer* 8 (April 1873): 97–98.

11. Ibid., 97–98.

12. Ibid., 97–98.

13. *Joyful News Co-operator*, February 1884, 1.

14. "Edenic Food Likes," *Woman's Herald of Industry and Social Science Cooperator* 3 (February 1884): 1.

15. A. T. De Learsey, "God's Food for Man," *Food, Home and Garden* 3 (January 1891): 6.

16. Annie Besant, "An Appeal for Reform," *The Animals' Defender* 8 (March 1903): 26.

17. International Vegetarian Congress, Chicago, *The Vegetarian Messenger* (September 1893): 282–298.

18. Anderson T. Hanson, "To Chicago!" *The Vegetarian,* 19 August 1893, 388.

19. International Vegetarian Congress, Chicago, *The Vegetarian Messenger* (September 1893): 282–298.

20. Ibid.

21. Alice Stockham, *Tokology: A Book for Every Woman* (Chicago: Sanitary Publishing Company, 1886), 124.

22. Susanna Way Dodds, *Diet Question. Health in the Household or Hygienic Cookery* (New York: Fowler & Wells, 1888), quoted in Hereward Carrington, *The Natural Diet of Man* (London: C.W. Daniel, LTD, circa 1910), 255.

23. M. L. Holbrook, *Eating for Strength; or, Food and Diet in Their Relation to Health and Work* (New York: M. L. Holbrook and Co., 1888).

24. R. A. Baker, "The Dining Room," *The Home Magazine,* April 1890, 14.

25. M. L. Holbrook, preface in *Fruit and Bread,* by Gustav Schlickeysen (New York: M. L. Holbrook & Co., 1877).

26. Howard J. Moore, "Why I Am a Vegetarian," *Chicago Vegetarian,* October 1897, 8.

27. Howard J. Moore, *The Universal Kinship* (Chicago: Charles H. Kerr & Co., 1906).

28. Laurence Gronland, "Why I Am Not a Vegetarian," *Chicago Vegetarian,* October 1898, 1–6.

29. J. Howard Moore, "Why Gronland Should Be a Vegetarian," *Chicago Vegetarian*, October 1898, 7–9.

30. Ibid., 7–9.

31. Ibid., 7–9.

32. Ibid., 7–9.

33. Henry D. Perky, "Experience Proves the Theory," *Chicago Vegetarian*, October 1898, 19.

34. "Vegetarian Thanksgiving Dinner," *The Vegetarian* 1 (November 1895): 89.

35. "The Picnic at Old St. Joe," *Chicago Vegetarian*, August 1898, 10.

36. "Mr. Angell's Inconsistency," *Chicago Vegetarian*, August 1898, 10.

37. *Henry S. Clubb, The Vegetarian Messenger and Health Review* 6 (April 1914): 130.

38. "The Growth of Humane Sentiment," *The Animals' Defender* 9, no. 3 (1904): 12.

39. M.L. Holbrook, "Vegetarianism," *The Journal of Hygiene and Herald of Health* 46 (September 1896): 228.

40. Ibid., 228.

41. "Vegetarian Notes," *The Animals' Defender* 8 (January 1903): 3.

42. John B. Miller, "A Vegetarian Colony in Missouri," *The Vegetarian and Our Fellow Creatures* 5 (April 15, 1901): 196.

CHAPTER 7

1. "Suffragists Have Meatless Luncheon," *The Vegetarian Magazine*, June 1903, 219.

2. "The Weak Vegetarian," *The Animals' Defender* 7 (June 1902): 15.

3. Menu, first vegetarian restaurant, New York City, circa 1901.

4. Charles William Dabney, A Memoir, University of Tennessee Collection.

5. Charles William Dabney to John Harvey Kellogg, 9 January 1923, contained in the John Harvey Kellogg Collection at the University of Michigan Library.

6. Advertisement for Sanitas Nut Food Co., *Chicago Vegetarian*, November 1898.

7. Publishers' Department, *Good Health* 33 (August 1898), 522.

8. *Biography of John Harvey Kellogg*, Scientific American Compiling Department, date unknown, contained in JHK Collection at University of Michigan.

9. "Mrs. Kellogg Leaves Record," *Battle Creek Moon Journal*, 15 June 1920, 20.

10. Mary Sanderson, "Substantial Meals Without Meat," *Good Housekeeping*, January–May 1909, 108.

11. "Notable Vegetarians," *The Literary Digest*, 24 May 1913, 1196–1199.

12. Ibid., 1196.

13. Elmer Vernon McCollum, *A History of Nutrition; The Sequence of Ideas in Nutrition Investigations* (Boston: Houghton Mifflin, 1957).

14. "Adventures in Diet," *New York Times*, 19 April 1936, sec. F, 4:2.

15. "Meat Made Heaviest Ducks," *New York Times*, 2 June 1912, 3.

16. "Personal Glimpses," *Literary Digest*, 1 September 1928, 43.

17. "Notable Vegetarians," *The Literary Digest*, 24 May 1913, 1197.

18. "The Salvation Army and Vegetarianism," *The Vegetarian Messenger and Health Review* 6 (April 1914): 79–86.

19. *The Vegetarian*, 15 January 1898, 2.

20. "The Weak Vegetarian," *The New England Anti-Vivisection Society Monthly* 5 (August 1900): 5.

21. "Does Meat Injure Athletes?" *The Literary Digest*, 13 February 1915, 313–314.

22. Bernarr McFadden, *Vitality Supreme* (New York: Physical Culture Publishing, 1915), preface.

23. Bernarr MacFadden, *Physical Culture Magazine*, September 1902, 344.

24. M. E. Jaffa, *Further Investigations among Fruitarians at the California Agricultural Experiment Station*, U.S. Department of Agriculture, Bulletin no. 132, 1901–1902.

25. Russell H. Chitteneden, "Physiological Economy in Nutrition," *Popular Science Monthly*, June 1903, 2–23.

26. Mikkel Hindhede, "The Effect of Food Restrictions During War on Mortality in Copenhagen," *Journal of the American Medical Association* 74 (February 1920): 381.

27. "A Great Scientist on Vegetarianism," *The New England Anti-Vivisection Society Monthly*, July 1900, 19.

28. Extract from lecture by Elmer Vernon McCollum at the Battle Creek Sanitarium, December 4, 1923, contained in the John Harvey Kellogg Collection at The University of Michigan Library.

29. Elmer Vernon McCollum to Roman, 24 April 1924, contained in the John Harvey Kellogg Collection at The University of Michigan Library.

30. Ibid.

31. Alonzo Taylor, "Is Vegetarianism Capable of World-Wide Application?" *Popular Science*, December 1911, 587.

32. Upton Sinclair, "Starving for Health's Sake," *Cosmopolitan*, May 1910, 739–745.

33. Upton Sinclair, "Mr. Sinclair Would Be Sued," *New York Times*, 4 May 1906, 8.

34. Hereward Carrington, "Scientific Cannibalism," *New York Times*, 4 June 1909, 6.

35. J. E. Fries, "The Cannibal's Diet," *New York Times*, 7 June 1909, 6.

36. "The Contributors' Club," *Atlantic Monthly*, June 1905, 855–858.

37. "Conversions to Vegetarianism, Topics of The Times," *New York Times*, 4 June 1906, 8.

38. Ibid.

39. B. O. Flower, "Ernest Crosby: A Civic Leader of the New Time," *Arena*, April 1901, 386.

40. Ibid., 386.

41. Ibid., 387.

42. B. O. Flower, "Ernest Howard Crosby: Prophet of Peace and Apostle of Social Righteousness," *Arena*, March 1907, 263.

43. Leo Tolstoy, "History of Vegetarianism," International Vegetarian Union, http://www.ivu.org, 2000.

44. Ernest Crosby and Elisee Reclus, *The Meat Fetish, Two Essays on Vegetarianism* (London: A.C. Fifield, 1905).

45. "Vegetarian Temple for Boston," *Boston American*, 1 February 1914, contained in the Millennium Guild clipping file at The Last Post, Falls Village, Conn.

46. Ibid.

47. M.R.L. Freshel, *Selections from Three Essays by Richard Wagner on a Subject of Such Importance to the Moral Progress of Humanity That It Constitutes an Issue of Ethics & Religion* (Boston: The Millennium Guild, 1933).

48. "Bar Turkeys, Feel Thankful on Vegetables," *Boston American*, 28 November 1913, contained in Millennium Guide clipping file at the Last Post, Falls Village, Conn.

49. Edwin Osgood Grover, *The Animal Lover's Knapsack* (New York: Thomas Y. Crowell Co., 1929), 229.

50. Morris Fishbein, *The New Medical Follies* (New York: Boni and Liveright, 1927).

51. Richard Schwarz, *John Harvey Kellogg, M.D.* (Nashville, Tenn.: Southern Publishing Association, 1970), 39–40.

52. "News," *The Vegetarian and Fruitarian*, February 1928, 26.

53. "America Going Vegetarian," *The Literary Digest*, 21 July 1928, 19.

CHAPTER 8

1. Frederick Damrau, "The Folly of Vegetarianism," *Hygeia* 5 (September 1927): 439.

2. Harriet Morgan, "Dietary Delusions: Past and Present," *Hygeia* 14 (April 1936): 313.

3. Celeste Turner Wright, "Much Taboo About Nothing," *Hygeia* 18 (December 1940): 1088.

4. *Meat Selection Preparation and Many Ways to Serve* [Booklet] (Armour and Company, 1934).

5. "We Eat Less Meat, Prices Drop; Industry Unites to Increase Use," *Business Week*, 4 March 1931, 16.

6. Otto Carqué, *Natural Foods: The Safe Way to Health* (Los Angeles: Carqué Pure Food Company, 1925), 289.

7. "Milk from Soybeans Is New Economy Food," *Washington Post*, 21 May 1933, 24.

8. Doris Gardiner, interview by the authors, November 1998.

9. "Special Rationing Plan for Vegetarians Studied," *New York Times*, 25 January 1943, 16.

10. "La Gaurdia to Seek U.S. Help on Meat," *New York Times*, 18 December 1944, 21.

11. "Heydays for the Vegetarians," *New York Times Magazine* (8 April 1945): 17.

12. Ibid.

13. *Is Meat Essential to Health?* [Booklet] (New York City: The League For Public Discussion, October 1946).

14. Jean Oswald, *Yours For Health: The Life and Times of Herbert M. Shelton* (Franklin, Wis.: Franklin Books, 1989).

15. "Normalize!," *The New Yorker*, 9 August 1947, 16.

16. Henry Bailey Stevens, *The Recovery of Culture* (New York: Harper & Brothers, 1949), 20–26.

17. "Biographical Note," Henry Bailey Stevens & Agnes Ryan Papers, 1898–1974, University of New Hampshire Library, 16 September 1998.

18. Stevens, *The Recovery of Culture*, 20–26.

19. Sarah Norcliffe Cleghorn, *The Seamless Robe* (New York: Macmillan, 1945), 149–150.

20. Ibid., 149–150.

21. "People: The Real Dark Horses Start Running for the Presidency," *Newsweek*, 26 April 1948, 43.

22. "Candidate: Salvation by Spinach," *Newsweek*, 8 November 1948, 25.

23. *Platform of the American Vegetarian Party—1960*, [handout] American Vegetarian Party, 1960.

24. "Vegetarian Unit Boils up in a Stew but Political Wing Calls It a Beef," *New York Times*, 4 April 1952, 27.

25. "Multi-Party System," *New York Times Magazine* 6 (15 June 1952): 5.

26. W.H. Sebrell, Jr., "Food Faddism and Public Health," in *What Can We Do About Food Faddism?*, Symposium conducted by American Institute of Nutrition, Atlantic City, N.J., 14 April 1954.

27. A.M. Liebstein, M.D., and Neil Ehmke, "The Case for Vegetarianism," *The American Mercury* 70 (April 1950): 398–407.

28. Muriel Golde, conversation with authors, June 2000.

29. Joann Scanlon, conversation with authors, June 2000.

30. Symon Gould, "Jottings from a Vegetarian's NoteBook," *The American Vegetarian* 12 (February 1, 1953): 1.

31. Mervyn G. Hardinge, telephone interview with authors, various times between March 1999 and September 2001.

32. Mervyn G. Hardinge and Frederick Stare, "Nutritional Studies of Vegetarians, I. Nutrition, Physical, and Laboratory Studies," *American Journal of Clinical Nutrition* 2 (1954): 73–82.

33. Mervyn G. Hardinge and Frederick Stare, "Nutritional Studies of Vegetarians, II. Dietary and Serum Levels of Cholesterol," *American Journal of Clinical Nutrition* 2 (1954): 83–88.

34. "Diet & Health," *Time*, 21 April 1952, 72.

35. Jay Dinshah, conversation with authors, various dates in 1998, 2000.

36. Freya Dinshah, conversation with authors, various dates in 2001.

37. "Diet and Stress in Vascular Disease," *Journal of the American Medical Association*, 176 (June 3, 1961): 806.

CHAPTER 9

1. "Radio Couple Garners Devoted Following Over 44 Years," *The Christian Science Monitor*, 13 January 1982.

2. Steve Allen, preface to *Bare Feet and Good Things to Eat*, by Gypsy Boots (Los Angeles: Virg Nover Printer, 1965).

3. Gypsy Boots, conversation with authors, January 2000.

4. Manley Witten, "The Safe House," *Los Angeles Times*, 15 October 1992, part J2.

5. Ibid.

6. Lisa Laws, telephone conversation with authors, August 13, 2001.

7. Lowell D. Streiker, *The Gospel of Irreligious Religion* (New York: Sheed and Ward, 1969), 76.

8. "The Kosher of the Counterculture," *Time*, 16 November 1970, 59.

9. Shanta Sacharoff, "Dr. Catgood (India Cuisine)," *Rags*, March 1971, 55.

10. William Hedgepeth and Dennis Stock, *The Alternative: Communal Life in America* (New York: Macmillan, 1970).

11. Stephen Gaskin, telephone interview by the authors, November 1998, August 2002.

12. Stephen Gaskin, *Hey Beatnik! This Is The Farm* (Summertown, Tenn.: The Book Publishing Company, 1974).

13. Edward B. Fiske, "Marijuana Part of Religion at Commune in Tennessee," *New York Times*, 17 February 1973, 27.

14. Helen Nearing and Scott Nearing, *The Good Life* (New York: Shocken Books, 1989), 142.

15. Helen Nearing and Scott Nearing, *Living the Good Life* (New York: Schocken Books, 1970).

16. Nearing and Nearing, *The Good Life*, 142.

17. "Helen and Scott Nearing," *Vegetarian World* 4 (March/May 1978), 30–31.

18. Francis Moore Lappé, *Diet for a Small Planet* (New York: Ballantine Books, 1971).

19. Colman McCarthy, "Hamburgers to Soyburgers" *Washington Post*, 13 May 1989, A19.

20. Victoria Moran, *Vegetarian Times.*

21. "Vegetarian Efficiency," *Vegetarian Voice* 2 (January/February 1975): 1.

22. "Telling Millions about Vegetarianism for Pennies," *Vegetarian World* (1975): 16.

23. Nellie Shriver, *Vegetarian Times* (1975), 5.

24. Nellie Shriver, correspondence with authors, August 1998.

25. "Being an Activist at Your College," *Vegetarian World* 3 (December 1977–February 1978).

26. Victoria Moran and Lucy Moll, *Vegetarian Times*, 1990.

27. Constantina Salamone, "Women, Are You Still Human Chauvinists?" *Majority Report*, October 1972, 16.

28. Constantina Salamone, interview by the authors, 1998, 2001.

29. Judy Klemesrud, "Vegetarianism: Growing Way of Life," *New York Times*, 21 March 1975, L43.

30. Peter Singer, ed., *In Defense of Animals* (New York: Harper & Row, 1986), 135.

31. Marcia Pearson, "Seattle Vegetarians Organize a Society," *Vegetarian World* 2, no. 8 (1976): 7.

32. "Vegetarians Set for a Seder," *Daily News*, 26 March 1980, 10.

33. Dudley Giehl, *Vegetarianism: A Way of Life* (New York: Barnes & Noble Books, 1979), viii–ix.

34. "Maine Magnificent!" special issue, pictorial record of the World Vegetarian Congress, *Vegetarian Voice* (September/October, November/December 1975): 1.

35. "Force Against Famine," *The Christian Century* (December 1975): 971–972.

36. Judy Klemesrud, "World Vegetarians Meet To Talk—And Eat," *New York Times*, 22 August 1975.

37. Judy Klemesrud, "Special Meals on Campus," *New York Times,* 10 March 1976, 47.

38. "But What About Protein?" *Life and Health* Supplement, Vol. 1, 2nd ed. (1973).

39. Dr. Doris Calloway, "Are Vegetarian Diets Safe?" *McCall's,* January 1972, 28.

40. Ibid.

41. S.B., "When a Vegetarian Diet Can Be Dangerous," *Good Housekeeping,* May 1976, 211.

42. Ibid.

43. Vic Sussman, "My Life among the Vegetables," *Washington Post Magazine,* 28 March 1993, W20.

44. Vegetarian Society, Inc., *A Vegetarian Primer* (n.d.).

45. William Blanchard, *Vegetarian World* (1975).

46. "Superman Part VI," *Vegetarian World* March–May 1978, 13.

47. "The Great Debates," *Vegetarian World* March–May 1978, 10–11.

48. "Food-Day Dinner at the White House Offers the Meat of Controversy," *New York Times,* 22 April 1977.

CHAPTER 10

1. Alex Pacheco, interview by the authors, April 2000.

2. Michel McQueen, "Poultry Store Picketed in Anti-Cruelty Protest," *Washington Post,* 26 June 1980, C1.

3. "Now It's Civil Rights For Animals," *U.S. News & World Report,* 22 December 1980, 55.

4. Ingrid Newkirk, e-mail and phone correspondence with authors, 4 November 1998, April 2001.

5. People for the Ethical Treatment of Animals (PETA), *Factory Farming: Mechanized Madness,* booklet, 1980s.

6. "The Year's 25 Most Fascinating Business People," *Fortune,* 1 January 1990, 62.

7. Michael Specter, "The Extremist; The Woman behind the Most Successful Radical Group in America," *New Yorker,* 14 April 2003, 52.

8. Colman McCarthy, "The Great American Meatout," *Washington Post,* 28 March 1987, A21.

9. Peter Burwash, *Vegetarian Primer* (New York: Atheneum, 1983), 10.

10. John Harvey Kellogg, "Pigarians," *Good Health,* no. 1 (January 1900): 51–52.

11. Harvey Diamond and Marilyn Diamond, *Fit for Life* (New York: Warner Books, 1985).

12. Lucy Moll, "Between the Lines of Fit for Life," *Vegetarian Times,* no. 109 (September 1986): 39.

13. Reynold Bean, "Confessions of an Ex-Butcher," *Vegetarian Times,* no. 167 (July 1991): 59.

14. *Beyond Beef* 1 (spring 1992): 2.

15. "How to Win an Argument with a Meat Eater," *New York Times,* 18 June 1989, advertisement.

16. Colman McCarthy, interview with the authors, 5 August 2003.

17. Colman McCarthy, "Of Meat and Machismo," *Washington Post*, 24 July 1990, E3.

18. Susan Reed, "Activist Ingrid Newkirk Fights Passionately for the Rights of Animals," *People Weekly*, 22 October 1990, 59.

19. *People Weekly*, 25 August 1997, 79.

20. Anita Manning, "A Beefed-Up Attack on Meat Eaters," *USA Today*, 10 September 1990, sec. D, 1.

21. Michael Bates, "Singer k.d. lang Takes Anti-Meat Stance, Cattle Country Retaliates," *Associated Press*, 28 June 1990.

22. *USA Today*, 9 July 1990, sec. D, 2.

23. Sandra Blakeslee, "Arteries Are Unblocked Without Drugs in Study," *New York Times*, 21 July 1990.

24. Mary O'Neill, "Unusual Heart Therapy Wins Coverage from Large Insurers," *New York Times*, 28 July 1993, A1.

25. Jane Brody, "Huge Study of Diet Indicts Fat and Meat," *New York Times*, 8 May 1990, C1.

26. Ibid.

27. William Castelli, interview by the authors, June 1994.

28. *Salon.com*, "People," http://www.salon.com/people/conv/2001/03/12/barnard/index.html.

29. Neal Barnard, M.D., "Editorial: U.S. Dietary Guidelines Victory in Court," *Physicians Committee for Responsible Medicine Magazine*, winter 2001, www.pcrm.org/magazine/GM01winter/GM01win8.html.

30. Marion Nestle, *Food Politics* (Berkeley: University of California Press, 2002).

31. Linda Roach Monroe, "Benefits of Milk Fall under Attack," *Houston Chronicle*, 30 September 1992, A8.

32. Gene and Lorri Bauston, e-mail interview by the authors, September 1998, 3 March 2001.

33. Ann Bancroft, "Group Trying to Keep Turkey Off the Table," *San Francisco Chronicle*, 25 November 1993, A23.

34. Clifford Rothman, "Last Frontier of Animal Rights? The Farm," *Los Angeles Times*, 6 July 1995, sec. E, 1.

35. Karen Davis, e-mail interview with the authors, December 2003.

36. Karen Davis, interview and correspondence with the authors, 15 April 2000, September 2001.

37. Sue Anne Pressley, "At This Thanksgiving Table, They Serve Turkey Dinners," *Washington Post*, 27 November 1991, D1.

38. Howard F. Lyman, *Mad Cowboy: Plain Truth from the Cattle Rancher Who Won't Eat Meat* (New York: Scribner, 1998).

39. Howard Lyman, telephone interview with the authors, 14 July 1999.

40. Pamela Rice, interview by the authors, 12 April 2001.

41. Michael Granberg, "Vegetarian Driver Plans to File Suit," *Los Angeles Times*, 15 June 1996, Orange County edition, Metro section, part B, 1.

42. "Vegetarian Wrongly Fired, Bias Panel Finds," *Los Angeles Times*, 24 August 1996, Orange County edition, Metro section, part A1.

43. Leslie Kaufman, "Children of the Corn," *Newsweek*, 28 August 1995, 60.

44. "How Many Teens Are Vegetarians?" *Vegetarian Journal* 20 (January/February 2001).

45. "Here's Who We Are!" *Vegetarian Times* (October 1992).

46. The Vegetarian Resource Group, "How Many Vegetarians Are There?" press release, 1 September 1997.

47. Ron Pickarski, interview by the authors, 4 March 2001.

48. Jeff Nelson, correspondence with the authors, 10 June 2001.

49. Scott MacKay, "Eat a Dog—Save an Animal—Porn Actress, Activist Promote Vegan Diet," *Providence Journal,* 3 July 2003, B.01.

50. John McDougall, e-mail interview by the authors, 8 March 2001.

51. Mervyn Hardinge, interview by the authors, September 2001.

52. Roberta Kalechofsky, interview by the authors, 20 March 2001.

53. Bruce Friedrich, interview by the authors, 19 March 2001.

54. Bill Broadway, "A Meatless Mission," *Washington Post,* 13 March 1999, B8.

55. Andrew Linzey, *Animal Gospel* (Westminster, England: John Knox Press, 1998), 127.

56. Quoted in *All in One Peace* by Colman McCarthy (New Brunswick, N.J.: Rutgers University Press), 171.

Index

About the Authors

KAREN IACOBBO is a journalist and researcher. She is also Adjunct Professor, Freshman Studies at Johnson and Wales University and Special Lecturer at Providence College.

MICHAEL IACOBBO is a journalist who has worked for the Associated Press, the *Providence Phoenix*, and other publications.